Puppy Parenting

Gail I. Clark, Ph.D.

Alpine Publications, Inc.
Loveland, Colorado

Puppy Parenting

Library of Congress Cataloging-in-Publication Data

Clark, Gail I., 1950-
    Puppy parenting / Gail I. Clark.
       p.   cm.
    Includes index.
    ISBN 1-57779-012-X (pbk.)
    1. Puppies—Training. 2. Puppies—Behavior. 3. Puppies.
    I. Title.
    SF431.C5175 1999
    636.7'088'7—dc21
                                           98-34718
                                              CIP

Many manufacturers secure trademark rights for their products. When Alpine Publications is aware of a trademark claim, we identify the product name by using initial capital letters.

For the sake of simplicity, the terms "he" or "she" are sometimes used to identify an animal or person. These are used in the generic sense only. No discrimination of any kind is intended toward either sex.

Alpine Publications accepts no responsibility for medical information, suggested treatments, or vaccinations mentioned herein. The reader is advised to check with their local, licensed veterinarian before giving medical attention.

This book is available at special quantity discounts for breeders and for club promotions, premiums, or educational use. Write for details.

Photos: © Kent and Donna Dannen
Edited by: Dianne J. Nelson
Design and composition by: Dianne J. Nelson, Shadow Canyon Graphics

First Printing 1998
1 2 3 4 5 6 7 8 9 0
Printed in the United States of America

CONTENTS

Preface v

Introduction ix

Chapter 1:
   Choosing a Breed 1
Chapter 2:
   Where to Find a Puppy 19
Chapter 3:
   Choosing Your Breeder and Puppy 27
Chapter 4:
   Puppy Body Language 37
Chapter 5:
   The Best Age to Bring Your Puppy Home 49
Chapter 6:
   Preparing for Your New Puppy 55
Chapter 7:
   Bringing Your Puppy Home 69
Chapter 8:
   General Puppy Care 85
Chapter 9:
   Socialization 97
Chapter 10:
   House-Training 121
Chapter 11:
   Communicating Proper Behavior to Your Puppy . . .139
Chapter 12:
   Understanding Body Language 151
Chapter 13:
   Disciplining Your Puppy 159
Chapter 14:
   How Your Puppy Learns 173
Chapter 15:

Chapter 15:
    Puppy Manners and Training 181
Chapter 16:
    Preventing Problem Behaviors 211
Chapter 17:
    Multiple-Dog Households 241
Chapter 18:
    Games and Exercise 249
Chapter 19:
    Puppy Obedience Classes 257

Afterword 265
Other Resources 267
About the Author 269
Index 271

Preface

Somewhere between the yank, jerk, hit-the-puppy-over-the-head-with-the-news-paper, rub-the-nose-in-the-poop methods of training and the canine psychologist, psychiatrist, behaviorist, psychic, and massage therapist, raising a puppy has become very confusing for the new puppy owner. Puppy raising can be easy when you use your natural and intuitive parenting skills and common sense. Even if you have never been a parent, you possess basic, innate nurturing and parenting qualities that can easily be tapped and applied for raising your puppy to be the best dog possible. Just as you nurture, communicate, educate, reward, discipline, supervise, and provide a safe environment for a young child, so must you do the same for a puppy. A puppy, like a child, will develop into a well-mannered, well-adjusted, devoted, loving member of the family if you use sensible parenting skills and good common sense.

Contrary to many puppy-raising theories of the twentieth century, you don't have to act like a dog to communicate with your puppy. Growling back at your puppy if he growls at you does *not* communicate dominance or make your puppy think that you are his mother, as some theorists suggest. Your growling is only a bad imitation of a dog, and if your puppy doesn't know that you are not his mother, then he has a serious identity crisis that will not be cured by your growling at him. Biting your puppy back when he nips you, as some methods dictate, is a good way to justify plastic surgery for the nose you wanted to change. Acting like a dog is not only unnatural for most of us, it does not make sense to your puppy. With a little common sense, a simple and introductory understanding of puppy behavior, and tapping your fundamental and intuitive parenting skills, you can raise a puppy to be well adjusted, behaved, and loving while you maintain your human identity.

Relating child rearing to raising a puppy is not to say that you should anthropomorphize and think of your puppy as a child. Instead, you utilize basic child-rearing principles in regard to reinforcement, positive guidance, and discipline. Positive reinforcement and guidance teach children and puppies proper behavior. If you want a child to learn how to tie his shoelaces, you teach him or show him how to tie his laces, praise him when he ties them by himself, and maybe even reward him by going for a walk to get an ice-cream cone. The same principle of positive reinforcement can be applied to your puppy when you teach him basic commands and proper behavior. For example, to teach your puppy to sit on command, you could show your puppy how to sit, praise him for sitting, then take him for a walk or give him a treat as a reward for sitting. Raising a well-behaved puppy simply involves motivating good behavior through positive reinforcement and discouraging inappropriate behavior through discipline. If your child was disobedient, you would constructively discipline him to discourage his repeating the behavior. A puppy also needs discipline to understand which behaviors are unacceptable. If your child started to pull you down the stairs, you would very likely pull him back, reprimand him for pulling, then show him the proper way to go down stairs. When your child walks down the stairs properly, he is praised. If your puppy pulled you down the street, you would also pull him back, show him how to walk properly on the lead, then praise him for walking on a loose lead. Children and puppies are more likely to repeat behaviors that are rewarded and avoid behaviors that produce reprimands or negative consequences.

Good parenting also involves providing a safe environment to prevent inappropriate behavior when you cannot supervise your puppy. When you can't supervise or prevent your young children from getting into things or running around the house or car, you might use a crib, a playpen, a harness, a car seat, or other device to control your child's movement. To control your puppy's movement when you can't supervise him, you use a leash or crate. Raising your puppy to be well behaved is easy when you learn how to provide a positive puppy environment.

I found the need for my first book, *The Mentally Sound Dog*, to focus on resolving behavioral problems and retraining the problem dog. There is, however, a great need for practical and easy-to-follow information on raising a puppy in a positive manner that prevents problem behaviors from developing. The majority of behavioral problems in dogs that have been presented to me through thousands of clients could have been avoided with early puppy training. Many people simply didn't know what behaviors to expect from their puppies or how to prevent misbehavior. Other clients who researched various informational sources became confused by the conflicting advice. Some clients who attended puppy classes were disillusioned by the lack of information on training and puppy problem solving. My goal is to provide sound advice and reliable information for choosing the right puppy, practical and useful insights about puppy behavior, and sensible, easy-to-follow methods for training your puppy. I will also answer some of the most common questions asked by puppy owners.

You are about to embark upon a step-by-step approach to nurture, socialize, and shape a mentally sound and well-behaved puppy through positive parenting and easy training techniques starting with the first day you bring your puppy home. Whether you are inexperienced, experienced, confused by conflicting advice, or an instructor, you will find the information and techniques discussed in this book valuable for positively nurturing, shaping, and training your puppy into a valued and loved companion and household member.

Introduction

When I got my first puppy, long before I committed to a career of working with dogs, I had great expectations that he would develop into a mentally sound, well-behaved, devoted dog—maybe another Lassie or Rin-Tin-Tin—a naturally heroic, obedient dog that would climb enormous mountains, forge great rivers, and share the last morsel of food to save my life. My great expectations quickly turned into disillusionment when the only mountain that my new puppy climbed was the kitchen counter, where he stole my steak and forged through the puddle that he left in the living room as he headed for a hidden corner to gobble his booty before I caught him. My disenchantment with my ill-mannered, less-than-devoted food hoarder of a dog launched me into an obsessive commitment to understand the canine species and how to raise a well-mannered, devoted canine companion. Through years of academic and empirical study involving canine behavior and the human-canine interaction, I discovered that successful relationships between dogs and owners are more likely to develop when prospective puppy owners research different breeds and choose a particular breed for attributes that are suited to their lifestyle, select a puppy based on a temperament that is compatible to their own, and start training at a very early age.

Natural behaviors that occur between dogs should not be directed toward children or other family members.

An unsuccessful relationship between a dog and his owner evolves from unrealistic expectations. If you expect your puppy to have a short coat, weigh ten pounds, and spend most of his life in your lap, you will be sorely disappointed if he starts to look like Rapunzel, weighs 100 pounds, and bounces off the wall as a form of entertainment. Researching the different breeds for traits that are desirable to you maximizes your chances of selecting a breed that will satisfy your expectations.

A successful canine-human relationship also depends upon a compatible match between temperaments. The meek dog owner who purchases the largest male Rottweiler of the litter as a brave companion and protector may feel a little more than disappointed after he finds himself backed into a corner in front of a set of pearly white teeth for merely having the audacity to ask the dog to remove himself from the couch.

While carefully selecting a breed and choosing a puppy for temperament improve your chances of building a satisfying bond with your puppy, your best expectations can only be fulfilled with early training. Learning how to teach your puppy to behave appropriately is essential for channeling natural puppy behaviors that may become problem behaviors. For example, inherent behaviors such as chasing, biting, and pouncing among littermates are functional, and necessary for your puppy to learn social, sexual, and canine survival skills. However, if these natural behaviors are allowed to be directed at humans, they become problem behaviors. While the chase game that your ten-week-old puppy played with his littermates may appear to be harmless to play with the kids, the game quickly turns into a problem when your puppy is eight months old and strong enough to knock the kids over as he snaps in an attempt to catch them. You must teach your puppy how to behave properly, and you must redirect potentially problem behavior in a positive manner before it develops into a serious problem.

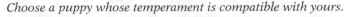

Choose a puppy whose temperament is compatible with yours.

Rhodesian Ridgeback pups.

If you have already chosen your puppy and problem behaviors have developed, it is not too late to implement a positive training program that will teach him correct behavior. With positive training, handling, socialization, and a safe environment, even an older puppy can reach his full potential and develop into a good canine citizen and companion. Whether you are in the process of selecting a puppy, or your puppy is eight weeks, eighteen months, or two years of age, the information presented in this book will help you to understand your puppy and develop a rewarding bond that will meet your highest expectations.

CHAPTER 1

Choosing a Breed

 There are more than 130 pure dog breeds and an infinite number of mixed breeds. Each breed or mixture of breeds possesses different characteristics, idiosyncracies, or behaviors that can either add to or detract from the ideal pet relationship depending on your preferences and expectations. When choosing a breed to fit your lifestyle and personality, size, sex, coat type, and temperament are important issues to consider. For example, the Great Dane may be too large to romp in the backyard with your kids. A Pembroke Welsh Corgi that sheds hair on your clothes and furniture and in your dinner plate may be more than you can handle if you are an aspiring fast-track executive who entertains clients frequently. The energetic Boxer may be a poor choice for the retired couple who enjoys puttering in the garden, and the avid jogger who buys a Saint Bernard as an exercise partner may be very disappointed to find out that his dog's idea of a long jog is a trip from the couch to the food bowl.

Second to choosing the right breed is selecting a puppy with a good temperament that is compatible with your own personality. A dog that challenges his owner's authority may be too much for a passive dog owner to manage. Choosing a puppy with traits and a temperament that do not fit your personality causes disappointment, resentment, frustration, and possibly abandonment of the pet.

1

TRAITS AND CHARACTERISTICS

It is important to research the different breeds and choose a breed that is compatible with your preferences and expectations. A dog bred to chase, dig, and burrow into holes for small game may not be the right choice if you have a prize garden. A Chow Chow, generally considered to be devoted to one person, may not fit into a household with lots of children and with people coming and going on a regular basis. Start your research with the American Kennel Club's *Complete Dog Book*. The American Kennel Club (AKC) has categorized breeds into seven groups: Sporting, Hound, Working, Terrier, Toy, Nonsporting, and Herding. Traits associated with these groups are generalizations, and any individual dog may or may not possess some or all of the characteristics of their breed. Generally, the sporting group—Spaniels, Setters, Retrievers, and Pointers—consists of bird-hunting dogs. The hound group—Bloodhounds, Dachshunds, Beagles, Rhodesian Ridgebacks, and Afghans—use their nose or eyes to hunt and chase down game. Breeds associated with the working group—Alaskan Malamutes, Samoyeds, Saint Bernards, Rottweilers, Great Danes, and New-foundlands—were bred to perform working tasks such as guarding, carting, and sledding. Terriers such as Cairns, Airedales, Bull Terriers, and Scottish Terriers were generally bred to hunt and furrow out vermin. Toys—Maltese, Pekingese, Papillons, and Miniature Poodles were bred for human companionship. The nonsporting breeds—Standard Poodles, Chow Chows, Chinese Shar-Peis, and Dalmatians—were bred for different tasks and possess many of the traits, such as retrieving, hunting, and guarding, found in the other groups. The herding group consists of breeds that were bred for herding sheep and cattle and include the Border Collie, the Australian Shepherd, the German Shepherd, the Bouvier des Flandres, and the Pulik. Narrow down the breeds that appeal to you and carefully read the AKC Standard for each breed.

Specific traits were perpetuated in each breed to enhance the dog's working ability or purpose. For instance, sporting dogs are more likely to naturally retrieve than dogs from the hound group. Therefore, if your desire is to have a dog that plays ball day in and day out, choose a natural retriever from a breed in the sporting group.

Each breed has certain characteristics that are potential problem behaviors if not channeled positively.

Check out the numerous books that are available on the different breeds, including the rare and foreign breeds. The information available from the AKC, from breed books, and from breeders and other sources can be very specific about the traits of each breed, thus helping you make the right choice in a puppy.

THE MIXED BREED VERSUS THE PUREBRED

There has been a long-standing controversy between dog lovers over which makes a better pet—the mixed-breed or the purebred dog. Mixed breeds, or hybrids, possess genes from totally unrelated parents, which is believed to produce healthy, resilient offspring. In spite of the heterogeneous genes, heredity diseases do occur in mixed breeds. Hereditary diseases are more likely to be prevalent and dominant in the purebred dog, because of the

Rhodesian Ridgebacks Hound Group.

Saint Bernards are part of the Working Group.

homogeneity of the genes, or the passing of pure or similar genes from generation to generation. Conversely, the hybrid dog is equipped with a larger degree of diversified genes, thus eliminating the perpetual passing of genes responsible for certain diseases.

While many professionals claim that hybrids are healthier as a result of their heterogeneous genetic makeup, the reputable breeder of the purebred dog is dedicated to researching and producing bloodlines that ensure their dogs' health, along with preserving breed type and traits. The homogenous, or "like" genes of the purebred, which may sometimes be responsible for perpetuating a disease, are also critical in eliminating a disease. This occurs because there is a small gene pool that is deficient of disease genes. Also, the dogs that are produced are similar in appearance and behavior. For instance, all Basset Hounds possess genes for short legs, while a hybrid may possess genes for short and long legs. With both genes present in the mixed breed, the outcome—whether the dog has short, long, or medium-length legs—is difficult to predict. The genetic arrangement of the mixed breed can be likened to shuffling cards—you never know the outcome. Generally, two purebred Dobermans bred together will produce puppies that look and act like Dobermans. If you purchase a purebred Great Pyrenees puppy, you can expect that he will be large, light colored, and more docile than an Irish Setter. The mixed-breed dog may look like a Labrador when he is a puppy but may only grow to be the size of a Shetland Sheepdog. The Labrador-Chow mix may possess more protective traits than retrieving characteristics.

Consider a purebred dog if you desire specific traits associated with appearance or working ability. Traits of a mixed breed may be difficult to predict as the puppy matures, as was the case with a man who purchased his three-month-old Beagle mix from a local animal shelter. In the market for a small dog, this man was told by the animal shelter that the puppy would only grow to be about fifteen inches. By the time the Beagle mix was eleven months old, the dog stood twenty-six inches at the shoulder. The Beagle and his owner, by demand of their landlord, had to find a new place to live. If you don't have explicit requirements about appearance or behavior, the mixed breed can make a very loving, intelligent, wonderful companion. Although research on particular mixed breeds

Puppies from the Sporting Group.

Gordon Setters are from the Sporting Group.

is somewhat complicated, there may be *some* predictability regarding appearance and temperament if you know the dog's parentage. For instance, a Golden Retriever–Labrador mix may exhibit traits of both breeds, and you may comfortably assume that the dog will not look or act like a Rottweiler.

SIZE

People generally consider the size of their new puppy in relation to their living space. For practical purposes, if you live in a one-room apartment, you would not want to sell your couch-bed in order to house a Great Dane. However, living space should not be the only consideration in determining the ideal size range of your prospective puppy.

As a young pup, Max, a Golden Retriever, roamed a very large house and backyard happily. Every morning, Max and his ninety-eight-pound owner went for a morning constitutional. Max loved going out for his morning walks, which pleased his owner because Max had been purchased specifically as a walking buddy. Unfortunately, as Max grew and became stronger, the walks became increasingly less enjoyable for his owner, who had difficulty controlling the ninety-five-pound Max. Max's owner attempted to maintain control with training but found the physical requirements painful regardless of the techniques and devices suggested by her trainers. In the end, Max was confined to his house and yard, and his owner unhappily went on walks alone. In this case, a smaller dog would have been a better choice as a walking companion. The size of the dog and your ability to maintain physical and general control are very important. The large, friendly, ten-month-old Labrador Retriever that loves children may need physical restraint occasionally to prevent an exuberant greeting from scratching or knocking over a child. If you cannot physically control your dog when necessary, a harmless situation may become serious and dangerous.

While physical ability and size are important, so, too, is choosing a breed that is capable of sharing your favorite activities. A five-pound Yorkshire Terrier may be a poor choice if you want your dog to join you on your weekly twenty-six-mile marathon. Although toy dogs are generally spunky and filled with energy, they may have difficulty keeping up with the enthusiastic athlete.

Bulldogs are from the Non-Sporting Group.

Another example of the Non-Sporting Group: the Shar-Pei.

Floyd, an avid bird hunter and marathon runner, chose a Gordon Setter as a running buddy. Floyd was disappointed when his predominantly black-colored Gordon Setter would wilt in the summer sun and lie under a tree after five miles of jogging. While some, including myself, would consider this Gordon Setter a smart dog for stopping, Floyd was frustrated and disappointed. After researching some other breeds, Floyd learned that German Shorthair Pointers were "big runners." Floyd purchased one, and the two of them enjoyed many marathon runs together.

COAT TYPE

Too often, coat type is not considered when a puppy is being chosen, and the shedding dog is relegated to the backyard where both the family and the pet are deprived of important social contact and a close relationship. Coat type is important to the fastidious owner or to a household where members are troubled with allergies. The only dogs that do not shed are the hairless breeds, such as the Chinese Crested, the Mexican Hairless, and the Peruvian Orka Inca. Curly-coated breeds, such as Poodle, Portuguese Water Dog, and Puli, have been erroneously depicted not to shed. These breeds shed into their own coat rather than all over the house. While this coat type might minimize allergic reactions and is a great option for the person who hates to vacuum, it is *not* a good coat for those who hate brushing hair. Brushing the coated breed is critical for maintaining good health and is a time-consuming task that cannot be neglected.

Short-haired dogs are not usually thought of as heavy shedders when, in fact, they may shed as profusely as Samoyeds. The short hair will get into your furniture, carpet, and clothing. However, the Doberman or Rottweiler that has a wash-and-wear coat and does not need to be brushed to control mats requires much less grooming time. Coat type is generally very predictable in the different breeds and is an important consideration in terms of maintenance and time commitment.

TEMPERAMENT

Dogs are bred not only for variation in appearance, but also for differences in temperament. The German Shepherd neither looks nor acts anything like the Irish Setter. The temperament and energy level of a puppy strongly contribute to his behavior. The reactive or nervous puppy may be easily traumatized by any event out of the ordinary and may dart around constantly, whereas the bold puppy may find the same event only worthy of a casual glance at the most. The puppy with pent-up, excess energy is more likely to chew the trees in the yard than the puppy that is content to lie at your feet.

Fortunately, a puppy often exhibits specific behavior and body language that can help you determine his temperament and energy level before you bring him home. A dominant or strong-tempered puppy is not a good choice for individuals who are uncomfortable with asserting their authority or who are reluctant to set rules and limits. From the time Cali, a Jack Russell Terrier, was a young puppy, Doug and Jill were "impressed with her expression of self-will." Doug and Jill encouraged Cali's free expression, and as she matured, she expressed her own rules and limits in regard to sleeping in bed. If she accidently got kicked or moved during the night, she growled and snapped. Doug and Jill

The West Highland Terrier, from the Terrier Group.

tried hard during the night not to kick or move Cali. If Doug went to bed late, he would sleep on the guest bed to avoid a confrontation with Cali. Although neither Doug nor Jill were particularly happy with Cali's rule over the bedroom, neither had the heart to exert their will until Doug made the mistake of getting up to go to the bathroom one night and was bitten fairly severely when he attempted to get back into bed. A permissive household will become a dog-dominated household if a dominant puppy is chosen and not handled properly.

A Pug, from the Toy Group.

Another frustrating scenario is the submissive puppy in a disciplinary home. Gary, a gentle man whose deep voice, body stature, and mannerisms projected total confidence, chose Rocky for his beautiful markings rather than for his temperament. Every time Rocky and Gary interacted, Rocky would dribble urine. When Gary became frustrated with Rocky, his voice would get deeper and louder, and Rocky would become even more submissive and would urinate a flood. Gary sought help, which included a physical exam and learning how to interact with Rocky without triggering or encouraging his submissive behavior. The submissive urinating did subside considerably; however, Rocky still acted like a submissive dog and this detracted from their relationship.

The energy level of a breed is also a very important consideration. For high-energy, active individuals who want a breed to keep up with them in fun and fast activities, a Mastiff may be the wrong choice. If you are an excitable, nervous person who wants a dog as

Papillion puppies, from the Toy Group.

a quiet companion to relax at your feet in front of the fire while you read a book, a Dalmatian is probably going to be a disappointment. High activity is a desired trait in some breeds but may not be appropriate for all households. For example, the Border Collie is bred to be an energetic, intense, willful, watchful worker, which, if not directed appropriately, can cause stress and irritability in a nonsheep, relaxed household.

When Whimpy first started watching television, his owners thought that it was pretty cute. As time went by, Whimpy became so fixated on the television that he would sit in front of the set for hours, blocking his owners' view. The family actually avoided watching television because Whimpy was so annoying, and they could not get his attention unless the set was turned off. When the set was off, Whimpy became fixated on anything that moved, including other dogs, which he attempted to herd. Whimpy's herding attempts were interpreted as aggressive gestures by the other dogs, and his owner found taking him out for walks very unenjoyable. Whimpy needed a job to direct his energy. Luckily, Whimpy and his owner found that they had a common interest in herding, and by following this interest, Whimpy appropriately learned how to herd sheep instead of dogs. His television addiction was thus redirected. In another household, where the family did not have the time to follow their dog's natural interest, the story might not have had as happy an ending.

Different breeds have different energy levels based on the tasks that they were bred to perform. Before you choose a puppy, honestly evaluate your own interests and personality. Choose a puppy with an appropriate temperament and energy level for your household that is more likely to meet your expectations.

MALE VERSUS FEMALE

Choosing a dog or bitch is generally based on behavioral traits possessed by the individual sexes, and on personal preferences in appearance—besides the obvious plumbing differences. Living with one sex rather than the other may be more tolerable to certain people. For instance, some pet owners would not feel inconvenienced by a bitch's heat cycle but may find a dog that has a potential to mark turf with urine totally impossible to maintain in their home. The differences between the sexes regarding behavior and appearance are serious considerations when choosing a puppy housemate.

The female is generally a smaller version of the male in all breeds.

Appearance

In all breeds, the dog is generally a larger version of the bitch in height, weight, and bone structure. The dog is usually thicker or heavier in bone mass than the bitch. The dog's features, as a result of the heavier bone, may be described as more masculine or coarser than the bitch's features, which most people describe as elegant or feminine. The overall larger size of the dog is often accompanied with more dominant or assertive behavior. The larger puppy often rules the litter based on the pup's ability to physically command. The established power or social status that the puppy earns in the litter serves to develop his personality, which is often carried over to his human family. Because dogs are generally larger than bitches, aggression or dominance is reported more often by owners of males. However, owning a bitch does *not* guarantee that aggression and dominance will be eliminated.

The temperament and energy level of a puppy strongly contribute to his behavior. Different breeds have different energy levels based on the tasks that they were bred to perform. Terriers are known for their expression of "self-will."

Personality and Behavior

Size and the puppy's social position or ability to assert power may be attributed to the male hormone testosterone. Testosterone has also been linked to sexual behaviors that produce urges for dogs to roam in search of bitches and motivate marking or urinating on objects. Marking behavior is similar to graffiti—the art is left everywhere for everyone to see or sniff and serves to notify intruders that they are stepping on occupied turf. As in the case of aggression, the incidence of marking in the house is much greater with dogs than with bitches.

Another hormone that has behavioral effects is progesterone. The hormone contributes to the bitch's heat cycle and to subsequent behavioral changes, commonly known as PMS. Bitches may have one, two, or, in rare cases, three heat cycles per year, which presents a very odoriferous calling card to any dog within what seems like a 100-mile radius. Dogs have been reported to break through doors and windows to court and mate a bitch in season. The heat can be a bloody mess, and regarding behavior, the bitch

A Shetland Sheepdog, from the Herding Group.

Mixed breed puppies can be adorable pets, but the genetic arrangement of mixed breeds is like shuffling cards—you never know the outcome. If you don't have explicit requirements about appearance or behavior, the mixed breed can make a very loving, intelligent, wonderful companion.

may become irritable, aggressive, and depressed. An in-season bitch may exhibit nesting behavior or digging at the carpet in preparation of a litter and may become extremely attached to a particular toy that she carries around constantly. Some bitches experience false pregnancy after the heat, which may produce behavioral and physiological changes such as teat growth, milk production, and weight gain. The behavioral changes connected with the heat cycle may precede the actual heat by three weeks and may last as long as two or more months after the heat.

Although bitches may exhibit aggressive behavior, the incidence of aggression from bitches, when not in connection with protecting a litter, appears to be less when compared to that of dogs. The natural tendency toward aggression in the dog often makes owning or housing two or more dogs in the same household very difficult. Dog owners have reported fewer aggressive incidents or fights between neutered animals and between a dog and bitch as opposed to unneutered animals of the same sex. Neutering both sexes early in their development, between four and six months, is a common practice to reduce health risks, aggression, and behavioral problems.

While some pet owners may find a dog's propensity toward aggressive behavior a drawback, other people are encouraged by assertive, strong-willed behavior. Aggression is considered a real asset in terms of a dog being used as a watchdog. Undeservedly, the bitch is greatly underestimated in her ability to protect or to perform the duties of a watchdog. My bitches are the better watchdogs in that they are the first to the door and create quite a ruckus, while my males conveniently position themselves as backups. While my dogs have caused a few second thoughts with a friend or two who arrived at my house earlier than expected and attempted to enter, my bitches convinced the people that waiting outside was a much safer proposition.

Trainability

Many trainers will express a preference for a dog over a bitch when it comes to training. The trainer may believe that the dog is more likely to bounce back from a hard collar correction, whereas a bitch may sulk or become temporarily unresponsive to a strong correction. The trainer who uses methods that can make any dog sulk should reevaluate the method rather than choose a puppy based on suspected pain tolerance. Any intelligent dog will shut down to harsh training methods. Both sexes are trainable.

Intelligence

Another reason why people may choose between a dog and a bitch is because they believe that one sex is more intelligent than the other. There is no evidence that supports a significant difference in intelligence between the sexes, and those who claim that there is a difference may be tainted by their prejudice or preference for one sex over the other. Intelligence is more apt to vary individually rather than by the sex of the puppy.

CHAPTER 2

Where to Find
a Puppy

 There are many resources for finding a puppy, such as breeders, pet shops, humane societies, and newspapers. If you are looking for a purebred puppy, the best resources are the *AKC Gazette*, published by the AKC; *Dog World*, which can be found at most retail magazine stands; and *Bloodlines*, the United Kennel Club (UKC) publication. These organizations and publications list breeders and clubs involved with the various registered breeds and rare breeds. Breeders of purebred dogs can also be found through local kennel clubs, dog shows, breeder-referral services, and the internet.

BUYING A PUPPY FROM A PROFESSIONAL BREEDER

Most professional breeders offer two types of puppies, show quality and pet quality. Generally, there is a significant price difference between the two categories. The traits that determine pet quality should be minor, such as undesirable eye color or bite inconsistencies that may make the puppy uncompetitive in a dog show, and not structural faults or other problems that affect soundness of body structure and mind.

The purchase of the puppy, pet or show quality, should always come with registration papers and written guarantees. The parents of the puppy should be health screened for problems common to

A reputable breeder is committed to the betterment of the breed and takes raising puppies as a serious responsibility.

the breed, and the results should be available to you. A reputable breeder will require a spay/neuter contract for pet-quality puppies. Show-quality puppies have been bred from a champion lineage usually consisting of at least one champion parent.

Reputable breeders never place puppies in new homes before eight weeks of age, and the puppies are usually very well socialized by the time they are sent to their new homes. It is by far the best policy to purchase your purebred puppy from a breeder who is committed to the betterment of the breed and who takes raising puppies as a serious responsibility.

BUYING A PUPPY FROM A PET SHOP
Pet shops provide easy access to many different purebred and mixed-breed puppies. Generally, the puppies found in pet shops are specifically bred to supply a demand to potential consumers.

The demand is high, which gives the pet-shop suppliers incentive to breed many dogs. These suppliers produce so many puppies every year that they are known as "puppy mills."

Puppy mills, and thus pet shops, are not the ideal source for a puppy, for several reasons. The sheer number of animals produced in a puppy mill makes the individualized handling and socialization, which are critical to healthy emotional development, practically and economically unfeasible. Puppies produced from mills and sold to pet shops are generally not good examples of their breed, because the only criteria for breeding two dogs may be that they can breed. Therefore, the mill and pet-shop puppies are often the offspring of ill-tempered parents and possess faults such as poor structure, incorrect bites, or undesirable markings.

The mill and pet-shop environments usually consist of very tight quarters, where several puppies are placed together in the same cage. The puppies are rarely taken out of the cage unless potential buyers remove them. The puppies live in these cages twenty-four hours a day, very close to their droppings. This does not facilitate housebreaking, nor does it support the puppy's natural desire to keep a clean den. The small quarters hamper healthy exposure to the environment, movement, and exploration.

Puppies sold for profit from pet shops or puppy mills may not be the best examples of their breed.

The puppies arrive at the pet shops at the peak of their sensitive period and may live there until sold for four or more weeks—a period when the puppies should be exposed to many different situations for healthy and diverse socialization.

The poorly enriched rearing environment is emotionally unhealthy, contributes to behavioral problems, and hinders a puppy from becoming a sociable, well-adjusted domestic companion.

The price for a purebred puppy in a pet shop is usually comparable to and often more than the asking price from a reputable breeder. Although the purebred pet-shop puppies are often sold with registration papers, the documents only serve as identification to register the puppy with a registry for purebred dogs. Registration "papers" enable an owner to show the puppy and do not guarantee quality. Other than providing a forty-eight-hour health guarantee, a pet shop typically sells puppies without a contract or guarantee against hereditary problems. Some pet shops sell puppies with a ninety-day health warranty. The warranty is useless for the majority of hereditary problems that cannot be detected until the dog is one to two years of age.

Mixed breeds are often consigned to pet shops for better sales exposure. These puppies are not generally produced from planned breedings, but rather from accidental breedings. The owner who did not expect to be blessed with a litter and chooses not to spend the time and effort involved in finding good homes for the puppies sells them to a pet shop.

HUMANE SOCIETY

The humane societies are overfilled with animals of all ages waiting to be adopted. Although abandoned litters will sometimes find their way to the humane society, the majority of dogs are six months of age and older. There seems to be no discrimination by breed in the dogs that people abandon, although the rarer breeds by nature of their small population are less represented at a shelter. The cost for a puppy from a shelter is generally less than $100. Registration papers for puppies are not available, even if the papers were surrendered with the dog. Puppies are adopted out with a mandatory spay/neuter contract. Some societies neuter the puppy before he leaves the shelter.

While many a wonderful puppy has been adopted from a shelter, many puppies are deprived of ideal rearing conditions, and the older surrendered puppies have often been abandoned because they have behavioral problems such as nipping, biting, and destructive tendencies. The shelter is not always privy to the puppies' temperament. The previous owners of these problem puppies rarely tell the shelter the truth about why they are surrendering their puppy for fear that the puppy will be put to sleep or not adopted. The well-meaning and hard-working shelter volunteers are either inexperienced in accurately evaluating temperament, or the puppies do not exhibit problem behavior during their stay at the shelter. Many puppies that end up at a shelter may have been abused or may suffer from the trauma of being abandoned, which can result in behavioral problems and severe separation anxiety. Abandoned puppies need

Surrendered or abandoned puppies from the shelters often need special care and patience.

special care and patience. If you are thinking about adopting an older puppy from a shelter, you should be prepared for the possibility of behavioral problems.

THE OLDER PUPPY OR RESCUE PUPPY

A rescue puppy or a puppy that is being fostered until a proper home is found can be located through the local or national breed clubs. To get in touch with these clubs you can contact the AKC, UKC, or do some research on the computer networks. Puppies that have been abandoned or given up may come equipped with some unusual or problematic behaviors. These puppies often have been neglected at the least and abused at the worst. Rehabilitation can be a long, slow process requiring patient handling and social-ization. Even if a puppy has not been neglected and abused, he may exhibit unusual behavior in a new home. Some rescued pups may have come from homes where they were never let inside the house, and they may not know that urinating in the house is unac-ceptable. You will have to be very understanding and patient in teaching your puppy the new rules.

BUYING A DOG FROM A PART-TIME
OR ONE-TIME BREEDER

Part-time or one-time breeders often advertise their litters in the local newspaper. These litters are often a result of an acci-dental breeding. The probability of novice breeders produc-ing a quality litter by researching bloodlines and choosing com-patible parent dogs is low. Accidental breedings or puppies bred by novice breeders may or may not come with registration papers. The parent dogs are usually neighborhood dogs or are owned by the same person and happened to be available for breeding. These dogs are rarely selected based on desirable traits, and in fact they often possess *undesirable* char-acteristics. The novice breeder almost always advertises cham-pion bloodlines based on distant descendants in the pedigree.

The price of the pup-pies is generally high but usually drops as the litter gets older and eats more. These puppies do not come with any guaran-

Part-time or novice breeders rarely produce quality pup-pies in that they generally do little research in choosing compatible parent dogs.

Choosing a reputable breeder increases your chances of getting a puppy that will be the best dog for you.

tees or a contract. Many of the inexperienced breeders begin to place their puppies at six weeks of age because they are uneducated about raising a litter, and the work involved in caring for and feeding the puppies becomes overwhelming. There may be meager attempts at socialization even though the puppies spend most of their time in the backyard or garage. Although these puppies are not raised in the very best of conditions, they stand a better chance of becoming good companions than the mill–pet-shop pups.

Finding a reputable breeder of mixed breeds may be difficult unless you can find a breeder-referral service, generally at a veterinarian's office in your area. If you are looking for a mixed breed, newspaper ads are the most common resource.

Ideally, your research will lead you to several breeders who have litters available. Choosing a reputable breeder increases your chances of getting a puppy that will be the best dog for you.

Understanding canine body language tells you what a puppy is thinking.
Identifying behavioral styles is critical for matching puppies with owners.

CHAPTER 3

Choosing Your Breeder and Puppy

T he knowledgeable, reputable breeder is as interested in selling you a puppy that will be perfect as you are in getting the best puppy for your household.

YOUR FIRST CONTACT WITH A BREEDER

The first contact with a breeder is often described by people as a less-than-wonderful experience. If you were to walk into a pet shop to buy a puppy, the most difficult obstacle would be writing a check for the puppy. When you contact a breeder to purchase a puppy, you will be asked so many questions about your lifestyle and background that you may feel like a victim of the Spanish Inquisition. The reputable breeder interviews all potential buyers in the interest of finding suitable, permanent, happy homes for their puppies with people who are prepared for the responsibility and commitment of owning a dog. The seemingly nosey breeder who cares enough about his puppies' future to screen buyers will often be very supportive and resourceful in helping you with puppy problems.

INTERVIEWING THE BREEDER

The breeder should be an expert on his breed and should be honest about the positive and negative traits. After observing a Kuvas at a dog show, Harry and his three young children fell in love with the large, sheep-guarding breed. The first and only breeder whom Harry contacted sold him a puppy. As the Kuvas puppy grew, she began herding the children fairly aggressively and became increasingly difficult for the family to handle. Harry sought help and was surprised to learn, contrary to what his breeder told him, that the aggressive guard breed was not considered a children's dog. When I met the family, they were very disappointed and frustrated and were seriously close to giving the puppy away. If Harry had asked more questions and checked referrals, he might have been saved much frustration and disappointment. A knowledgeable, honest breeder can help you determine which breed or puppy is a good choice for your home.

To ensure that you are choosing a knowledgeable, reputable breeder, ask for referrals, then check them out. Inquire about the general physical health and temperament of your prospective puppy's lineage. Is everyone happy with their puppy and why? Are the puppies healthy? Has the breeder been supportive? Encourage these contacts to talk about the breeder and about the line's general behavioral traits. Inquire about temperament and hereditary problems for the particular breed and line so that there will be no surprises and you can make informed choices. All breeds have problems. There are no perfect dogs. However, some problems are easier to live with than others. For instance, bite problems where the teeth are not exactly straight are a lot easier to live with than temperament or health problems, such as juvenile cataracts in which the puppy may become blind by the time he is two years old. Compare the information from referrals with the material given to you by the breeder. If your breeder is reputable and honest, you will be told about the problems within the breed and the particular line.

COMMUNICATING CLEARLY WITH THE BREEDER

Before looking at puppies, discuss your expectations with the breeder. These should include physical characteristics that are important to you and the purposes you have in mind for your puppy, such as companionship, hunting, showing, etc. These expectations need to be clearly stated so that neither you nor the breeder will be disappointed. Breeders do not want to sell a show dog to someone who is not sure if he wants to show. In the same light, you would not want to buy a dog for hunting that may be a closet pacifist. Describe to the breeder your living environment and interests that you plan to share with your puppy. This information will be helpful in matching your personality with that of the puppy. The breeder, who has spent a lot of time with the pups, will have an intuitive feeling as to the personality of each puppy and the type of home that will be best suited for each one. The breeder who understands your expectations and preferences can make a more informed choice about which puppy will fit best into your household.

PUPPY CONTRACTS

If a contract is attached to the puppy, ask to read it before you look at the puppies. The round, soft eyes and wagging tail of a puppy can make any intelligent adult compulsively sign anything, only to experience remorse later. Some contracts are unreasonable and impossible to fulfill. Kathy bought a Bernese Mountain Dog with a contract that stipulated release from all responsibility on

Carefully read your contract and guarantees. Be open with your breeder so that he can help you pick the right puppy for your lifestyle and expectations.

the breeder's part in regard to structural problems if the puppy was fed any food besides the breeder's recommendation or if he was allowed to go up and down stairs before he was eighteen months old. Kathy lived in a four-level house, and the particular dog food mentioned in the contract was very difficult to obtain in her area. Read, understand, discuss, and clarify the terms of the contract before you look at the puppies. Have a third party or professional read the terms of the contract and help negotiate changes that you can all live with when the excitement of the new puppy wears off. If both parties are flexible and reasonable, a long and supportive relationship may evolve, not only between you and your puppy, but between you and the breeder as well.

After the breeder is familiar with you, your goals, and desires for a puppy, ask him to show you the pups along with a list of the strong and weak points of each puppy. If none of the puppies appears to be what you had in mind, do not settle for less. Remember—this puppy will be your roommate for twelve or more years, and if you and the pup are not compatible, everyone, especially the dog, will lose. If you do not find the puppy of your dreams in one litter, be honest and ask for other referrals.

BREEDER'S RESPONSIBILITY

The appearance of the puppies and the area in which they spend most of their time are good indicators of the breeder's dedication in raising a healthy, sound litter. The well-socialized puppy is outgoing and energetic. All of the pups should look well fed, clean, and groomed. The puppy area should be fairly clean. However, to expect the area to be immaculate is unreasonable with a large litter when droppings may occur every few seconds. The puppy quarters should not be isolated in the backyard or garage. If this is the case, ask if the puppies have been allowed in the house to experience household activities and noises. The knowledgeable breeder knows that puppies must be exposed to many different people, situations, and objects from a very early age.

At eight or nine weeks of age, the vaccination program should have been well started and recorded, in addition to testing for and controlling worms. Ask to see the sire and dam. There should be no excuse not to see the dam, while the sire has often deserted the

A knowledgeable breeder takes extra time to socialize the puppies.
There should be no excuse for not seeing the dam.
A good-tempered dam is tolerant of visitors.

The puppies and the area in which they live should be clean.

nest for other potential dams. The parents should have been screened for health problems such as hip dysplasia and progressive retinal atrophy. The results of any screening should be available for your review and confirmation. Contact the dog's owner and ask about the sire's accomplishments, traits, and previous offspring. Confirm that the sire is of sound mind and body. A healthy lineage, responsible breeder, and good rearing environment maximize your chances of picking the perfect puppy.

SELECTING YOUR PUPPY

Selecting a spouse with a good temperament is often an easier task than selecting a puppy. At least when you choose a spouse, you get to see and know your prospective mate through dating, whereas you choose a puppy on the first date. Most breeders will let you visit several different times and spend as much time as you need to make a decision about a puppy. Professionals are available for hire as consultants to help new pet owners pick out the right puppy. If you don't have a qualified counselor, at the very least, bring a good friend. Love at first sight is not always lasting or happy love. A helper who makes unbiased comments and may constrain you from blind love and choosing the first pup that falls into your feet is well worth the price of a consultation fee or a lunch.

There are circumstances where you may not have the luxury of choosing your own puppy, and you must rely on the breeder to send you a good puppy sight unseen. In this case, being honest with the breeder about yourself, your family, and your lifestyle is very important. Some breeders will send pictures and videos of the available pups, and you can state your preferences for particular ones. When a pup is bought sight unseen, the breeder should guarantee your right to send the pup back within a predetermined amount of time if the puppy does not meet your standards. One person who had severe reservations about buying a puppy sight unseen from me stated that he was actually relieved after the pup arrived. He fell in love with her immediately and did not have to go through the stress of indecision to pick out the pup from eight adorable puppies. A reputable breeder can be trusted to fill your order if you clearly and honestly give him an assessment of yourself and your expectations in a pet.

Ask the breeder to show you the entire litter,
as well as the individual puppies.

OBSERVING THE LITTER

If you have the opportunity to observe the litter and pick your puppy, you will want a clear idea of the traits that you seek in a puppy. The pup's physical structure is also important for building a good relationship. If your puppy does not appeal to you physically, the bonding process will be slower. A puppy with structural problems or physical traits that you find distasteful may not fulfill your expectations.

Handle and examine each puppy individually, and write down the structural points that you like or dislike; for example, pretty head, good bite, dark eyes, tail set where it looks like it belongs, unattractive markings, etc. Discuss each trait and how it conforms to your standard and/or the breed's standard. The experienced breeder has probably seen and followed the structural idiosyncracies and development in other pups or litters and is often able to predict which traits will be more likely to change for better or worse. Your expectations may include a large, bold male, and if you are not careful or don't check your list, the little male in the corner may steal your heart.

A good way to avoid the pitfall of being picked by a puppy, instead of *you* picking your puppy, is to stick to your guns and look at the whole litter, not just the ones that catch your eye from the start. Arrange to view the puppies after they have taken a nap, with a reasonable time lapse after the nap to allow the critters to wake up and drink a little. Ask the breeder to let you see the pups together, as well as separately.

If you have the opportunity, make several visits to the litter before you decide on a particular puppy. The physical and social developmental changes in young puppies occur practically hourly, and certainly daily. The small male that appeared to be laid back a few days ago may be a big bully on your next visit. If you can arrange several visits to the litter during the developmental phase,

Observe the interactions between the puppies. The puppies to which you should give less consideration are the ones that are off alone in the corner or that appear to be bullies.

Make several visits to the breeder so that you can observe the puppy as he develops both mentally and physically.

you will be able to observe physical and temperamental differences between the puppies and increase your chances of picking the right puppy for you.

View each puppy objectively, and write down your observations so that you do not forget which characteristics belong to which puppy. Include behavior that you may want to note, such as whether a puppy seemed frightened or unsure. Did the puppy have interest in you, or did the pup just whine? Was the puppy playful or lethargic? After you have evaluated and identified traits in each pup, watch the litter interact together. The puppies that you may want to consider with serious reservations are the ones that are noticeably different from their littermates. The pup that bowls over the entire litter with one swat of the paw may never stop trying to challenge your social position as leader. Contrary to the bully, the pup off to the side that avoids you may be timid and may spend his entire life under your bed.

Many breeders perform temperament tests as an attempt to predict the pup's adult personality in terms of submission, fearfulness, and dominance (see Chapter 4). Although there is little evidence that these temperament tests do indeed predict adult temperament in all pups, they are helpful in predicting the extreme temperaments, such as excessive fearfulness and confidence. If the breeder has not already done a temperament test, you may want to request that one be performed. If a temperament test is not available, discuss and compare your observations of body language and litter interactions with the breeder so that the two of you can identify traits that are most likely to be compatible with your personality and lifestyle.

If you use objective criteria, such as preferences in sex, temperament, and energy levels, you won't be sorry when you walk out the door with that special pup.

CHAPTER 4

Puppy Body Language

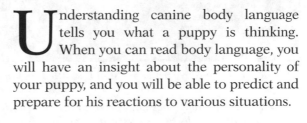

Understanding canine body language tells you what a puppy is thinking. When you can read body language, you will have an insight about the personality of your puppy, and you will be able to predict and prepare for his reactions to various situations.

BODY LANGUAGE OF THE DOMINANT PUPPY

The largest and strongest puppy is usually the most dominant of the litter. The dominant pup is the one that gets the best teat and that gets to lie on the top of the heap when the puppies huddle in a pile. The dominant puppy is often called the top dog, because during play, sex, aggression, or feeding, he is either on top or first in line. The dominant puppy stands erect and moves around fearlessly. He spends the majority of his time romping and bowling over littermates. The dominant puppy is usually the first to greet people and is aggressive in grabbing toys from his littermates. The puppy that earns and enjoys the position of litter leader will not be willing to relinquish this prime post readily and will need structure and an authoritative, strong, confident, experienced owner.

The dominant puppy spends most of his time bowling over his littermates.

The fearful puppy does not approach people readily. A fearful puppy will typically avoid eye contact and is often observed with his tail between his legs and his ears flat to his head.

BODY LANGUAGE OF THE FEARFUL PUPPY

Generally, the fearful puppy is observed off alone much of the time. Unlike the dominant puppy, the fearful puppy does not easily or comfortably approach people. A fearful puppy avoids direct eye contact and either throws quick glances or appears to look at a threat from the side of his eye. The ears of a fearful puppy are held close to his head, and his tail is usually held tight or tucked under his rump between his rear legs. Without early, positive intervention, the fearful puppy is at risk of becoming a problem dog. The fearful puppy needs empathy instead of sympathy and does best with an owner who can provide positive socialization, consistency, structure, and lots of patience.

BODY LANGUAGE OF THE SUBMISSIVE DOG

A submissive puppy is not necessarily a fearful puppy. The submissive puppy may be apprehensive when approached, but, unlike the fearful puppy, he is likely to approach people. The submissive puppy will often approach people with his head lowered in a tipped position as he either scoots along the ground in a sit position or rolls over on the ground to expose his belly and genitals.

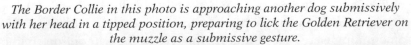

The Border Collie in this photo is approaching another dog submissively with her head in a tipped position, preparing to lick the Golden Retriever on the muzzle as a submissive gesture.

Typically, the submissive puppy urinates during the approach display and avoids eye contact. A gentle, sensitive, patient owner who is willing to provide positive training to build the puppy's confidence is a good match for a submissive puppy.

TEMPERAMENT TESTS

A temperament test can be a useful tool in identifying a puppy's behavioral style or reactivity level and potential ability to adapt to new environments. It can increase your chances of choosing a puppy that will fulfill your expectations. Some puppies inherently cope with the environment and stress better than others. A puppy that is prewired or born with a particularly low stress threshold exhibits submission, anxiety, or fear to novel stimuli. Fearful puppies have great difficulty adapting to the constantly changing environment. The opposite of a fearful puppy is one that is prewired with a high stress threshold and that exhibits extreme confidence and fearlessness. A puppy with a confident, fearless behavioral style exhibits dominant traits and often aggression.

Identifying behavioral styles is critical for matching puppies with owners. If a highly confident puppy is placed in a home that employs appropriate discipline, the aggressive tendencies could be snuffed out early and the puppy would in all likelihood develop with a good companion personality. On the other hand, if this same puppy were placed in a permissive home without discipline, he would probably develop into a fearless, aggressive dog. Temperament tests provide novel and mildly stressful circumstances in which a puppy's reaction or body language can be observed to predict temperament or behavioral style.

There are several tests that can be conducted in litters as young as seven to ten weeks of age. Temperament testing should be performed at any age after seven weeks. A puppy's personality changes constantly as a function of his environment and experiences, and the older the puppy is when testing is performed, the more accurate the information will be about his developing behavioral style.

The test below uses heart rate—a good predictor of an individual's behavioral style—as an objective measure with the traditional temperament test that was developed by several professionals for predicting potential working dogs. The differences in heart rate between puppies can give the tester important information. It takes longer for the heart rate of a startled, fearful puppy to return to normal than it does for the heart rate of a startled, bold puppy. Although the brave puppy may experience an increase in heart rate and may jump fifteen feet into the air, bark, and raise his hackles at an unexpected rattle of a bag, his heart rate will return to normal within approximately thirty seconds once the stimulus is removed. The fearful puppy will freeze, tremble, or try to escape, and it will take several minutes for his heart rate to return to normal after the stimulus has been removed. The amount of time that it takes for a puppy's heart rate to return to normal is a good indicator of his behavioral style and ability to cope with the environment.

The basic temperament test shown below was generated from the works and publications of Campbell (1975) and Bartlet (1982). Any behavioral test may be used with heart rate.

Testing Materials

A novel item for the sight/object test can be a hairpiece, wig, or any object that the puppy has not seen before and that can be tied to the end of a four-foot string and made to flop and move. A black piece of cloth, one inch wide and six inches long, with the ends sewn together, can be used as a tourniquet for the restraint test. A writing pen can be used to tighten the tourniquet. You can use plastic or paper sandwich bags that can be blown up and popped for the noise test. You will also need a stopwatch to measure six-second intervals of heartbeats.

The plastic bag in the background that is about to be popped is used to measure noise sensitivity.

Procedure

Two people are required. If you do not have an experienced temperament tester, practice the test exercises on a few adult dogs before you test puppies. Each subtest contains six possible reactions to score that describe confident and anxious behaviors. Low scores are an indication of confident reactions, and high scores indicate anxious reactions. The total possible points for the test ranges between eight and forty-eight. The puppies should be tested individually in a quiet room that they have not been in before and they should be isolated from the rest of the litter.

Once the puppy is brought into the testing room, measure and record his baseline resting heart rate. To do this, gently hold the puppy in place on the floor with one hand between his front legs on his chest cavity and the other hand gently on his rear leg at the stifle. You should be able to feel a pulse in both areas. Choose the pulse that is easier for you to feel and count. Once you find the pulse and are ready to begin counting, cue your assistant to activate the stopwatch. After every six seconds, your assistant should cue you to report the number of heartbeats that you counted during the six-second interval. This procedure does take practice for you to become accurate. The heartbeats are counted every six seconds for one and one-half minutes. The lowest heart rate from the six-second samples is used as the baseline or resting heart rate. The average resting heart rate for puppies in the testing I conducted was ten to thirteen beats per six-second interval. Heart rate is only measured in tests 3 through 8.

Once the resting heart rate is recorded, place the puppy in the center of the room a few feet away from the person performing the test.

1. Reaction to People. Kneel down and attempt to coax the puppy to come by quiet hand claps and a happy, encouraging call such as, "Puppy, puppy." Circle the number that best describes the puppy's reaction based on the list of behaviors.

Note: In tests 1, 2, and 3, it is important to determine from body language whether the puppy does not follow because he has something else to do or because he is apprehensive and trying to avoid people. If you and your assistant suspect that the puppy was just distracted or too busy exploring to come or follow, score the puppy with a lower score to indicate confident behavior.

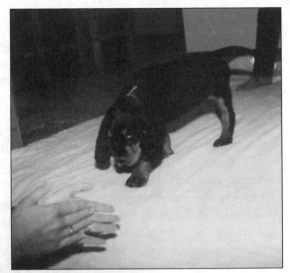

Call the puppy with soft hand claps to get his attention and measure his reaction to people.

The manner in which a puppy follows, or does not follow, a person may give some indication of his confident or fearful personalilty.

2. Encouraging the Puppy to Follow. Pick up and place the puppy next to your leg. Make sure that the puppy glances at your leg. Then, with a happy voice, encourage him to follow you as you walk away. Circle his reaction.

3. Petting the Puppy. Kneel next to the puppy and place him in a standing position next to you. Your assistant should start the stopwatch on your signal as you loom over the puppy and gently stroke him from head to rump for thirty seconds. At the end of thirty seconds, your assistant records the puppy's reaction as you release him and position your hands to measure his heart rate. As soon as you feel the pulse, cue your assistant to start the stopwatch. Every six seconds, your assistant cues you to report the number of heartbeats and records the number that you report on the evaluation sheet in columns 1 through 6 until the pulse is at resting rate or for one and one-half minutes, whichever comes first. The measuring and recording of the heart rate is done in the same manner for tests 3 through 8.

4. Cradling the Puppy Above Ground. Bend over and cradle the puppy a few inches from the ground, holding him under his belly with your fingers interlaced and palms up. Signal your assistant to start the stopwatch and elevate the puppy for thirty seconds. At the end of thirty seconds, your assistant should record the puppy's reaction as you release him and position your hands to count heartbeats.

For this puppy, cradling does not appear to be a traumatic event; however, his heart rate after the test may give a good indication about how he copes with different situations.

5. Rolling the Puppy on His Back. Kneel on the floor and gently place the puppy on his back. Signal your assistant to start the stopwatch. You hold the puppy on his back by placing one hand on his chest cavity, applying enough pressure to keep him on his back. Hold the puppy in place for thirty seconds. At the end of thirty seconds, your assistant should circle the puppy's reaction as you place him upright and position your hands to measure the heart rate.

Few puppies enjoy being rolled on their back initially. The amount they struggle and how they make eye contact can be important to the tester in predicting personality and reaction under restraint.

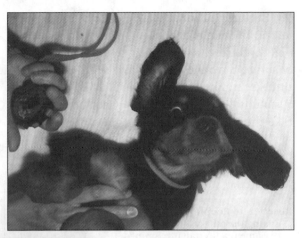

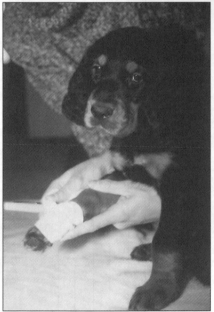

A piece of cloth is used to tighten around the puppy's paw to measure reaction to restraint and physical sensitivity.

6. Holding the Puppy's Paw. Place the tourniquet around the puppy's paw. Insert and twist a pencil until the cloth is fitted to the puppy's paw, tourniquet-style. Twist the pencil in complete turns, counting each turn, until the puppy responds with a whine or bite, or you have made five turns. Remove the tourniquet. As your assistant circles the puppy's reaction, position your hands to measure his heart rate.

7. Sudden Noise. Place the puppy in the center of the test area. Have your assistant blow up a plastic or paper sandwich bag and move away from the puppy. On your cue, the bag is popped to create a loud, sharp noise. Your assistant should circle the puppy's reaction as you position your hands to measure his heart rate.

8. Sight of a New Object. Place the puppy in the center of the test area and move away from him as your assistant tosses the object tied on a string in front of the puppy. Once the puppy is observed or believed to have seen the object, jerk the object three times to make it appear as if it is moving on its own. Have your assistant circle the puppy's reaction as you position your hands to take the heart rate.

Puppy Identification _____ Age_____
Sex:___ Resting Heart Rate (HR)___

Test Reaction	Score	HR	1	2	3	4	5	6 or more
Reaction to People								
1. Calling the puppy								
Came readily, tail up, jumped, bit at hands	1							
Came readily, tail up, pawed, licked at hands	2							
Came readily, tail up	3							
Came readily, tail down	4							
Came hesitantly, tail down	5							
Did not come at all	6							
2. Encouraging the puppy to follow								
Followed readily, tail up, underfoot, bit at feet	1							
Followed readily, tail up, underfoot	2							
Followed readily, tail up	3							
Followed readily, tail down	4							
Followed hesitantly, tail down	5							
Did not follow or went away	6							
Reaction to Light Restraint								
3. Petting puppy								
Went away	1							
Jumped, pawed, bit, growled	2							
Jumped, pawed	3							
Stands, licked at hands	4							
Cuddles up to tester and tries to lick face	5							
Rolled over, licked at hands	6							
4. Cradling puppy above the ground								
Struggled fiercely, bit, growled	1							
Struggled fiercely	2							
Struggled, relaxed	3							
Struggled slightly, settled	4							
No struggle, licked at hands	5							
No struggle, froze	6							
Reaction to Heavy Restraint								
5. Rolling puppy on back								

Test Reaction	Score	HR	1	2	3	4	5	6 or more
Struggled fiercely, flailed, bit, eye contact	1							
Struggled fiercely, flailed, eye contact	2							
Settled, struggled, settled, some eye contact	3							
Struggled, settled, little or no eye contact	4							
No struggle, no eye contact	5							
No struggle, straining to avoid eye contact	6							
6. Holding paw								
Putting on tourniquet	1							
One turn of tourniquet	2							
Two turns of tourniquet	3							
Three turns of tourniquet	4							
Four turns of tourniquet	5							
Five turns of tourniquet	6							

Reaction to Noise
7. Sudden noise

Reaction	Score
Listens, locates sound, walks toward barking	1
Listens, locates sound, barks	2
Listens, locates the sound	3
Startles, tail down	4
Cringes, backs off, hides	5
No apparent reaction, froze	6

Reaction to Novel Object
8. Sight of new object

Reaction	Score
Looks, attacks, and bites	1
Looks, barks with tail up	2
Looks curiously, attempts to investigate	3
Looks curiously, investigates, backs off	4
Looks, barks, tail tucked	5
Runs away, hides	6

Test Score Interpretation

Each puppy's test score in the litter is totaled and added to calculate an average litter score. Each individual puppy's score within the litter is compared to the average score of the litter. The puppies that scored a high average on the test relative to the other puppies in the litter and that exhibited longer heart-rate recovery periods to resting heart rate are identified as "anxious/fearful." For example, if the litter average was 33, and a particular puppy scored 44, and more than thirty-six seconds were required for the puppy to recover to resting or baseline heart rate whenever he was stressed in the test, the puppy is identified as anxious/fearful.

Puppies that score low and show a recovery rate of thirty-six seconds or less after stress are identified as "confident/fearless." The puppy that scores twenty-five and returns to a resting heart rate on the average of eighteen seconds is identified as "confident/fearless." Less emotional puppies return to their baseline heart rates in less time than puppies that are more emotional. Puppies that score close to the average litter score and return to a resting heart rate within thirty-six seconds are identified as "balanced puppies."

There may be situations where a test score indicates confident behavior, while the heart-rate recovery score suggests anxious tendencies. A good example of this inconsistency is a puppy that does not overtly startle when the plastic bag is popped, yet maintains an elevated heart rate for longer than thirty-six seconds. Puppies that fall into this borderline area may be good candidates for early positive intervention, because they may be at risk for developing anxious behavioral styles depending upon their environment.

In the absence of a formal temperament test or heart-rate measure, you can determine if a puppy recovers quickly from a startling stimulus when you understand the body language of a fearful or dominant dog. Other obvious signs or body language that indicate nervousness are panting, pacing, and sweating through the pads. The recovery period is possibly a better indicator of potential behavioral styles and of the puppy's ability to cope with his environment.

Although the temperament test does not tell you which puppy will be the super obedience trial champion or the best retriever, the test can give you insight into a puppy's potential temperament so that you may better choose the right personality for your lifestyle.

CHAPTER 5

The Best Age to Bring Your Puppy Home

The age at which a puppy is separated from his litter and introduced to his new home is very important to his future development. The optimal age to bring your new puppy home is ten to twelve weeks.

DEVELOPMENT

The six-week-old pup is too young to be removed from the litter. He is very dependent upon the litter and dam and has not learned the important social canine skills that he can only learn from his own dam and littermates. As a canine behavioral consultant, I have had the opportunity to collect many case histories on problem puppies and older dogs. My records indicate a definite correlation between aggression, fearful behavior, and separation anxiety and puppies being separated from their litter at six weeks of age and earlier.

Puppies that are separated from their litter before ten weeks do not get the opportunity to learn and practice appropriate canine body language associated with behaviors such as aggression, play, and sex. A puppy that is separated from the litter too early typically learns to be very mouthy and snaps when something displeases him, instead of posturing to ward off a conflict or submitting to authority. The puppy that remains in the litter and learns body language understands that snapping to get his way is met with a fast snap back from a littermate or the dam. The puppy also learns to inhibit snapping, because it only results in retaliation from the opponent rather than personal gain. Therefore, the puppy subsequently learns

*The six-week-old puppy is too young to leave the litter
even if he is weaned.*

*After seven weeks of age, the social structure becomes
highly observable and littermates begin
to establish their social hierarchy.*

how to use and interpret body language to ward off a snap or submit to authority.

At seven weeks of age, the social structure of the litter becomes highly observable, and littermates begin to establish a strong social hierarchy that is critical in the development of their future canine and human relationships. In the litter, puppies learn discipline and critical canine body language soon after weaning. As they become more playful and annoying, the dam's corrections become stronger and more meaningful. At the same time, the littermates establish a hierarchy of power and body language to communicate social position. The puppies learn how to read body language through playing, fighting, eating together, and passing in a close and limited area. These interactive experiences between the dam and other littermates prepare and teach a puppy how to exhibit appropriate body language to other dogs.

Learning about canine body language during the litter experience also helps your puppy understand human body language.

As the puppies become more playful and annoying, the dam's corrections teach the puppies about body language and limits.

Once a seven-week-old puppy learns from his dam or littermates that a growl signals displeasure, your natural, low, throaty voice of reprimand that sounds similar to a growl becomes a familiar signal to your puppy.

Although past literature has suggested that a six- to seven-week-old puppy will bond more strongly with people, recent research indicates that the bonding process is better influenced by a nurturing environment with a loving breeder and by the social behavior that a puppy learns in the litter. Therefore, a puppy does not have to leave the litter at or before seven weeks to maximize bonding. In fact, a puppy that is placed at seven weeks will be robbed of social experiences that are important for his development into a well-socialized adult dog. While socialization within the litter is important for the seven- to eight-week-old puppy, the familiar surroundings and the comfort of littermates are important to the eight-week-old puppy in helping him cope more efficiently and comfortably with the environment during a very sensitive developmental stage.

At eight weeks of age, a puppy moves into a fearful or sensitive period in which all of his senses become acute and he suddenly becomes more aware of his environment. At this time, a puppy can be traumatized relatively easily by the most ordinary events. Kola, an outgoing, rambunctious Bernese Mountain Dog puppy, arrived at her new home at seven weeks old. During her eighth week and sensitive period, Kola accidentally brushed past a broom standing against the wall. The broom fell and Kola startled. Thereafter, the mere sight of a broom produced a nervous reaction from Kola. The sensitive period, combined with added stress from a new environment and a sudden noise, had a profound effect on Kola. Any frightening event that occurs during a puppy's eighth week may have a profound and possibly lasting effect on his personality. This is a very inopportune time to remove a pup from the comfort and stability of his litter environment

During this sensitive phase, a puppy's immune system is further compromised by a visit to the veterinarian for the customary health check and puppy shots. Housebreaking, which is stressful for the new puppy owner, is more stressful for the eight-week-old puppy, particularly if his new owner is not taking the inevitable accidents on the carpet in the best possible frame of mind. A new home,

At eight weeks of age, the puppy enters a sensitive stage where the most ordinary events can traumatize him.

By ten weeks of age, puppies show more confidence, curiosity, and willingness to learn.

no matter how wonderful, is a drastic change for a young puppy and is inherently stressful, especially during the sensitive period.

The physiological system of the nine- or ten-week-old puppy is fairly mature, and the pup is generally past the sensitive period. Puppies begin to display independence and increased exploratory behavior at this time. At this age, a puppy steadily and gradually shows more confidence, curiosity, and willingness to learn. His ability to cope with a new environment is increased. An older puppy will whine and cry less after being separated from his litter, and he will be more prepared to learn. House training will be easier, because the pup will have better control of his own body. Consequently, interactions with your puppy will be more positive and nurturing at this age. In general, taking home an older pup will be less stressful for him, for you, and for your household. While nine and ten weeks of age may be an appropriate time for puppies to handle stress and learn about their surroundings, they still need gentle guidance and time to adapt.

Good preparation and planning for your puppy's arrival will help him manage the drastic changes more comfortably. Arrange to bring your puppy home on a weekend or when you have several days at home, and when the household is not in an uproar with visitors or other out-of-the-ordinary busy activities. The first few weeks in a new home are stressful on a puppy, and he will require lots of your attention and patience. Good planning can make the transition for you and your puppy much easier.

Plan a good time to bring your puppy home when you will have the time and patience to give him extra attention to help him socialize and adjust.

CHAPTER 6

Preparing for Your New Puppy

Preparing for your puppy's arrival includes puppy proofing your house, buying food care items, and finding a veterinarian.

PUPPY PROOFING THE HOUSE AND YARD

Puppies are curious little creatures. They are like a two-year-old child who gets into everything and eats anything that does not eat him first. Picking up prized possessions that you do not want to become teething toys and placing them out of your puppy's reach will save you a lot of running after your puppy. Knickknacks, shoes, socks, and kids' toys are all potential chew items.

Electrical cords, plants, and chemicals, which are very danger-ous to a puppy's health, can be attractive teething items and need to be out of his reach. Place dangerous plants and chemicals, such as antifreeze and cleaning products, on high shelves or in cabinets where your puppy does not have access. Unplug any unnecessary electrical cords. For unremovable objects, cords, or furniture, use a taste repellent such as Bitter Apple Gel to deter your puppy from chewing these items. Don't wait for your puppy to start chewing on electrical cords or furniture—use the deterrent as a preventive and reapply it often. When your puppy gets into his serious chew-ing stage, around four and one-half months, reapply the deterrent daily until he gets through the chewing and curious stage.

Preparing for your puppy includes puppy proofing your house.
Put away those items that are dangerous or irreplaceable.
Bitter Apple is a good deterrent for items that you cannot put away.

Restrict or block your puppy from areas where items are hard to remove from your puppy's reach and where deterrents cannot be used. Block any tight areas where your puppy can get stuck, such as behind the waterbed. Child safety gates are very useful for either keeping a puppy out of a particular room or keeping him in the room so that you can keep an eye on him and prevent chewing or pottying in the wrong places.

Your yard is another area that must be prepared and puppy proofed. A yard that offers no shade provides a perfect opportunity for your puppy to dig down into the cool earth for relief from the heat. Make sure that your puppy has shade and shelter from the weather, such as an insulated dog house. All possible escape routes, such as spaces between fence boards, must be closed, and a secure spring lock should be placed on all exits so that the gate is never accidently left open. Walk your yard and remove or protect objects that you don't want chewed, such as hoses, child toys, and lawn furniture. Research whether your plants and shrubbery are safe if your puppy begins to chew on them. Trees and shrubs can be protected from the teething puppy with light wire fencing.

A puppy will take almost anything into his mouth, including rocks and wood chips, so block off any areas that have decorative landscaping. At fourteen weeks old, Snorkel decided to snack on rocks in between meals. Snorkel, having eyes bigger than his stomach, was miserable for three days when he chose a rock that had a very difficult time passing. Many times, rock eating results in rock-removal surgery. If your puppy does eat rocks, consider clearing the yard of rocks, building a spacious pen, or fencing off rocked

Dogs naturally seek covered, denlike places for security.

areas. If you have a deck, crawl space, or other area in your yard that your puppy can crawl under or into, block all of the entrances so that he can't get stuck. The space underneath a deck may seem like a nice private den at first, but as your puppy grows, that space can become a trap.

When you cannot supervise your puppy and he has to be left alone, a crate is the safest and best place for your puppy. In a crate in the house, your puppy will be protected from weather, from children who may enjoy teasing a puppy through the fence, and from other dangerous activities. The crate is just one of the essential puppy-care items that you will want to purchase before your puppy arrives (see below).

PUPPY-CARE ESSENTIALS

Purchase your general-care items before your puppy arrives. One less errand to run gives you more time to be with your new puppy, to make good decisions about products, and to comparison shop.

Crates

The crate is an essential item that is the most effective tool for raising a well-mannered dog. By nature, dogs prefer denlike structures, and the crate provides the covered, isolated security that puppies naturally seek. The crate will keep your puppy out of trouble when you cannot supervise him. With proper reinforcement and training, your puppy will either come to love the crate, or, at the very least, tolerate it. The crate is a safe way to transport your puppy, particularly if you don't have anyone to ride with you. Using a crate in the car prevents your puppy from running around the vehicle and distracting you. If your puppy gets sick or has to eliminate, shredded paper towels are absorbent and can be placed on the floor of the crate to keep your puppy comfortable and your vehicle clean. The pup may even get engrossed in shredding the towels and be distracted from the trauma of the new experience. A loose puppy in the car or in your lap is an accident waiting to happen, as Kathy found out when her puppy's paw got stuck in the steering wheel when she was turning. The crate is also handy for safely transporting the older energetic puppy.

By nature, dogs prefer denlike structures, and the crate provides security for a puppy. The crate will also keep your puppy out of trouble when you can't supervise him.

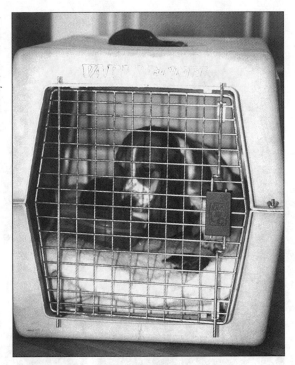

Crates can be purchased wherever a complete line of pet supplies are sold. There are various heights and widths of crates for different size dogs (see size chart). A crate that is just large enough for your puppy to lie down, turn around, and stand is a good fit. The crate should only be tall enough to allow your puppy to stand with his head at shoulder level. If you buy a crate to fit your ten-week-old puppy, it may not be big enough after he grows to full size. Although crates are very saleable used, you can avoid having to purchase several crates to keep up with your growing puppy by buying one that you anticipate will fit your puppy when he is full grown. You can place an adjustable, removable partition inside the oversized crate to make it smaller and more secure for your puppy.

Crate Sizes and Types. Commercial crates are made either of smooth, molded fiberglass or of wire. Fiberglass crates are completely enclosed with the exception of two small wire-mesh windows for ventilation on each side and a wire-mesh door. These crates are

Crates are made to house dogs as small as a Toy Poodle to as large as a Great Dane. There are several different styles to accommodate the various breeds and the dog owner's preferences.

specifically designed so that a puppy cannot chew or get caught on any sharp edges and are more similar to a den than the wire crates. They are easy to take apart for cleaning, and the top half fits snugly into the bottom half for easy transportation and storage.

The wire-mesh crate folds up compactly for easy transportation. A steel pan inside the crate provides a solid base and can be easily removed for cleaning. You can cover the top and/or any side(s) of the crate with a sheet or blanket to give your puppy additional security and privacy. You can also put a washable blanket or pad on the floor of the crate. However, remember that anything you place in the crate is fair game for being chewed up. Small stainless-steel water and food dishes specifically made for the crate are available.

SIZE CHART

Kennel Size	Dog Size
16"W x 21"D x 15"H	Toy breeds (toy poodle)
20"W x 27"D x 19"H	13-inch Beagle, Lhasa Apso
22"W x 32"D x 23"H	Shetland Sheepdog, Corgi
24"W x 36"D x 26"H	Labrador Retriever, Setter
27"W x 40"D x 30"H	Rottweiler, Greyhound
32"W x 48"D x 35"H	Great Dane, Borzoi

If you want to foster a positive relationship with your puppy and rear a well-behaved dog, the crate is a humane and critical piece of equipment for this purpose.

Equipment

Your next purchase should be a suitable collar and lead for the trip home in case you have to stop and let your puppy out to relieve himself. The safest collar, a "Greyhound collar," tightens up when your puppy pulls so that he cannot back or pull out of the collar. These collars are not choke collars. The collar is adjustable and, when fitted properly, it only tightens enough so that your puppy can't get his head out if he decides that he doesn't want to go in the same direction as you or he becomes frightened and

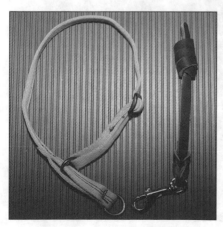

wants to run. An inexpensive fabric lead for your puppy to drag around as he gets used to the feel of it is more practical than leather.

The Greyhound collar is shown on the left. Another important piece of equipment is the handle, which is a short leash that allows you to keep a "handle" on your puppy's behavior when he is in the house and not wearing a leash.

Toys

Good chewing items for your young, curious, teething puppy are essential. In helping a customer choose appropriate toys for her five-month-old puppy, I picked up a nice plush squeak toy. My customer said that her puppy loved the stuffed toys but destroyed them within a week's time. I tried to explain that a good toy appropriately channels the puppy's chewing, directing the destruction away from the sofa. In the end, replacing toys weekly is much cheaper than replacing the sofa. An indestructible toy is of little value if your puppy does not like it. Dog toys are for the puppy's pleasure, and if pouncing and ripping them apart is part of the game, the toy has served well.

There are many different types of safe toys, such as plush toys, Gumabones, rope bones, sterilized bones, and Kong's. Hard rubber toys, such as the kong toys that have holes in the middle, are also good for hiding special treats inside to keep your pup's interest. Peanut butter or cheese spread can be smeared on the gumabones or stuffed in the sterilized bones and Kong toys to motivate your puppy

Appropriate, safe chew toys are essential for the young teething puppy to channel his need to chew as his teeth cut through the gums.

to chew on these items. Ice cubes are good chew items for teething discomfort, or chew toys can be put in the freezer for fifteen minutes to help relieve the itch and pain of teething. Latex toys keep your puppy busy but are not as good for gnawing purposes. Puppies enjoy tossing these toys, however. If tossing turns into ripping apart, supervise your puppy's play so that he doesn't swallow the pieces.

Puppies love rawhides. Concern has been raised about the danger of giving puppies rawhides, because they become soft after they are chewed, and the puppy may attempt to swallow a large piece. Although the rawhide material is safe for consumption, the large pieces can become stuck in your puppy's throat and choke him. Do not leave your puppy unsupervised with rawhides if he has a tendency to swallow large pieces.

Hoofs are generally safe gnawing objects, and you can spread cheese or peanut butter inside for a really special treat. Periodically check the hoof to make sure your puppy is not chewing on sharp edges or pieces. Knuckle marrow bones from the butcher or the natural bones that are sold at pet-supply stores are chew items that puppies really enjoy. Steak or meat bones are dangerous for your puppy, because he will be able to break off and swallow sharp pieces.

A tennis ball inside a sock makes a fun toy for your pup to toss around and for the two of you to play tug-of-war. If your puppy gets confused between his play sock and your sock, just exchange the play sock for yours and he will learn quickly which socks are toys. The play sock has your puppy's scent, and your socks have your scent. I found that there is one advantage to letting my puppies play with abandoned socks. After twenty-five years of puppies, my family is almost trained to put their socks away!

Racquetballs and pantyhose are dangerous for your puppy. A racquetball can compress inside your puppy's mouth and obstruct his airway, and hosiery can be swallowed and get caught in your puppy's intestines.

Encourage your puppy to play with his toys, and keep him interested by supplying him with a variety of toys. My dogs have a full toy box, and half of the fun with the toys is pulling them out and later helping me put them back in the box. Rotate the toys every week to add variety. The rotation not only keeps your puppy from getting bored with his toys, but the toys will last longer.

Food

Puppies can be very sensitive to dietary changes, so it is important to know which brand of food your puppy was eating. Many breeders send at least a day's supply of food with the pup. If you plan to switch brands, purchase a small bag of the food that your breeder was using to mix in with the new brand. This will help prevent your puppy from getting diarrhea. A good plan for changing diet is to start by mixing a small quantity of the new food—no more than 10 percent of the total amount fed—to the breeder's food. Slowly decrease the breeder's brand while you gradually increase the new food each day.

Food and Water Bowls

The size of your puppy's food bowl is determined by the amount of food that you anticipate your puppy will eat at maturity. Plastic bowls are not recommended, because they can sometimes affect the black pigment on your puppy's nose. Heavy ceramic bowls for both food and water decrease spillage and bowl tossing by the playful and/or clumsy puppy.

Treats

In the dog-food section of the store there is always a large variety of treats and biscuits. Biscuits are good treats for asking your puppy to perform simple tasks such as sit. Special high-value treats such as liver or beef jerky should be used for training or calling your puppy to come. A few delectable treats a day for training, or every time you call your pup to you, will endear him to you quickly. Treats can also be used to turn negative experiences such as grooming into positive sessions. Most puppies are not thrilled to stand or lie still for grooming, whereas a few well-timed treats may make standing still for brushing much more pleasurable.

Cleaning Products

Good planning includes having the proper cleaning products on hand before accidents occur. To expect that your puppy will not have any accidents is unrealistic. You will need a good carpet cleaner, a pet-waste neutralizer, and a repellent, all of which can be found at pet-supply outlets. A general cleaner will take out the

The size of your puppy's food and water bowls is determined by the amount of food and water that you anticipate your puppy will consume at maturity. Plastic bowls are not recommended because they sometimes affect the black pigment on a puppy's nose.

All members of the family should offer the pup a treat.

odor so that you can't smell the waste, and a neutralizer will eliminate the odor for your puppy. If your puppy can smell the odor, he will be stimulated to use the area again. After the area is cleaned, a dog-repellent product will prevent your puppy from being attracted to the area. A general spraying around the house with the repellent is also helpful. The spray will not repulse your puppy from being in the room—it will just make the carpet an undesirable place for him to sniff and relieve himself.

Some lifestyles or situations dictate that paper training is easier than training a puppy for the outdoors at the start. If this is the case, get a good supply of papers and place them over a plastic drop cloth so that the urine does not soak into the floorboards. If the odors become a part of the floor, your puppy will be attracted to the area even after the papers are removed. Plan the area where your puppy will be allowed access, and close the doors or purchase child gates to block the rooms where your puppy will not be allowed.

PUPPY IDENTIFICATION

The energetic, curious puppy will begin to expand his world by exploring the environment independently, and a hole in the fence is a temptation that most puppies cannot resist. Pick a name for your puppy right away so that you can prepare identification for him in case he gets out of your sight or feels adventurous and slips away accidentally. The safest and most complete identification is comprised of tags and a tattoo or microchip. While tags give people immediate information to get your puppy back home, the tags alone are not fail-safe because they can fall off or your puppy can lose his collar. A backup identification system, such as a tattoo or microchip, will always be with your puppy. The tattoo or microchip is usually a number, and when the number is filed with its respective registry, the dog's demographic information is kept on file and is available to veterinarians and humane societies. Shelters and many veterinarians now regularly scan found dogs for microchips or tattoos to locate the lost dog's owner and will have information about identification for your puppy.

GROOMING SUPPLIES

The grooming supplies that you will need depend upon the size and coat type of your puppy. Your breeder or reputable pet retailer should be able to suggest the best items for you to purchase. You want to start grooming your pup right away to get him used to baths, toenail clipping, brushing, and handling. Even if your puppy doesn't need a brushing yet, you will be wise to get him used to being brushed from the start. It is much easier to teach a 10-pound puppy about grooming than a 120-pound hulk.

If you do not plan to groom your puppy yourself, you may want to research and contact a good groomer who will set aside some special time for your inexperienced pup. Ask the groomer about proper equipment and maintenance in between appointments to keep your puppy well groomed and healthy. If you plan to groom your puppy yourself and his coat requires scissoring or clippers, ask a groomer or your breeder to help with the first session, because clipping and scissoring a moving target takes some practice. For a fee, a groomer may be willing to teach you how to groom your puppy.

Your grooming-equipment purchases should include toenail clippers, blood stop for nails, a toothbrush, and doggy toothpaste. Clipping toenails and brushing your puppy's teeth are important for raising a healthy dog. Your breeder, groomer, or veterinarian can show you how to brush teeth and clip nails.

THE PHYSICAL

You will need to arrange an appointment for your new puppy to have a physical. You are entitled to a forty-eight-hour rescission period from your breeder, allowing time for a veterinarian to examine your new puppy for illnesses, disorders, or congenital defects such as heart murmurs. The recession period entitles you to return the puppy for a full refund if the veterinarian finds him unhealthy.

Finding a Veterinarian

Ask for referrals from friends or from the humane society, or contact the American Veterinarian Medical Association. Feeling comfortable with your veterinarian and the staff is important. Ask about office policy for checkups, emergencies, general care, and billing so that you do not get any surprises during a critical time. If you do not have a good working relationship with your veterinarian and the staff during routine visits, emergencies can become disasters. Go to the clinic to make the appointment so that you can check out the facility, the staff, and their qualifications. Although most people do not interview a veterinarian before their first visit, there is nothing wrong with doing so for your peace of mind. The veterinarian who is compassionate, who takes time to answer your questions, who treats your puppy like he is the star patient, who is willing to refer you to specialists, and who isn't grouchy if you call for an emergency in the middle of the night or on Christmas day is very special. A good veterinarian has a knowledgeable, competent, friendly staff who can be a good resource for other essential information about dog care and products.

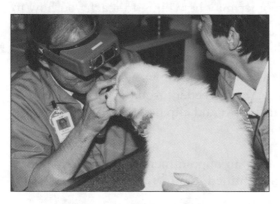

Arranging for a veterinarian to examine your puppy within two days of purchase is required by most contracts.

CHAPTER 7

Bringing Your Puppy Home

Arrange for your puppy to start his trip home on an empty stomach or several hours after a light meal to reduce motion-sickness problems and minimize travel stress. Plan as short a trip as possible, avoid rush-hour traffic, and run your errands before you pick up your puppy. When flying your puppy on an airline, a direct flight is much easier on a puppy than a layover or a plane change.

SHIPPING A PUPPY BY AIR

Flying a puppy on a commercial airline cannot always be arranged conveniently. Weather conditions, temperature, and availability of space will dictate whether an airline will book a puppy on any particular flight. Reservations can be bumped at the discretion of the airline, and you may not have a guarantee that your puppy is getting on a particular flight until forty-five minutes before the flight is scheduled to leave. If you are picking your puppy up at the airport, call to confirm that your pup got on the flight.

The extra cost to fly a puppy on a nonstop flight with special services is well worth the money and the safest way for your puppy to travel on an airline. Nonstop flights and special counter-to-counter services eliminate much of the time spent on the tarmac waiting for several takeoffs or loading and unloading. The

When you arrive home with your puppy, take him outside where you will expect him to relieve himself, such as the backyard. Then, introduce him to his new toys and chew items.

less time your puppy spends traveling, the lower the risk that something will go wrong. Remind the person who is shipping your puppy to mark the crate clearly with the destination and origin, and to put both his and your address and telephone number on the label. When you get your puppy, carry him out of the terminal in his crate to an area where he can relieve himself and have a drink of water. Place his lead on and give him several minutes to walk around and get his ground legs before the drive home. Bring along paper towels to clean up messes that may have occurred during the flight. Also, take along cleanup bags so that you can clean up after your puppy on public grounds. All dog owners should be committed to picking up after their dog in public places. An easy way to pick up feces is to carry plastic bags. You can place your hand in the plastic bag as if it were a glove and pick up the droppings without touching them. Pull the bag over the feces, tie it shut, and dispose of it in a waste container. Disposable plastic gloves are another good option. If dog owners don't become more conscientious about cleaning up after their dogs, dogs will continue to be banned from more and more public places.

DRIVING HOME WITH YOUR PUPPY

If you don't have someone to hold your puppy while you are driving, place him in his crate for the ride home. The crate is the safest way to travel in the car with a puppy. Bring along a cooler with ice cubes to place in the crate dish so that your puppy can have small amounts of water during the trip. Stressed puppies need water, and ice cubes provide enough water without filling a puppy's bladder too fast. Place a safe chew toy in the crate for your puppy to gnaw. If you have a long ride, plan a couple of stops for your puppy to get out, stretch, and relieve himself. If your puppy whines or barks in the crate, ignore him and chances are he will fall asleep for the rest of the trip home. If your puppy's barking is too distracting, bang on the top of the crate and tell him "quiet." No matter how sorry you feel for the little one, do not take him out of the crate until he is quiet, or you will set yourself up for crate problems later.

Show your new puppy where he is to relieve himself.
After he has done a little exploring and emptied his bladder,
kneel down and call him to give him a treat. A tasty treat from
each family member is a good way to introduce him to everyone.

INTRODUCING YOUR PUPPY TO HIS NEW HOME

When you arrive home, take your puppy out of his crate in the area where you expect him to relieve himself, such as the backyard. When he relieves himself, calmly praise him. Follow him around inside the house as he explores to prevent him from getting into trouble. Show your puppy to his water and food. If he drinks or eats, take him out within half an hour. If he does not relieve himself half an hour after a food and water binge, place him in the crate for another half hour and try again. Review the chapter on house-training for reinforcing good toilet habits from the very start.

INTRODUCING THE PUPPY TO THE FAMILY

Sit on the floor with your puppy and introduce him to his new toys and chew items. Have family members sit on the floor, and let your puppy go up to each person on his own. A delectable treat from each family member to entice him over is a good tactic. Call your puppy's name as you offer him a tasty treat. When you use a treat, your puppy will learn his name after just a few times of calling him. My puppy, Snorkel, learned his name with just three repetitions of praise and a liver treat. After the third liver treat, he would come running as fast as he could from anywhere in the house when he heard his name.

To teach your puppy his name and to come, say his name and tell him "come" as you show him a treat by placing it right in front of his nose. Draw the treat close to your body so that he has to come close to you to get the treat. Your puppy's eyesight and olfactory systems are still developing, and you may need to move your hand around a lot to help him track and follow the treat. When he comes to you, praise him and give the treat. The fastest way to a dog's brain is through his stomach. I give all of my new puppies delectable treats such as cheese, liver, hot dogs, and other specialty items from the start to accustom them to different foods. This allows me to

To teach your puppy his name and the come command, show him a treat, call his name, and command "come" as you draw the treat close to you. Your puppy will follow the treat. When he is close, give him the treat and praise him.

switch motivators occasionally during training. My husband started giving two of my puppies a carrot when they became curious about what was in his hand on his daily walks through the yard to the horse barn. The puppies chewed the carrots out of curiosity at first, while the older dogs spit the carrots out. The puppies that got carrots as youngsters still enthusiastically follow my husband to get their morning treat, while the older dogs turn up their noses. Like a young child, if your puppy does not experience the taste of different foods early, he may become finicky about new foods.

Never grab at your puppy or pick him up to hand him over to another person. Grabbing and picking up to hand puppies over to people does not promote confidence. If your puppy has no choice in being passed from person to person, he may become insecure and fearful. Let your puppy go to each person before that person picks him up. If he doesn't go over on his own, give him time and keep trying with a tasty treat. If you do pick up your puppy and he struggles and yells, do not put him down until he relaxes or gives up fighting. If you put him down while he is struggling, you are reinforcing his fighting when he does not want to be handled by rewarding him with letting go when he fights. There are times, such as during grooming, where he will have to be handled against his wishes, and you do not want to promote his fighting with you to get released.

Regardless of how energetic a puppy seems, he can become overwhelmed by the whole experience of leaving his happy litter and traveling to a new world. Young puppies sleep a lot, so make the introductions and playtime short to give him the opportunity to relieve himself and nap in the crate. Prevent problem behavior from the start by placing your puppy in the crate for naps if you cannot keep an active eye on him rather than giving him the run of the house.

INTRODUCING THE PUPPY TO OTHER HOUSEHOLD DOGS

Although you may have experienced love at first sight toward your puppy, this may not be the case when your other dog sees him for the first time. A resident dog often perceives his house, yard, toys, and family as his territory and may feel a need to aggressively defend his possessions from intruders or a new puppy. Occasionally, older dogs may appear frightened or apprehensive of young puppies because the odor of a puppy may be so novel and strange that your dog may not comprehend that your puppy is a canine. Your older dog may be so confused or threatened by the wiggly little creature that he may lash out with a snap.

Even if you are fairly certain that your older dog will not have a negative reaction to your new puppy, it is a good idea to exercise caution. Arrange to have a helper. Before you bring your puppy into the house, pick up all items that your older dog may perceive as his possessions, such as toys, bones, and food dishes. Contain your older dog in another room or in the yard so that you can bring your puppy into the room without interference. When you are ready to introduce your puppy, place him in his crate. Introduce each animal individually, one at a time. Attach a lead to your older dog and let him sniff the puppy through the crate openings. If your dog paws at the crate, correct him with a pop of the lead and a "stop it." You may need to pop the lead several times before he ceases pawing at the crate. Letting pets sniff through the vents will not only get the heavy, obnoxious sniffing over with, it is a safe way to prevent injury and allow time for both animals to calm down a bit from the novelty of the event. If you note any fear or aggression, don't let your puppy out of the crate until the other animal calms down or is corrected and is responding appropriately.

If you are unsure how your older dog will react, or if he does display aggression, a head halter is a good investment to control his behavior. The halter is very similar to a horse halter; however, the strap that fits around the dog's muzzle can be adjusted and tightened so that he cannot open his mouth wide enough to bite. This device is also an excellent precaution if you do not have someone to help you introduce the dogs.

In the absence of aggression, place your older dog on a sit-stay. When he settles down have your helper take the puppy out of his crate and attach a lead. Your helper should sit your puppy a foot or two in front of your older dog to give the dogs an opportunity to make eye contact and orient. To start your older dog investigating, form a touching chain by placing a hand on each dog and petting them at the same time. If you touch your puppy, your older dog will become curious and will want to investigate the new crea-

The touching chain will encourage your dog to investigate and places your scent on the new puppy, which may help ward off an attack.

Letting your older dog sniff the puppy from your lap gets the heavy sniffing out of the way so that your older dog does not chase and paw your puppy.

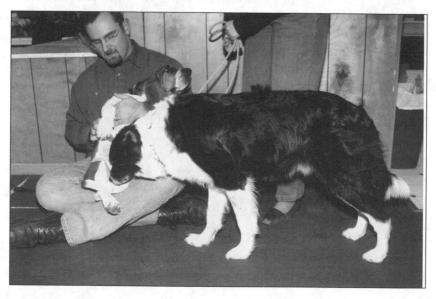

ture. The touching chain also places your scent on the puppy, which may help ward off a possible attack. Have your helper place your puppy in his lap, tummy up, and let your older dog sniff his underside and genitals. If you place your pup on his back, you will eliminate the older dog from chasing or pawing your puppy to get to the underside—the most sought-after sniffing area. If the greeting is amicable and their tails are not tucked, their bodies are not stiff, and teeth are not bared, a little play romp on lead is acceptable. Keep the play period fairly short and keep watching for potential altercations. You don't want either dog to get too tired or irritable, which may provoke a snap and lead to a pattern of tiffs.

If the inexperienced puppy is very obnoxious and fearless, he may not heed the warnings or signals from the older dog to settle down. If your puppy ignores signals or body language to stop playing, he may receive an angry bite. Conversely, the older dog may also relentlessly badger the puppy to play, making him apprehensive or fearful. Leave the leads on both dogs, and monitor their play or interactions until your puppy is understanding and responding to your older dog's language.

Introducing your resident dogs to the new pup on neutral territory or in a place other than your home will often prevent aggression associated with territorial behavior that can interfere with a positive first-time greeting. However, meeting on neutral ground does not necessarily eliminate territorial behavior when you get home, so you will need to continue to exercise caution by keeping the leads on and monitoring interactions.

Although your dogs may have played well together the first time, your older dog may snap at your puppy out of annoyance or to ward him off, but with no intent to hurt him. Some dogs may welcome the new pup into the home at first, and then, when the pup becomes rambunctious or takes a little too much liberty with toys or territory, the older dog may begin to resent him. In my house, any new dog is welcomed by my dogs and given a lot of leeway for three days. After three days, my dogs are very prompt to teach the rules and set the social position in the pack, which usually places the newcomer on the bottom of the heap.

When Snorkel arrived at my house, he thought that he had

Meeting on neutral ground does not guarantee that when you get home your older dog will accept the new pup into the house unconditionally.

entered doggy heaven. He immediately decided that the five dog bowls meant a smorgasbord, the three bitches were his harem, and the two males were his compatriots in keeping the harem in line. My five dogs had a high tolerance level at first, but when Snorkel got too close to an occupied food bowl, chew toy, or bone, he was met with a loud bark, then a growl, and finally an air snap. Snorkel found this amusing, particularly with the bitches, and would immediately go into a play bow. He would then bark and dart toward them. If the bitch ignored him, he would mount her. The bitches quickly added a lunge with their air snaps that sent Snorkel on the run across the room. If he returned, they repeated the lunge and stepped up the growling and snaps as they ran after him a short distance. This immediately cooled his desire to sexually molest the bitches. When Snorkel got too annoying for Skinner, a formidable ninety-three-pound male, Skinner would slap

Even if your dogs appear to be friendly and start to play, keep the lead attached in case they change their minds.

Snorkel to the ground with his paw and hold him there, growling intensely until Snorkel cried uncle. Neither Skinner nor the bitches ever attempted to bite Snorkel, and as long as there was no sign of carnage, I allowed my dogs to set their rules within their pack.

If your older dog snaps at your puppy but does not connect, do not correct your older dog. He is communicating to the puppy, and your puppy must learn to heed such warnings. If your older dog delivers an actual bite, the puppy probably did not pay attention to the warnings and your older dog stepped up the correction. If your puppy continues to ignore the meaning of the first bite, multiple bites will ensue, and you will need to intervene. These animals must be supervised closely, and your older dog must be corrected for the overly aggressive correction.

Scuba was not as tolerant of Snorkel as the bitches were and backed up his initial air-snap warnings with a harrowing growl and very fierce displays of teeth. Perceiving that Snorkel did not take the initial warnings seriously enough and that Scuba's next step was a serious bite, I intervened before a fight started with a sharp "stop it." I popped both of their collars, then distracted Snorkel with something else to do. Snorkel, having received a correction from both of us, gave up trying to torment Scuba. Supervise your puppy so that you can intervene when he becomes too annoying to the older dog. Do not wait for a fight to begin. When your older dog makes eye contact and growls at your puppy, and you suspect that a bite is coming, give a strong reprimand and command for the older dog to "settle." Give your puppy a verbal correction and distract him from your older dog with a toy, or crate him if he gets too wound up pestering the older dog.

Reading and interpreting the body language of your dogs so that you know when to step in requires an observant, trained eye and knowing your own dogs' communication. Glaring and a stiff body backed up with a serious growl indicates a fight. If you are unsure about the meaning of the interactions between your dogs, you would benefit by seeking a professional who could observe your dogs.

Debbie had just bought a new Golden Retriever puppy to keep her older Golden bitch company. When the puppy became obnoxious, the bitch would give the puppy the riot act by placing her mouth on his neck and growling. The puppy would scream and Debbie would run to comfort him. Her puppy would continue to scream in her arms for a good five minutes as she consoled him. Although there was never a mark on the puppy, Debbie became really concerned that her bitch would hurt him and contacted me. I spent an hour observing their play and general interactions. I was able to assure Debbie that the bitch was teaching the puppy the rules and did not intend to hurt him. However, if Debbie kept intervening or separating them, the puppy would not get the messages that the bitch was sending. I instructed Debbie not to console her puppy and only to interfere if the bitch increased the correction. The puppy has aptly learned to tread softly when the bitch gives a warning snap or growl. Debbie learned to let them communicate, and the two dogs are great buddies. If you don't feel in control or are uncertain about being able to control the situation, call a professional.

There are two schools of thought about managing or living

with the social structure of canines. One school of thought pro-
fesses that the dogs work out their social structure themselves
without interference, even if a fight breaks out. Although I agree
that the dogs need to work out the social structure between themselves, the situation must not get out of hand. If ranking-order tiffs
only involve verbalizations, body language, and air snaps, there is
no reason to interfere. However, I do not advocate empowering a
dominant dog by allowing him to be pushy or permitting fights
that are obviously going to cause injury to one or both of the dogs.
Would you allow an older sibling to beat up a younger one without
interference? In my pack of dogs, *I* am the final authority. If a situation begins to get out of control and I suspect that a fight will
ensue, I command the dogs to "knock it off," which means for
them to separate. If they don't separate immediately, I correct
them with a sharp pop away from each other. Both dogs are then
commanded to settle so that they can calm down. I enforce a fif-
teen- to thirty-minute settle until they decharge and the fight is
defused.

In cases where dogs can work out their own disputes without
injury, the message will be much more effective than any interference or point that you attempt to communicate. Recently, I
observed Snorkel badgering and lunging at Casino, causing quite a
ruckus. Casino was displaying body language suggesting that
Snorkel should stop, but Snorkel was ignoring her messages and
she wasn't backing up her threats. Piper, a very dominant bitch
and clearly agitated, charged after Snorkel from across the yard
and bowled him over to the ground with quite the verbal reprimand. When Piper finished her discussion with Snorkel, he got
up, shook himself off, and found a toy to pounce on instead of
chasing Casino. Piper communicated "stop it" much more effectively than I could have, and my intervention was unnecessary.
However, if any of the dogs' body language had indicated serious
aggression, I would have intervened.

The social structure between dogs changes constantly. As your
puppy grows, develops, and gains confidence, fighting may erupt.
Do not leave your puppy alone with older dogs until you are sure
that they are best buddies and your puppy can hold his own if a

fight breaks out. To prevent fights, make sure that you supervise playtime, feeding time, and any situation that causes the dogs to become very excited or to compete with each other, such as running to the door when someone rings the bell. In these excitable situations, it is important to use obedience training to obtain and maintain control of the dogs and to eliminate fights caused by competition for possessions and attention.

CATS

Puppies are naturally curious about cats. When introducing a puppy to a cat, first place your puppy in the crate for the cat to sniff. When the sniffing is over, place the cat in the crate to give your puppy a chance to sniff the creature. At this point, most cats will exhibit aggressive hissing and swiping, which will teach your puppy that the cat can be a formidable foe. The crate will prevent the cat from actually making contact with your puppy. When the hissing and clawing cease, place your puppy on a lead to prevent him from lunging at the cat, or take your puppy out of the room before you let the cat out of the bag, so to speak. You do not want your puppy loose in the room when you let the cat out of the crate, because in all likelihood, the cat will run and you don't want your puppy to chase the cat. If your puppy starts to chase or lunge at the cat, command "leave it,'" and pop him back with the lead. If he does not pay attention to the collar correction, have a squirt bottle filled with cold water handy. Pop your puppy back on the collar and squirt him in between his eyes with the water. Immediately after delivering the correction, command your puppy to sit, and gently place him in a sit so that you can praise him for good behavior. After your puppy misbehaves and receives a correction, always give him an alternative behavior like "sit" to earn your approval.

The cat will probably stick to high ground for awhile. If your puppy attempts to jump up to get to your cat once his lead is off, let the cat display his defenses to discourage the puppy. Most dogs will keep a safe distance from a cat that does not run. If your cat is declawed or will not stand his ground and protect himself, put the lead back on your puppy and use pops on the collar and a squirt in the puppy's face to discourage his chasing behavior. If the first squirt does not discourage him, continue to squirt him until he reacts and turns his attention from the cat.

THE FIRST NIGHT

Rarely does the first night with a new pup include a good night's sleep. In fact, the first three nights can be fairly trying. When your puppy was in the litter, he could get up and relieve himself on adjacent papers, or if he wanted to play, he probably didn't get a serious rebuff if he woke up a littermate. Your puppy will whine and fuss at the loss of his littermates and probably need to go out very early in the morning.

As tempting as it is to just let your puppy sleep in bed with you, he should first learn how to sleep alone in a crate. Lower the chances of your puppy awakening in the middle of the night by feeding and watering him several hours before your bedtime. This will give him several hours to empty out so that his colon and bladder do not become full during the night. Your puppy can make it through the night without being fed or watered after 6:00 p.m. However, if your puppy is very thirsty at night—and I have two of them that are big drinkers—use the guinea-pig waterers or ice cubes. The small amount of water will quench your puppy's thirst without filling his bladder too fast.

Bedtime and the Crate

Place the crate next to your bed where your puppy will be comforted by the sound of your breathing. In addition, you will be able to discourage whining and barking promptly rather than running to another room. Throw a treat in the crate and put your puppy inside. Throw another treat in as you close the door. If your puppy appears stressed in the crate, exhibited by panting constantly, place a few ice cubes in his crate tray for water to keep him comfortable. Most crate trays are plastic, which can be a tempting chew toy for a pup. You can purchase metal crate cups, small ceramic dishes, or a guinea-pig bottle that hangs from the crate door.

Give your puppy toys and chew items in the crate to keep him busy just in case he is not ready for bed when you are, or he wakes in the middle of the night and needs something to do. The toys that you put in the crate should *only* be given in the crate so that they are special, making your puppy feel that being in the crate is positive.

Most nine- to ten-week-old puppies can go through the night. However, the new experience is stressful, and you should expect that your puppy will be a little anxious the first night and will have to relieve himself before morning. Have your puppy go out just before you go to bed. When your pup wakes up and whines in the middle of the night, take him outside to relieve his bladder. If he does relieve himself, calmly tell him "good," and place him back in the crate. If he continues to wake you each night to go out, he may not have a mature bladder and you will have to patiently try to extend the time between each outing in the middle of the night. Each time your puppy whines or barks to go out, tell him to be quiet the first time and wait about fifteen minutes before you take him out. Each time he wakes, try to extend the time that he has to wait before he is taken out so that he will learn to hold the urge for longer periods of time. Extending the time before you take him out, fifteen minutes each time, will help him build bladder capacity.

This method also works well for the young pup that is an enthusiastic early riser. If you take your puppy out and he starts playing rather than getting down to business, put him back in the crate. If he complains, correct him with "quiet" and bang on the top of the crate.

Often a puppy will verbalize the urge to go out even though he has the ability to hold off longer. If you take your puppy out of the crate every time he whines or barks, he will not learn to hold his bladder and will learn that whining and barking will get him out to play. Most puppies will go back to sleep if you do not respond to their first vocalization. When your puppy wakes in the morning, take him out immediately.

CHAPTER 8

General Puppy Care

Your puppy's physical condition influences his behavior, and a healthy mind depends upon a healthy body. If your puppy is sick, he will likely be lethargic and irritable. A puppy with matted fur or nails that are too long will be uncomfortable and irritable. Providing quality care includes giving your puppy quality dog food, grooming him regularly, and monitoring his health.

DOG FOODS

The quality of your puppy's food is important to his health. While cheaper dog foods have the essential vitamins and minerals, the quality of these sources may be inferior and make digestibility and efficient use physically expensive for your puppy. Some foods may supply nutrients through grain, while others use animal products or by-products. Low-quality foods may contribute to intestinal and skin allergies, as well as to behavioral problems such as coprophagy and hyperactivity. A premium dog food will be cheaper in the end if it keeps your puppy healthy by providing quality nutrients and a balanced diet.

Diet and Energy

A dietary program customized for your puppy's lifestyle to minimize excess energy levels makes controlling and directing his behavior easier. Feeding the excitable, nervous, high-energy puppy a high-

A healthy puppy's mind is influenced by his physical condition.

calorie puppy food packed with extra nutrients devised for the performance working dog will not help to calm your puppy. Instead of high-energy puppy food, I feed adult foods labeled "approved for all stages of a dog's life" that contain the minimum recommended nutrients. Consult your veterinarian and breeder about foods that are best for your puppy.

How Much to Feed

Generally, young puppies are fed three times a day, and the amount of food varies according to your puppy's activity and size. The amount of food that a manufacturer suggests on the food bag cannot apply to every individual puppy's metabolism, so if you are not sure how much to feed your puppy, start with the lowest recommendation and divide it into three portions. Monitor your puppy's weight and adjust his food accordingly. Puppies should not be fat. Excess weight is stressful on growing joints and bone structure. You shouldn't be able to see your puppy's ribs, but you should be able to feel them.

When your puppy loses interest in one of his meals, eliminate that feeding and add the food to the other portions. Feeding a puppy twice a day is usually adequate. As your puppy grows, frequently weigh and observe his waistline and adjust his food accordingly. If his waistline disappears, you will want to slightly decrease his food. Conversely, if your puppy is looking a little too lean, increase his food. Free feeding or leaving food out all day is not conducive to monitoring your puppy's intake, especially in a multidog household where you will not be able to tell how much each dog is eating. If you are not aware of how much your puppy is eating, you might not notice a loss in appetite, indicating that he

*Demand feedings or leaving the bowl of food out all the time not only
promotes poor eating habits but can also give your puppy
something to protect, thus promoting aggression.*

is feeling poorly. Free access to food makes house training more
difficult because your puppy will have to relieve himself more
often. A full bowl on the floor all the time may also promote
aggression by providing something for your puppy to protect from
other dogs or people. To avoid problems associated with food,
place your puppy's meal down, and after fifteen minutes, pick up
the bowl whether your puppy has eaten or not.

Changing Diets

Some people feel that their puppies become bored with the
same food day after day, and others report that their puppies love
the same food from birth to death. If you change diets, switch to a
comparable food rather than to something totally irresistible such
as canned food. If your puppy starts receiving a gourmet diet, he
will probably not go back to the original basic diet. For instance,
try giving your puppy half a bowl of the chicken recipe with half a
bowl of the lamb recipe from the same dog-food company. If the

foods are from the same manufacturer, they may be similar enough not to cause intestinal upsets. When you switch brands, you increase the risk of intestinal upsets. Gradually introduce the new food by adding a small amount of it to the old. Increase the amount daily over one week as you decrease the old food.

Most puppies love canned or semi-dry food. A diet of solely canned or semi-moist food is not recommended for sound teeth and general good health. If your puppy refuses to eat dry food, try adding one tablespoon of canned food. If your puppy does not eat his food, do not give him treats or scraps. Persevere in getting your puppy to eat dry food. A healthy puppy will not let himself starve to death.

Scraps and Tidbits

Feeding scraps is a controversial health issue and should be discussed with your veterinarian. Some veterinarians feel that scraps are detrimental to the nutritional balance of dog food, while other veterinarians believe that scraps in moderation are not harmful. If scraps do not disrupt your puppy's eating habits or diet, they can be desirable treats or an occasional welcome change from the same old dog food.

GROOMING YOUR PUPPY

While some breeds require more grooming than others, every puppy needs to have his nails clipped and his ears and teeth cleaned. Although several videos are available that teach you how to groom, there is nothing like having a mentor and hands-on experience. Your breeder and/or a professional groomer are good resources for teaching you how to perform maintenance grooming. Your veterinarian can show you how to clip nails, clean ears, and brush teeth. A grooming table, arm, and noose are necessities to save on your back and to keep your puppy from wiggling around if you are scissoring or clipping him. Never leave your puppy on the table unattended.

Nail Clipping

Your puppy's nails should be clipped at least weekly. If nails are allowed to grow too long, your puppy will not be able to walk properly on the pads of his feet. This can cause discomfort and

A puppy's nails should be clipped weekly. The first few times, ask someone to help you so that the puppy does not learn that he can struggle free and avoid having his nails clipped.

structural damage to his legs. Nails can grow so long that they curl and grow into a dog's leg if they are not clipped. I clip my puppies' nails every few days so that they get used to having it done.

Most dogs have an aversion to their nails being clipped because clipping isn't done often enough or the nail gets qwicked. Qwicking a nail means cutting the nail at the blood and nerve supply. In order to prevent nail cutting from becoming an uncomfortable activity, ask a groomer or veterinarian to help you the first few times. Many groomers will charge a nominal fee to either trim on a regular basis or show you how to trim nails. If your puppy has white nails, you will be able to see where the blood supply begins by the pink color. Unfortunately, on black nails you cannot see the blood line. Cutting toenails takes practice, and very few people are able to do it without occasionally qwicking a nail. Start by just cutting the tips of the nails every few days. Purchase a blood-stop product from a pet-supply store, read the instructions, and keep it close by when you trim nails.

If your puppy has dewclaws, you need to cut them as well. The dewclaws are digits located on the inside of your puppy's leg at about what you would consider the ankle on a puppy. Some puppies have dewclaws on the front and rear legs, while others have dewclaws only on the front legs.

Ask someone to help you hold your puppy and give him treats the first time you clip nails. Make sure that you have a good hold on your puppy, because if he gets away just once, he will learn that he can be successful and will continue to try to get away. If your puppy nips at you while you are cutting his nails, correct him with a cuff so that he does not learn to bite whenever he does not want to be handled. If you do not win the battle when he is young, the battles will become more forceful and impossible to win when your pup is full grown.

Ear Cleaning

Your groomer or veterinarian should help you clean your puppy's ears the first time, especially if you have a breed like a Poodle that needs to have hair removed from the ear canal periodically. If the hair is left in the canal, moisture and dirt collect, causing nasty ear infections. Floppy-eared puppies are more prone to ear infections. I inspect and clean my dogs' ears once a week. If you take your puppy swimming, it is a good idea to clean his ears and use antibacterial ear powder after each swim.

Brushing Your Puppy's Teeth

Many people are under the false assumption that if they give their puppies enough hard biscuits, rawhides, bones, and chew products, they don't have to worry about their puppy's teeth. Dogs, like humans, get plaque buildup if their teeth are not cleaned. Although dogs generally do not get cavities, you should clean your puppy's teeth and inspect his mouth frequently to make sure that there are no sores, abrasions, or other problems.

Your puppy's baby teeth will fall out before you have to worry about them rotting; however, your puppy should get used to having his teeth cleaned from a very early age. Most veterinarians recommend that a dog have his teeth cleaned daily. You may also want to talk to your veterinarian about proper teeth cleaning and options such as periodic teeth scaling. The veterinarians use electronic tooth scalers, which generally require having your puppy under anesthetic. Skinner, my Gordon Setter, is so used to having his teeth cleaned that when he finally needed to have his teeth scaled, I commanded him to sit-stay and the veterinarian was able to scale Skinner's teeth without placing him under anesthetic.

Brushing the Coat

Although short-haired dogs do not appear to need much coat brushing, frequent brushing will keep a shedding coat under better control. The shed hair will be in your brush instead of on your furniture or clothing. There are many different types of brushes on the market, so take your puppy with you to the groomer and ask which is the best brush for your puppy's coat. If you have a heavy or long, furry-coated breed that requires a lot of brushing, your money will be well spent if you ask a groomer to teach you how to care for the coat. If you don't brush properly or just brush over the top of the coat, the fur will snarl and matt.

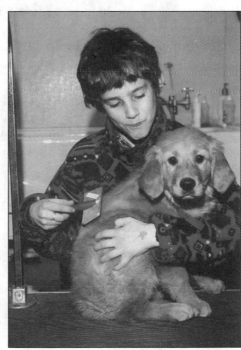

Frequent brushing will keep a shedding coat under better control. If your puppy has long fur, brushing just the top of the coat will not prevent matting. Ask your breeder or a professional groomer about coat care for your puppy.

My worst experience in grooming was with a dog that was matted to the skin. Although the owner was brushing the dog weekly, she was brushing over the top of the coat and not through the hair to the skin. We wound up shaving the coat because the knots were so tight, and it would have been painful for the dog to have his fur brushed and pulled on for hours. As we shaved the coat, we uncovered cuts and sores that hadn't healed under the mats. As if the infected cuts and sores weren't bad enough, two of us had to leave the room when we uncovered an infected sore that had maggots crawling in it. After we recovered from our sick stomachs, we completed the shaving and found a new dog. While we were working on this guy, we would have sworn from his behavior that he was a senior citizen even though he was only two years old. Once he was shaved, he bounded and bounced around acting like a puppy again.

Fur has a purpose for your puppy, and the only way to avoid having to shave him is to keep him well brushed. Keeping your puppy's coat brushed out is important for his health and helps him keep cool in the summer and warm in the winter. There will be less breakage of the hair, more luster to the coat, a pleasant odor, and fewer tangles in between brushings if you spray a coat conditioner on the hair as you brush. Always brush the coat out before you give your puppy a bath. If you bathe a snarled coat, you will have worse mats.

Place your puppy on a grooming table or on the floor and command him to down-stay while you brush his coat. Anytime he gets up, patiently command him to down-stay and place him down again. Only when you decide that the grooming session is over is your puppy allowed up. Make the sessions short at first, and reward your puppy with a treat when he is lying quietly. If your puppy has knots, be very gentle when you untangle them.

Bathing Your Puppy

Dirt caked on your puppy's coat or a strong doggy odor are probably good indications that your puppy needs a bath. My puppies get a bath within the first week of their arrival and about every two to three weeks thereafter, partly out of necessity and partly to get them used to the process before they are too big to

Frequent bathing or giving your puppy a bath when he is dirty will not destroy natural oils or dry out a coat as long as you use a quality dog shampoo and conditioner.

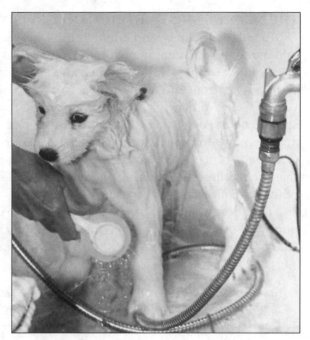

handle in the tub easily. Bathing a puppy often will *not* destroy the natural oils in his coat when you use a quality dog shampoo and conditioner to protect and enhance the coat. Warm water is necessary to clean your puppy's coat properly. Flea and tick shampoo should only be used upon recommendation by your veterinarian. For the winter months, you may want to try the dry shampoos that will get your puppy clean and smelling good without soaking him down with water.

Even though I have never owned a dog that wagged his tail for a bath, I am told that there are dogs in this world that enjoy their baths. Make the experience tolerable by acting jovial, giving him treats, and being patient. Even if your puppy doesn't enjoy his bath in spite of the treats, or you do not intend to do the bathing after he gets older, teach him to behave in the tub. Do not let your puppy get out of the tub or he will learn to battle the bath if he is rewarded with an escape route. A puppy that learns to tolerate the bath will be a welcome client for a groomer.

THE PUPPY'S FIRST VETERINARIAN VISIT

Regular checkups and inoculations by your veterinarian are important for maintaining your puppy's health. Checkups may alert you to any physical problems, and yearly inoculations protect your puppy from diseases. Puppies may become nervous at the veterinarian's office for a combination of reasons, such as the strange odors, other dogs, the whimpering or crying of other dogs, and the new atmosphere and people. Take your puppy along to the veterinary office when you make your first appointment, rather than scheduling it over the phone. This will expose him to the office without having to be examined.

The first visit will involve the veterinarian touching your puppy all over his body, and giving your puppy an injection of vaccine to protect him from certain diseases. To prepare your puppy,

Your puppy's first veterinary visit will involve the veterinarian touching your puppy all over his body. Bring along some delectable treats for your puppy to make the visit a positive expeience for him.

handle and inspect him on a regular basis so that the veterinarian's exam will seem routine rather than a traumatic experience. Even with regular handling, the ambiance of the medical office may still make your puppy apprehensive, and dropping in occasionally for a treat without an examination will make the veterinary office less threatening. Take along some tasty treats, such as a couple of pieces of liver or cheese for the receptionist, veterinarian, and staff to give your puppy. The gift of a few delectable treats rarely fails to endear you to the puppy.

Health Precautions

Ask your veterinarian about giving you a list of household items that are dangerous to your puppy. Certain products and foods that people routinely keep in their house can be very toxic to puppies, such as chocolate, onions, antifreeze, electrical cords, and cleaning products, to mention a few.

Your veterinarian can also show you how to take your puppy's temperature. The normal temperature for a canine is generally between 100.5°F and 102.0°F. If you suspect that your puppy is ill, taking his temperature can help you decide whether a veterinary visit is necessary or provide important information for your veterinarian. Let your veterinarian show you how to run your hands all over your puppy's body to check for lumps and bumps that may cause concern and that should be brought to his attention. Ask how to inspect your puppy's teeth and mouth and what changes to look for. The color of the gums is an important sign of illness. If the gums are pale, rather than pink, your puppy may be ill. Learn how to check ears for infection. Yeast infections in the ear often have an odor that is quite detectable even to the novice nose. And finally, ask about emergency procedures and canine first-aid kits in case your puppy gets injured or poisoned.

Socialization begins at the breeder's kennel and should continue after you bring your puppy home. Positive exposure to different people, objects, animals, and circumstances in a non-threatening manner is critical for developing a well-behaved puppy.
PHOTO © KENT AND DONNA DANNEN

CHAPTER 9

Socialization

 S ocialization begins at the breeder's kennel and should continue after you bring your puppy home. Positive exposure to many different people, objects, animals, and circumstances in a nonthreatening manner is critical for developing a well-behaved and mentally adjusted puppy.

POSITIVE SOCIALIZATION

Until your puppy has all of his inoculations and it is safe to take him out in public, socialization can begin at home with grooming. A gentle grooming can be as satisfying to your puppy as being petted and can prepare him to be handled by different people. Your puppy must allow you to open his mouth and inspect his teeth. If your puppy is teething, keep your mouth exams very short. If you examine or handle your puppy's mouth too frequently during the teething stage when he is uncomfortable, you will set a negative association with mouth exams.

Handling should not always be limited to calm stroking. A gentle squeeze of the paw, a pat, or a mild tug on your puppy's ear or tail can help desensitize him to children and other people who do not always pet puppies gently. Devise games for tough patting, shoving and pulling of his tail, ears, hair, and skin so that he will

*Grooming is a good way to teach your puppy
to accept handling all over his body.*

not be threatened if someone accidently hurts him. If you act
playful, your puppy will accept the rough playing as a game. If
your puppy becomes fearful, you may want to start out with
firm touching and gradually build up the roughness. If your
puppy nips or becomes aggressive, correct him with a cuff
under the jaw.

Invite children into your home to visit and play with your
puppy. Have friends give treats as they gently touch your puppy all
over his body. The more people who handle your puppy positively,
the less threatened he will be around people. When your puppy is
comfortable around other people, leave him to play with a person
and go out of his sight. A puppy that plays with other people when
you are out of sight will learn not to be dependent upon you
around other people and new situations.

*Desensitize your dog to rough petting and playing
by pulling his ears gently or rolling him over.*

*When your dog is accustomed to being handled roughly,
he will not be threatened by rough petting.*

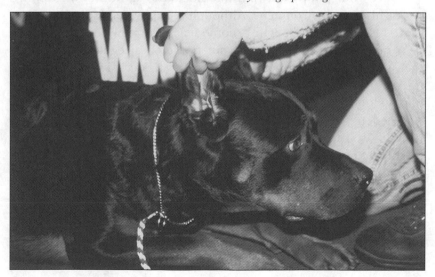

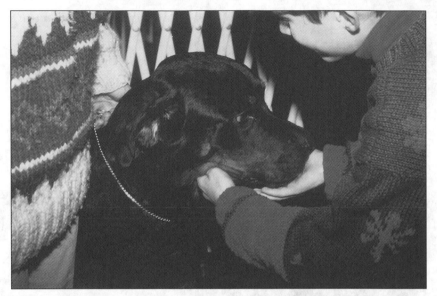

Have your child offer your puppy a treat in each hand. When the puppy is eating the second treat, your child can pet him under the chin.

PROPER HANDLING

Once your puppy has had his inoculations, he should venture out of his safe environment. Although a puppy generally starts out brave and outgoing, he will become fearful of new surroundings if he is not socialized outside of your home on a regular basis. Even the well-socialized, outgoing puppy can occasionally become uncertain or afraid. Your behavior and how you handle your puppy's uncertainty or fear in the presence of new stimuli will set a precedent for his reactions to the outside world for the rest of his life. For example, talking to and stroking your puppy in a sympathetic manner rewards him for acting fearful. Although you intend to communicate to him that you will take care of him and protect him, your puppy interprets your stroking, soothing tones and attention as approval for his fearful behavior.

Fearful behavior may further be rewarded if you avoid or remove your puppy from a perceived scary situation. Snorkel, at fourteen weeks of age, immediately became overwhelmed by the sounds and people at a busy car wash. His tail went down and he tried to hide between my legs. Instead of removing him from the situation or petting him, I talked to him in a jovial voice. He keyed into my voice and started wagging his tail. The minute he wagged his tail, I petted him and gave him a treat. He finished the treat and looked back at the commotion of the car wash without much concern. I then walked Snorkel over to one of the workers and asked him to give Snorkel a treat. Snorkel cautiously took the treat at first and then decided that things weren't so bad after all. In spite of the movement and strange noises, Snorkel walked around with his tail up and received a treat from all of the employees. Snorkel did not continue to behave fearfully, because he was not rewarded for it; instead he learned how to enjoy the environment. Socialization means exposure and positive and patient handling to teach your puppy how to cope with his environment.

SENSITIVE STAGES

All puppies appear to go through one or more sensitive stages where they may have episodes of uncertainty or mild fearfulness. These stages generally appear around the ages of eight weeks, eight months, and fifteen months. Sensitive periods may be associated with hormonal changes, such as the onset of a heat cycle or a male reaching puberty.

Casino, my Gordon Setter, was a fearless puppy and the first one in the litter to investigate any new situation. Her boldness continued in my house until she was just a few days short of eight months of age. She was sleeping a few feet away from me as I was folding laundry in the bedroom. When I picked up a pair of crumpled jeans to snap out the wrinkles, Casino flipped out when the jeans made a loud, hollow crack, and she ran from the room as if a demon was chasing her. When I brought a very reluctant Casino back into the bedroom, she ran behind the waterbed. The situation was pitiful—my eight-month-old Gordon Setter was crammed behind the waterbed, shaking. I couldn't reach or convince her to come out. Luckily for me, my cat was also behind the bed, sleeping. My cat, in her very special feline way, convinced Casino that the space could not be occupied by both of them at the same time. When Casino came out, I tied her to my waist so that she could not escape and avoid the situation. I ignored Casino as I folded laundry and she eventually calmed down. Even the most admirably bold dog can have startle reactions over the most ordinary things.

If your puppy has never had a startle reaction, he has just not been exposed to everything. Although one startle reaction does not mean that your puppy will become fearful of everything, proper handling is critical to prevent your puppy from generalizing his negative or frightening experience to other situations. Careful handling or systematic socialization to introduce your puppy to new people and novel surroundings positively teaches him how to cope with his environment, particularly during the sensitive stages.

SOCIALIZING YOUR PUPPY WITH NEW PEOPLE

Puppies must be allowed to approach people at their own pace and on their own accord. When puppies initiate approaching a person without being handed over or pushed, the experience is positive. If your puppy has a negative experience because he is pushed, pulled, forced toward a person, or approached too quickly, the traumatic event may instill a lasting fear of people in him. Even the outgoing puppy needs space and time to sniff, check out, and establish a feeling of trust before he approaches a new person. To prevent improper approaches toward your puppy, always make sure that your puppy has time, space, and treats to make socializing with people a positive event.

When you introduce your puppy to people, place him in a sit-stay and keep your lead loose. A lead that tightens when people approach, even though your intentions are well-meaning to prevent your puppy from jumping, communicates tension. A tight lead is uncomfortable, and your puppy will naturally form a negative association with greeting people.

If you puppy does not know sit-stay yet, you can either gently hold him in place by the collar or seek out people who do not mind your puppy jumping on them. When I begin socialization with my young puppies, I purposely seek out people who do not mind my puppy jumping on them. A puppy that jumps up on people is demonstrating his excitement and confidence around people, and correcting him for jumping destroys confidence.

*A puppy needs space and time to sniff and check out a person
before he feels comfortable approaching him.*

To prevent my puppy from jumping on people, I teach him
"off" at home. When my puppy has confidence around people, and
when I am certain that he understands "off" because he responds
correctly when he attempts to jump on me, I use the command if
he jumps on other people. If you correct a puppy for jumping
before he has confidence around people or before he understands
"off," he will associate the correction with people and will form a
negative association when people approach.

To discourage jumping, I also ask the person to hold out a
treat at my puppy's level. When my puppy approaches, he is
rewarded with a treat. If his body language is relaxed and he
approaches close, happy, and friendly, the person can pet him
under the chin. If I have a young puppy that does not know "off"
or "sit-stay," and having him jump is inappropriate in the situa-

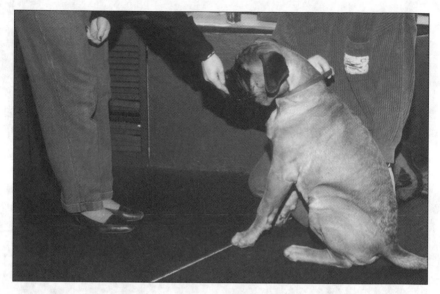

When introducing your puppy to new people, hold him in the sit and ask the person to offer him a treat. Do not let people simply approach without offering a treat.

tion, I simply sit my puppy and gently hold him in place. Once my puppy is in place, I ask the person to hold his hand out, palm up, and offer a treat without moving forward, staring into the puppy's eyes, or attempting to pet him. After my puppy takes the treat, has time to appraise the person's eyes and body language, and appears relaxed and accepting of the situation, I let the person reach forward and pet my puppy under the chin.

Never allow a person to approach if you do not have control. If your puppy becomes threatened and the person persists in approaching because he has either misread or ignored your puppy's body language, a defensive snap is probable. Worse yet, if the person backs away from your puppy in reaction to a growl or snap, your puppy learns that snapping controls human behavior and he can therefore avoid being handled when he chooses. Even if your puppy only backs away to avoid contact, the distance will reduce his fear and he will be reinforced to back away and avoid people.

To avoid the risk of overwhelming your puppy or having him learn avoidance tactics when you introduce him to people, do not let people approach him; rather, encourage your puppy to approach on his own free will. If your puppy does not approach people readily and is not interested in treats, invite your guest to sit down and ask him to ignore your puppy. As time passes, and your unsure puppy is ignored, he will eventually become curious and will sniff your guest. After he has sniffed and feels more comfortable, have your guest offer him a tasty treat. Your guest should avoid staring into your puppy's eyes, he should keep his body movements smooth, natural, and slow, and he should not attempt to pet your puppy. Even if your puppy does not take the treat, have your guest keep offering the treat periodically, or have him drop it on the floor. If the treat is tasty enough and your puppy picks it up from the floor, as most puppies will do, he'll realize that the person is not trying to kill him, and very likely will not resist the next offering from your guest's hand.

Sometimes the fearful puppy becomes so comfortable with people that he starts jumping on them to get the treat. Correct the jumping only with "sit." The treat is only given when your puppy is in the sit position. If your puppy is corrected for jumping instead of being given another command, he may associate the correction with the person and may become fearful again.

Another method that can be used to help your puppy investigate people or objects is the "touching chain." Give your guest a treat in the palm of his hand, and cup one of your hands under his. Have your free hand touch your puppy as he is offered the treat. The puppy will see that you didn't melt or die, and he will become curious and will want to venture closer. As your puppy moves closer, praise him. The food must have a high value—steak, cheese, or anything that your puppy loves enough to tempt him in spite of his fear. If your puppy is not a serious chow hound, withhold his daily meal on socialization days so that he is hungry.

When your puppy is taking the treat confidently from the cupped hands, have the person place a treat in each hand and offer both hands to your puppy. When your puppy takes the first treat and begins chewing the second one, have the person scratch your puppy under the chin with his empty hand. Chewing on the

*Puppies should be petted under the chin. If a person attempts to pet the
puppy's head, the puppy may feel threatened as the hand
comes toward him and blocks his vision.*

treat as the person is petting begins a pleasant association. After
your puppy allows petting, praise your puppy and give him more
treats as reinforcement for his social behavior. Repeat the touching chain when you introduce your puppy to people until he does
not respond apprehensively or fearfully. Touching should be
extended to all parts of your puppy's body very gradually, and only
when your puppy is relaxed and accepting— perhaps over a period
of a couple of months for some puppies. Once your puppy accepts
petting for a treat, allow petting before he gets the treat.

A puppy that shows signs of timidity or fear when people are
around must be exposed repeatedly to people in short, positive sessions. Barbara, who owned a timid, twelve-week-old Rhodesian
Ridgeback, had dreams of him becoming a show dog and sought

my help on how to socialize him. I went through the positive systematic approach with Barbara, and she was very excited that her puppy was responding during our lesson. Barbara was so anxious for improvement that she spent the next day at a dog show socializing her puppy. Barbara was confused when toward the middle of the day, her puppy refused to take treats and started to avoid people. Barbara had overwhelmed and fried her puppy's brain. The session was so long and stressful that the experience became very negative for her puppy. The most positive learning experiences are developed in short sessions before your puppy becomes overwhelmed, tired, and full from treats.

There are times when a puppy, regardless of what you do, will not go up to a certain person. In this case, accept your puppy's discriminating choice. Even if your puppy refuses to approach everyone, it is a choice that you may have to accept. You cannot force a puppy to love everyone, but you can make sure through obedience training that he is obedient around people and does not bite them.

Teach your puppy a sit-stay, and do not allow him under any circumstances to hide or back up. Command your puppy to sit-stay, and if he backs up, give him a collar correction. If he growls, tell him "quiet." The correction will be associated with disobeying the sit-stay. The correction will also distract your puppy and at the same time require that he pay attention to you. If your puppy is not on a stay command and is corrected for moving when a person offers a treat, he will associate being corrected with the person, and his fear will be affirmed. When your puppy stays and is quiet, praise him verbally.

PLACES TO SOCIALIZE PUPPIES WITH PEOPLE

Initially, socialization should take place with people who know how to approach puppies in a nonthreatening manner, such as at a training school, a veterinarian's office, or dog events. When your puppy is comfortable with greeting people, other favorite social grounds are nursing homes, ballparks, playgrounds, and open-air restaurants or ice cream parlors. I always have treats with me when my puppies accompany me in public. I also make a point of listing the banks and fast-food restaurants that give treats to dogs at the window. Getting a treat from a drive-through window makes riding in the car really fun for a puppy that may be unsure of road trips. Whenever I get in the car to go someplace where I can take my dogs, such as the pet-supply store or the car service center, one or more get to come along for socialization regardless of their age.

I am very careful not to take my dogs with me if they have to be left in the car unattended. Leaving a dog in the car unattended on a hot day is extremely dangerous. A car can heat up and your puppy can suffocate in a very short time. Do not leave your dog in a car or anyplace without shade and water. If you leave your puppy unattended in the car, make sure that he is in a crate so that you don't come back to find your gear shift eaten, as one of my clients experienced. As soon as my puppies are confident with people and different places, I call a local school and arrange to bring my puppy to a class and talk to the students about how to handle and nurture puppies.

SOCIALIZING CHILDREN AND DOGS

Puppies that live in households without children are commonly frightened or nervous around children and must be purposefully and systematically socialized to children in a positive way to feel comfortable with them. A puppy must learn how to properly interact with children, and children must have guidance, discipline, education, and supervision to learn how to interact appropriately with dogs. Children and puppies are curious, active creatures, and the combination left unsupervised can spell out serious problems.

The typical scenario that teaches a puppy to be aggressive is when a child and puppy are left in the yard alone. The child is running and playing, and the puppy joins in and starts chasing the child. At first, the child may think that this is fun until the puppy starts nipping at him to catch him. When this happens, the child may attempt to kick the puppy away, which causes the puppy to get more aggressive with his catch or to play tug-of-war. When the puppy gets aggressive and nips harder, the child screams and tries to pull away, causing the puppy to hang on harder. If the game continues as the puppy grows, it usually results in a bite. The puppy learns to play by chasing and biting whenever children are around.

Every dog that has teeth is capable of biting, and the best way to prevent injury is to supervise interactions between dogs and children. Even the most tolerant puppy may have bad or sick days and may lose patience with a child. He may at first try to escape; however, a persistent child who does not understand or does not heed the dog's body language and warnings may eventually receive a nasty bite. Children inclined to chase, tease, or be rough with a puppy must be taught to treat and interact with dogs properly. Children must be taught how to read and react to body language that signals fear, pain, and aggression. Supervision, management, and the modeling of nurturing behavior will protect children from dog bites much more effectively than correcting the puppy or child after the fact.

A dominant puppy often views a young child as a subordinate and a good subject to control. He may chase, herd, jump on, and injure a child. The puppy may even go so far as to push a child to the ground and mount him. Most children do not know how, nor do they have the coordination and muscle, to correct and stop a pushy puppy. A supervising adult must be available to correct the puppy immediately. To prevent your puppy from viewing your child as a subordinate, give your child status in your puppy's eyes by having him take an active role in feeding, grooming, and training the puppy. Even if your child is not old enough to train your puppy by himself, he can take part by giving commands and helping you hold the leash. If your puppy doesn't respond to your child's commands, you can enforce the commands while both of you hold the lead to teach your puppy that he must obey your child. Teach your children to play appropriate games with your puppy, such as fetch, and avoid games that may provoke too much excitement or aggression.

As responsible dog owners, we must socialize and teach our dogs to approach and play with children appropriately. Even if you don't have children, sometime in your dog's life he will come in contact with a child and he must learn to behave appropriately around children in a positive way. Ideally, socialization to children should begin in puppyhood before fast movements and unusual mannerisms by the children are interpreted as threats.

Ask the child to stand, relaxed, about a foot from your puppy. Explain to the child that he should not stare into the eyes of your puppy, but to look at his whole face. Have the child hold out a treat in the palm of his hand and cup your hand underneath his. The open palm eliminates any possibility of the puppy nipping the child's fingers as he takes the treat, and your hand protects the child's hand from the possibility of a bite. Cupping your hand underneath also prevents the child from pulling his hand away, which may provoke your puppy to chase the treat and inadvertently nip. It never fails to amaze me that children will put their hands in the most dirty and slimy substances, but a little dog slobber causes them to pull their hands away in disgust. Your hand cupped under the child's hand not only prevents the child from pulling his hand away too quickly, it also forms a touching chain that encourages trust for your puppy, and motivates him to investigate and approach. The child must not approach the puppy, and the puppy must not be forced or pushed toward the child. The idea

is to get your puppy to approach the child on his own and at his own pace. When your puppy is reaching toward the child and taking the treat confidently, have the child place a treat in each hand and offer both hands to your puppy. After your puppy takes the first treat and begins chewing on the second one, the child may scratch your puppy under the chin with his empty hand. Explain to the

When introducing dogs to children, always cup your hand under the child's hand as the puppy is offered a treat.

child that he should scratch the puppy under the chin because petting on top of the head before the puppy feels comfortable covers his eyes and can make him fearful. Chewing on a treat and being petted under the chin will encourage a pleasant association with the child. After your puppy feels comfortable with taking treats from the child's hand without your cupped hand underneath, give the leash to the child and instruct him to give your puppy an easy command, such as "sit." When your puppy sits, have the child give him a treat and praise. Having the child give your puppy commands and praise teaches your puppy to respect and obey children and you have modeled appropriate behavior around dogs. In addition, when a puppy obeys the child, the child feels empowered and confident. Touching and petting the rest of the dog's body should begin gradually and only when your puppy is exhibiting relaxed or happy body language. Supervise the touching all over the body, keeping a watchful eye for changes in his body language.

FEAR EPISODES

Dog owners often react improperly to their puppy's fearful episodes and unintentionally reinforce or reward fear. You may hold your puppy with a tight lead or collar, push the puppy closer, thus intensifying his fear, or comfort him, thus reinforcing fearful behavior. Fear may further be reinforced if you talk in a soothing voice and/or stroke your puppy or allow him to hide behind your legs. The more comforting you are, the more rewarding the fearful behavior is for your puppy, and the more likely the fear reaction will reoccur.

Avoiding a fearful situation does not teach your puppy confidence. A puppy must be positively exposed or socialized through repeated pleasant interactions for him to become brave and confident. At the least, a fearful puppy must learn through exposure not to bite or run away. Once a fearful puppy learns to be aggressive, his attacks will become more severe and frequent with little predictability. The prognosis for rehabilitating a fearful-aggressive puppy is bleak. You must not place your puppy in such a fearful position, particularly by allowing people to approach when he feels that there is no alternative but to snap. Socialize your fearful puppy very slowly and positively with treats.

Be observant of any signs that indicate fear or aggression. A sharp collar correction and "no" are appropriate if your puppy lunges or growls.

SOCIALIZING TO OTHER DOGS

Many of the social problems between dogs are the result of removing puppies from the litter too early. These puppies do not get adequate time during their most formative social period to learn proper canine etiquette. Puppies must learn how to approach other dogs appropriately.

When two dogs are brought together, each animal should sit at his own handler's side until they have had a minute to observe each other from a distance. Be very observant of any signs that indicate fear and/or aggression, such as staring or hard eye contact, raised hackles, and low growling. When no sign of aggression is evident, permit the dogs to sniff each other on a loose lead. Carefully observe the dogs and watch for a stiff and slow-moving body, which will signal you that a fight is about to happen. Be ready to use your snappy recall command in case either dog becomes tense. If the dogs sniff each other and accept the close contact without any evidence of an impending altercation, they will usually play together or ignore each other. If your puppy lunges, growls, or mounts, harshly command"no!" as you give him a sharp collar correction and call him to you. Place your puppy in a sit or down-stay at your side. If your puppy moves, correct him with a collar correction that puts him back into the original stay position spot.

The dogs should not be allowed to stare at each other, because staring intensifies aggression. If your puppy continues to stare and growl, a water correction will break eye contact, defuse the aggression, and distract your puppy. Praise your puppy when he is quiet. Keep the dogs in a sit or down and remaining a safe distance from each other—three to four feet apart.

Constant exposure to other dogs that are also under control, along with corrections to discourage aggressive behavior when necessary, will teach your puppy to cope with being around other dogs. Dogs cannot be taught to love other dogs, but puppies can be trained to *behave* in the presence of other dogs. Isolating your puppy from other dogs will *not* teach him to behave around other dogs.

*Give your puppy time to calm down when
something scares him before you move closer.*

NEW EVENTS

Unfortunately, many things that startle and frighten dogs are not within your control, such as cars that backfire, fireworks, or thunderstorms. When your puppy becomes startled, he will naturally attempt to run in the opposite direction. If he is allowed to run, his fear will decrease and he will thus be rewarded for bolting.

To help your puppy overcome a startle reaction when there isn't an opportunity to systematically desensitize him, promote a happy mood switch to distract him. Your puppy cannot be fearful and happy at the same time. Puppies cannot fully concentrate on two things at once, and by preventing your puppy from focusing on the frightening situation, there is a greater chance that the upsetting experience will not imprint on or remain with him. If your puppy is not distracted and focuses on the frightening situation, his fear may increase or intensify, and the memory of the event will become strong and lasting. Without intervention, there

If your puppy becomes frightened, do not remove him from the situation while he is hysterical or frantic. Wait until he calms down. Strange, looming objects that move often frighten puppies.

is a great risk that the strong negative memory will generalize toward any similar situation.

Kodiak, a fifteen-month-old male, became fearful when two boys sporting rollerblades passed on the street. Kodiak bolted and ran in the opposite direction. Thereafter, Kodiak's owner noticed that Kodiak appeared nervous on his walks and startled at any-thing that moved or made noise, including fast-moving teenage boys, strollers, and shopping carts. Kodiak's owner was instructed to distract him by talking in a very happy, jovial voice and initiat-ing play whenever a potentially startling event approached or Kodiak exhibited signs of nervousness. Kodiak, enthralled with his owner's playful manner, learned to turn his attention to his owner instead of bolting in the presence of noisy, moving objects.

Good Distractions

I toss a treat in the air to distract my puppy from a negative event. A puppy has to use quite a bit of eye and mouth coordina-tion to catch or chase a treat, and the concentration to catch a treat keeps my puppy's mind busy and off the scary stimulus.

Occasionally, a puppy may become so frightened that he refuses to be distracted no matter what you do. If your puppy is extremely frightened or stressed, his system shuts down to such an extent that even the chow hound will turn up his nose at a gourmet treat. If you cannot distract your puppy from the fright-ening stimulus, remain calm and talk to him in a normal voice as you command him to sit-stay or to perform some other obedience exercise to distract him. Command your puppy to heel or to sit and down several times in a row, and enforce the obedience even if you have to physically help your puppy by using his collar. Handle your puppy firmly but without anger. If you require that your puppy be obedient, he will learn to concentrate on obeying your command rather than focusing on the fearful event. Your puppy will also learn that even if he is frightened, he must be obedient. Praise your puppy only for obeying your command, even if you had to physically help him perform the exercise.

Do not remove your puppy from the frightening situation while he is hysterical or frantic; instead, wait for him to calm down so that he learns that frantic behavior does not open an exit.

If the event was extremely frightening for your puppy, do not place him back in the same surroundings for at least three weeks to give him ample time to forget the unpleasant incident. If you dwell on the problem, the event will become very prominent in your puppy's memory. After three weeks, you may again gradually introduce the scary stimulus. Take your puppy into the particular situation for short periods of time, implementing a game or using an obedience exercise to keep his attention on you. Gradually increase the time that your puppy is exposed to the scary event over several repetitions. In some cases, no matter what the effort, your puppy will never be rid of his fear associated with a particular incident. In these cases, using your obedience is very important to teach him that even if he feels hysterical and out of control, he must be obedient.

DESENSITIZATION TO NOISES

A noise can be created in another room, across a field, or at some distance while you distract your puppy with food or play. If your puppy shows no reaction to the noise, shorten the distance in small increments—a couple of feet at a time. If your puppy has a startle reaction, talk happily to him, distract him, and wait until he is relaxed and engrossed in a pleasurable activity before repeating the sound. Depending upon the severity of your puppy's reaction, the noise should be repeated either farther away or at the same distance. The noise must not be made louder or closer until there is no response from your puppy. If noises are repeated often enough, your puppy will eventually become accustomed to them and will ignore them.

At one time, I moved into an apartment next to an elevated train system. Trains passed every ten minutes or so, and I thought that I would never get used to the noise of a speeding train coming through my living room. After several months in my apartment, I was visiting with a guest from out of town when the express came roaring by as usual. My guest nearly jumped out of her skin. For the first time, I realized that I had grown accustomed to the sound of the trains passing and had not even noticed the noise in several weeks.

Desensitization to noises does not have to be accomplished in one day. As a matter of fact, if the training session is too long, your puppy's stress level may rise. I expose my puppies to loud and sudden noises very early when they are engrossed in pleasurable activities. For example, I clumsily handle metal food dishes or slam cabinet doors when my puppies are eating or while I prepare their dinners. If they react, I talk happily and they soon wag their tails and go back to eating.

Recently, while visiting New York City, I was fascinated with the dogs walking down the noisy streets. I happened to be watching a little West Highland Terrier eagerly and happily sniffing the ground when suddenly a loud boom shook the street. The dog owner and I jumped about four feet off the ground. The little Westie looked up for about two seconds before he returned to his sniffing. City dogs are constantly exposed to noise and thus become desensitized. The sounds of the city, which may send a country dog running with his tail between his legs, become commonplace or a part of the city dog's environment, worth little more than a mere glance or head turn. Frequent exposure to noises and a positive attitude will teach your puppy to cope with loud sounds.

NEW SURFACES

Unusual surfaces, such stairs, grates, or slippery floors, can scare a puppy. Puppies will often balk the first time they are faced with stairs. Most puppies do not seem to have as much hesitation in going up stairs as they do in going down. If your puppy is reluctant to go up stairs, coax him with a treat. If he still does not go up, place him in the middle of the staircase, holding onto him so that he doesn't fall backward, and try again to tempt him up the stairs with a treat. Your puppy will have little choice but to go up or down. Talk happily and praise him when he starts off in the right direction. If your puppy goes up the stairs but won't go down, place him on the third step and go down the stairs while you tempt him with a treat. Praise him when he follows you. With each repetition, place him further up the staircase and coax him down.

Approach flat surfaces slowly and permit your puppy the time and space to investigate the flooring. After your puppy has had ample time to inspect the surface, start across and command, "Let's go." If your puppy does not go across with you, tempt him with treats. If he still will not walk on the surface, gently take him across by the collar, talking in a happy voice. Praise your puppy when he walks across even if you had to lead him. Lead your puppy back and forth repeatedly over the surface until he walks on it by himself without jumping across or going around.

FEAR OF OBJECTS

When Scuba was a puppy and accompanied my husband and me to the city for the first time, he became unglued at the sight of a fire hydrant. A male dog that was afraid of fire hydrants was *not* something that my friends would let me live down, so on one cold winter night, Scuba learned about fire hydrants and scary objects. I set Scuba about ten feet away, where he showed only mild fear, and I commanded him to sit-stay. If I had to correct Scuba for backing up, he would associate the correction with disobeying and not with the hydrant. I let him sit there and look at the hydrant until he calmed down or, on this cold night, slowed his panting. Panting is a good indication of stress. Hard, fast panting even in the heat indicates that a dog is emotionally and physically stressed. Once Scuba calmed down, I released him, praised him, told him to heel, and took a step toward the hydrant, where I repeated "stay" and waited for him to calm down. Each step we took closer toward the hydrant would renew his anxiety, and I would wait for him to calm down or to realize that nothing was going to kill him. Then I would take another step. When we got to the hydrant forty-five minutes later, I touched it, forming a "touching chain." Scuba, seeing that I didn't get eaten, became curious at what I was touching and decided to sniff it. We got back into the car and proceeded to the next hydrant, and this time it only took me twenty minutes to encourage Scuba to sniff it. When we finally got to the fourth fire hydrant and my husband was ready to divorce me, Scuba went right up to the hydrant and sniffed it. The happy ending to the story is that Scuba never misses a fire hydrant these days, and because he learned that things aren't as scary as they look, he is always eager, or at the least brave enough, to investigate unusual objects.

Fearfulness may never be totally eliminated, but socialization is the best tool that you have to help your puppy tolerate and adjust to his environment. Because there are always new circumstances

Socialization is the best tool that you have to help your puppy adjust to his new environment.

for your puppy to encounter, socialization is an ongoing process. Puppies should be taken to different places and meet different people at every opportunity. Even if your puppy appears socialized and brave, his adult personality doesn't develop until around two years of age, and he can still become fearful if deliberate socialization is relaxed too soon. The more positive experiences your puppy has over time, the more bold he will become. Socialization and obedience training are critical for developing an outgoing and well-behaved dog.

A puppy has a natural tendency to keep a clean living area and not eliminate where he sleeps and eats.

CHAPTER 10

House-Training

Apuppy's natural tendency to keep a clean living area and not eliminate where he sleeps and eats can be effectively utilized in house-training with the use of a crate. The crate is a positive approach to house-training and an effective tool for keeping your puppy out of trouble when you can't watch him.

CRATING

The crate is an enclosed space much like a den environment and is a much safer option for confining your puppy than a small room or chaining him up in the yard. Puppies seek protective, enclosed places to rest and sleep. They will lie under a table or next to a wall or piece of furniture for security rather than in an open area or the middle of the room. Even a small room is too large to seem like a den to a young puppy, and as a result, he will feel insecure and will become anxious. By the time an insecure, anxious puppy is five months old, he will begin to chew, scratch, and destroy doors, walls, and everything within his path if he is confined to anything short of a crate. Leaving your puppy outside in the yard alone is not safe because windstorms may blow down fences, he may dig out, or people may intrude on your property. Left alone in the yard, a puppy is vulnerable, and he may become frightened, frustrated, and possibly prey to another dog or animal. One morning I received a call from a very hysterical client who had

121

just arrived home to witness her Yorkshire puppy, which was left alone in the yard, being carried off by an owl. Chaining a puppy is also a poor solution. A chained puppy feels anxious, vulnerable, and trapped. The chained puppy will learn to bark excessively, dig, chew, and circle in frustration and anxiety. Crates provide the protective, secure, denlike experience that dogs naturally seek.

If you leave your puppy in his crate, he cannot relieve himself on the carpet, damage your home, get into mischief, or disturb the neighbors. Your relationship with your puppy will be stronger and more positive without the stress, expense, and frustration of puppy behavioral problems. The crate, used properly, can prevent accidents and misbehavior from becoming serious, hard-to-fix habits.

Crating and House-Training

The secure, small, denlike crate discourages accidents because puppies generally detest having to lie near their own urine or feces. A puppy that has the freedom of the house will not make the effort to control his bodily functions, because he can leave a mess in one room and eat or sleep in another room where the offending mess does not spoil his appetite. To make matters worse, the unconfined puppy is richly reinforced for soiling when his bladder and sphincter muscles are relieved of pressure. In addition, if the soiled area is not cleaned properly, the odor will attract and stimulate your puppy to return to the spot to eliminate again. The crate prevents your puppy from messing in the house and provides a good incentive for him to control his bodily functions because the offensive mess is inescapable.

The crate is also used to prevent accidents when you cannot watch your puppy. If your puppy relieves himself in the house when you are not watching, you will not have the opportunity to show him the error of his ways, and he will learn that soiling in the house is acceptable. If you correct your puppy after the fact, he only learns that when urine or feces are on the floor, you are to be avoided. Although your puppy may certainly recognize his mess on the floor, he cannot grasp that if he holds the mess until he is let out, he will avoid your wrath later. A correction is only effective when the discipline is delivered *during* the misbehavior. To properly house-train and prevent confusion for your puppy:

The exercise pen is a good option for paper training and for keeping your puppy in a safe area when you are away from home.

1. Never leave your puppy unattended or unsupervised, even for a minute, until he is definitely house-trained.
2. Confine your puppy to his crate when he is not supervised, which includes at night when you are sleeping.

Crate Training

With proper reinforcement and handling, your puppy will more than likely come to love his crate as a secure den. Never use the crate to punish your puppy. Always place your puppy in the crate with praise, a treat, and a normal-toned command. If the crate is used as punishment, your puppy will find it aversive and will avoid it. If you must crate your puppy after a scolding, the negative association between the crate and scolding can be broken if you command him to do a simple exercise such as sit, then praise him for sitting before placing him in the crate. While walking into the kitchen with a glass of water in my hand, one of my dogs bumped me and the glass crashed to the floor in hundreds of pieces. In reflex mode, I yelled a loud expletive, and in my panic to get my puppy into the crate to keep her from getting cut as I cleaned up the glass, my voice and actions were not exactly positive. I realized that she was almost cowering and was looking very dejected. To prevent a negative association from being formed with the crate, I simply commanded her to sit and praised her profusely before I put her inside. Her tail came up, and she happily went into the crate for her treat.

During the day, position the crate, with the door open, in a room where your puppy will be able to freely explore his new den. At bedtime, place the crate next to your bed so that you can teach your puppy to stay in the crate quietly overnight. Place the crate next to your bed for about three days or just long enough for you to complete the crate-training process. After three days, you can put the crate in any part of the house that you wish or leave it by your bed.

At bedtime, throw a treat and/or toy into the crate as you command your puppy to "crate," "bed," or whatever word you wish to use. If your puppy does not go into the crate on his own, physically stuff him into it, if necessary. Do not fuss, voice sympathy, or show that you feel sorry for him. Close the crate door and give your puppy another treat through the door before walking away. A fuss when crating or when letting your puppy out of the crate makes the event an emotional affair that may cause anxiety for your puppy.

Whining and Barking

If your puppy whines or barks, hit the top of the crate and command in a firm, disciplinary voice, "Quiet." When your puppy is quiet, verbally praise "good." You will very likely have to repeat this reprimand several times before your puppy catches on that the whining and barking produce your banging on the crate. If he doesn't figure out the pattern after several bangs, get a little tougher and shake the crate, earthquake style, every time he makes noise. Do not open the crate or let him in bed or you will be setting the pattern that whining, fussing, and barking produce an open-door policy. If banging on the crate is ineffective, place a squirt bottle on top of the crate and squirt your puppy right between the eyes with cold water as you command very harshly, "Quiet." Once he is quiet, praise him with a soft verbal "good dog." Too much praise will cause him to become excited and will start him barking and whining again.

If your water correction does not work the first time, try it again several times before you step up the intensity by using more water. If the squirt bottle does not work at all, use several glasses of water. I once had to use a four-quart pot of water to get the point across to one of my ten-week-old pups. If the first glass of water had really bothered him, I would not have had to use a pot of water. The water did not harm him, but it bothered him enough to not want the process repeated. Not only did he survive the correction, he learned not to whine and bark in the crate.

Even if your puppy appears to like water, a harsh command paired with the water is quite aversive to a puppy and he will stop barking if you persist in your corrections. My youngest pup used to swim in the toilets every chance she got, and yet, a strong squirt of water and verbal correction were enough to discipline her in spite of her love for water. Very few puppies will cease barking without a correction. Recently, I had a puppy in a crate in my car and stopped to talk to someone. The puppy that was accustomed to my car and crate started barking and I ignored him. He barked continuously for the entire thirty minutes until I returned to my car. Ignoring a barking puppy does not cure a barking problem. If your corrections are not effective in stopping the barking, consult with a trainer to ensure that your technique and timing are appropriate.

The first few nights, many people feel really guilty about correcting their puppies for whining and barking and often don't correct them. However, after the third night of interrupted or no sleep, the guilt passes and they finally correct their puppy, only to wonder why they didn't do it the first night. I promise, after you correct your puppy, he will still love and respect you in the morning! If you don't get a good night's sleep, you won't have patience or energy for the next day when your puppy is really going to be a handful.

Crate Schedule

The crate schedule for house-training will vary with the age of your puppy. As your puppy gets older and physically becomes more reliable in controlling bodily functions in the house, he will spend less time in the crate. During the night, letting a puppy sleep in a crate for eight hours is perfectly reasonable.

The crate is used whenever you cannot supervise your puppy, such as when you are sleeping, when you are not at home, or when you are too busy to watch him. During the day, place your puppy in the crate when you run your errands or spend time in another room. When he's quiet and you can watch him, let him out of the crate. Place the crate in busy parts of the house during the day to ensure that your puppy is around people and the goings and comings of the household. Although the crate is not the most expensive-looking piece of furniture, you can place a decorative cover over the top of it and have it double as a side table.

Another advantage of the crate is that it can provide a break from that rambunctious critter when you are too tired to watch him. Snorkel is the Eveready battery cliché—he keeps going and going and going. He never sleeps outside his crate and loves to rip paper. I have actually resorted to stockpiling magazines for him just to keep him busy. The stockpile reminds me of when my son was two years old and got into my kitchen pots and pans. Instead of locking the cabinet, I arranged an entire safe compartment for him to pull out pots, pans, and Tupperware to keep him busy. I haven't decided whether keeping a child busy with messing up the kitchen, or a puppy with ripping papers, is a good idea, since my son is twenty-four years old and never cleans up the kitchen, and Snorkel is now an adult that still commits "hit-and-run by magazine ripoffs" while my husband is reading his magazines.

During the day, the crate is mandatory for the person who must work to buy puppy food. Until your puppy is trained, the crate is necessary to prevent accidents and destruction. If your puppy is left out of the crate when you cannot watch him, you can bet he will get into trouble. Ideally, your young puppy should be let out to relieve his bladder during the day after approximately four hours. If you cannot go home on a lunch hour to let your puppy out, you might want to think about asking a friend or hiring someone to do the job. When your puppy is six months old, he should be fine for eight hours in the crate under normal circumstances. Most dogs sleep sixteen hours a day and if they are not sleeping, they are soiling the house, barking, chewing, or digging. While you may wince at the thought of your puppy in a crate for eight hours during the day and eight hours at night, you surely expect your free-roaming, housebroken dog to constrain his bladder during the night or when you are at work. Of course, anytime there is an opportunity to come home, or have someone come in and let your puppy out in the yard for awhile, regardless of his age, take advantage of it. If your puppy is crated for long hours, he must have evening time and weekends for a lot of running in the yard, playing, training, socializing, or just relaxed touching time.

If you are consistent and persistent in putting your puppy in the crate and correcting his verbal protests, your puppy will adjust to the crate eventually. Your persistence and patience will pay off with the comfort of knowing that your puppy is in a safe environment while you are asleep or away. You will be comforted to know that when you wake in the morning, you will not step in a pile of unmentionables, and your household will be in the same condition as when you went to sleep. Even the most resistant puppy will be happier complaining in his kennel than sitting in an animal-shelter cage awaiting a very unfortunate fate because of behavioral problems.

Crating does not have to be a lifetime sentence or a permanent solution. When your puppy is housebroken and grows out of his chewing stage, he may then have the freedom of the house or yard if you wish. Although some of my puppies have been trustworthy as young as ten months of age, most of my dogs were not left unsupervised in the house until they were two years old.

When your puppy is reliable in your presence and is not having accidents or chewing anything that does not chew him first, you can test his good behavior by leaving him out of the crate for short periods of time while you get the mail or take a shower. If he is responsible, gradually increase his unsupervised time outside of the crate. Do not rush the process of leaving your puppy out of the crate. Occasionally, a puppy may let temptation get the best of him, and he may have an accident or redesign a shoe. Reintroduce the crate and wait several weeks before you give your puppy freedom again.

The best approach to house-training your young puppy is through use of the crate and supervision. Every time your puppy eliminates in the house without being caught in the act and shown outdoors or to a proper place, he learns that eliminating in the house is okay. A young puppy must be taught gently and positively where to eliminate. In addition to the crate, a strict feeding and exercise schedule, clear direction, and patient vigilance are positive approaches to house-training your puppy.

FEEDING SCHEDULE

The feeding schedule can very effectively regulate how much your puppy processes from the back end. The puppy that has access to food all day and eats a bite here and there will always have something to get rid of in the house. Feed your puppy at regular times, and pick up any food that he does not finish within fifteen minutes. Your breeder very likely fed the puppies two or three times a day. You will want to maintain the same schedule the first few days before you adapt the feeding times to your schedule. Feeding a couple of small meals a day rather than one large meal is healthier for your puppy, particularly for the larger breeds that eat four or more cups of food a day. Feeding three times a day may be difficult for some people and is unnecessary for many puppies. Eliminate the feeding that your puppy is least excited about, which is often the midday feeding.

EXERCISE SCHEDULE

After feeding, immediately take your puppy outside to the area where you want him to relieve himself. If he does not empty within five minutes, place him in the crate for fifteen minutes before you take him outside again. If he still doesn't relieve himself, put him back into the crate, and try again every fifteen minutes until he eliminates. Keep track of the time that your puppy takes to empty after he eats. If your puppy empties after twenty minutes, take him out twenty minutes after every feeding. When a puppy is fed on a regular schedule, you can develop a reliable schedule to take him out before any accidents occur.

When a puppy is fed on a regular schedule, you can develop a reliable schedule to take him out before any accidents occur.

Until your puppy's system matures, he will require several walks a day in between meals to prevent accidents. Young puppies need to be taken out before and after a play session or when they awake from a nap, and several times in between for good measure. Play and activity stimulate elimination. The totally engrossed puppy at play may suddenly squat to urinate or defecate without any apparent forewarning. As your puppy gets older, he will be more capable of controlling his bodily functions, and you can decrease the frequency of walks to perhaps three times a day for the young adult.

Go outside with your puppy on a leash to make sure that he empties instead of playing. Often a puppy will become distracted and will not empty himself outside, only to finish the business when he is let into the house. When your puppy begins to eliminate outside, take the opportunity to pair a command to the process. If your puppy learns a command to eliminate, many walks in the snow and rain may be shorter. Use creativity for coming up with an appropriate command. A "hurry" seems to work well without eliciting snickering from bystanders. When the puppy finally eliminates, give quiet verbal praise, such as, "Good dog." Avoid excited praise or treats, because the expectation and excitement over a forthcoming treat will distract him from completely emptying his system, and he will finish the job in the house when he calms down. If your puppy decides to play outside instead of getting down to the business at hand, confine him in his crate and wait fifteen to thirty minutes before you try again. Do not let him loose in the house until he empties outside.

For the first few weeks during house-training, gate off a large portion of your living area to keep your puppy in a small area near the door that he uses to go outside. A young puppy may not be able to control himself through a big house on the way to the door. When I lived in an apartment and had to go down six flights of stairs or use a slow elevator to get outside, I carried my puppies until we were outside to eliminate any extra physical activity that would have stimulated a premature urge. After a few times of taking your puppy out on a leash, he should get the idea. Once you are sure that your puppy understands where to relieve himself, let him start going out off leash by himself in your enclosed area.

PAPER TRAINING

Extenuating circumstances or different lifestyles may warrant that a puppy be paper trained. When I lived in an apartment in New York City, my husband was always burdened with taking our puppy out in the middle of the night because he worried about my safety. I was just as worried about his safety in the big city, so I decided to paper train my puppies. In those days, the Sunday *Times* had more use than just keeping us informed. Paper training also solved other problems, including giving my puppy an option when I was delayed at work or by public transportation. A plastic drop cloth under the newspaper protected my floors. Today, the invention of puppy pads with plastic backing to protect carpets and wood floors eliminates having to use newspaper.

Do not place the pads in the crate, because you do not want to encourage your puppy to eliminate in the crate. An exercise pen is a better option. This device consists of folded wire panels that, when opened, stand on their own; it is similar to a child's playpen.

You can attach the two open sides of the exercise pen to your crate, making a sort of run for your puppy. You can place papers in a portion of the exercise pen and leave the crate door open so that your puppy can go in and out at will, without having access to the rest of the house. At first you may want to put down papers in the entire pen area. Calmly praise your puppy every time he relieves himself on the papers. Once your puppy gets the idea to use the papers, you can decrease the papered area.

Give your puppy the opportunity to go on walks to relieve himself in the street and on grass in case you want to travel with him or train him to eliminate outside. Once my puppies grew up and didn't need fifteen walks a day, and when they could intimidate a potential villain on a dark night, I transferred the paper training to the outdoors. Most puppies will detect other dog odors outside and be stimulated to eliminate. If your puppy is reluctant to eliminate outside, take a portion of used paper and place it on the ground for your puppy to use and sniff where eliminating is acceptable. Remember to clean up after your puppy. The only thing worse than a dog that is not house-trained is an owner who is not trained to clean up after his or her own dog.

Accidents

Most puppies have occasional accidents due to illness or not being able to get outside in time. The accidents must be cleaned up properly to discourage repeated incidents in the same spot. If the odor of the urine and feces is not neutralized, it will attract your puppy and stimulate him to relieve himself in the same spot. Standard carpet or floor cleaner is not enough to discourage a puppy from returning to the same spot. A 50/50 mixture of vinegar and water, applied after cleaning with a basic carpet or floor cleaner, has been reported to be a good pet deodorizer. Sprinkling baking soda on the damp, washed spot will also help. Club soda helps to remove stain in the carpet. Several pet deodorizers are available that are reported to be very effective if you do not want to mix the vinegar solution. After you have cleaned the spot, spray a pet repellent to discourage your puppy from returning to the spot.

Catching Your Puppy in the Act of Soiling

An accident can be a teaching and learning experience. Catching your puppy in the act of soiling in the house provides an opportunity to teach him that the house is off limits. When your puppy eliminates outside and you praise him, he learns that relieving himself generates praise and your approval. Your praise outdoors does not teach your puppy that pottying indoors is unacceptable. Only after your puppy is praised outdoors and disciplined for an accident indoors will he learn that pottying outside earns praise and eliminating indoors is inappropriate.

Catching an accident and giving constructive discipline is a positive learning experience for your puppy. When you catch your puppy soiling in the house, do not run up to him. If you do, he will startle and run in the opposite direction, trailing the mess throughout the house during the chase. Instead, briskly walk up to your puppy and voice your disapproval without anger. A word such as "stop" may be useful to distract your puppy and convince him to hold whatever is left. A puppy will generally halt the flow of urine or feces if he is swooped up or taken by the collar for a trip outside. If you catch your puppy before he totally empties, he will have a little left over to spend in the yard, and you will have the opportunity to praise him if he finishes outside. The "stop" communicates to your puppy that the house is not a proper place to leave droppings, and the praise outside signals the yard as a good place to empty.

Do not give your puppy a harsh scolding. This only teaches him to be afraid of you. If your puppy does not appear to have anything left and you bring him back into the house, tie him to your waist or keep an eye on him. The trauma of being caught in the act may have temporarily suppressed his urge to finish the job outside. After half an hour or so, take him outside again to eliminate. If you cannot watch your puppy, place him in the crate to be sure that he does not slip off somewhere to finish the job.

While a young puppy will squat whenever the urge strikes, the older puppy will often return to the spot where he last soiled. In either case, it is very important to deodorize and spray a dog repellent to discourage your puppy from returning to the area. To encourage your puppy to use the proper area, pick up the feces and place it where you want him to eliminate. A urine-soaked paper towel or rag that you used to clean up a mess can be placed in the area that you want your puppy to use to encourage him to return to the appropriate spot. Puppy pads, which are sold in most pet stores, are supposedly scented to attract and stimulate a puppy to urinate and defecate. Place one of these pads outside to motivate your puppy to use the yard. Make the pad smaller and smaller each time you place it outside until the pad is eliminated altogether.

If your puppy is resistant to house-training in spite of a strict regimen, and he continues to have accidents in the crate or house, consult a veterinarian to rule out physical abnormalities.

Vigilance

Keeping an eye on a loose puppy in the house for several hours is not an easy task. An alternative to the crate for keeping track of your puppy and preventing him from slipping off into a corner for a quick mishap is to tie him to your waist with a six-foot lead. Your puppy will not have any unnoticed accidents, and as an added advantage, he will learn to keep close to you without getting underfoot. Although tying your puppy to your belt buckle sounds a little inconvenient, amazingly, it is not. Your puppy will adapt very quickly and will follow you around without getting stepped on. Tell your puppy, "Let's go," and go about your business. If he is reluctant to follow at first, just keep walking and encouraging him with your voice and a treat. Your puppy will learn that following you on a loose lead is more comfortable than fighting a tight lead.

Warn your puppy before you move, especially if you haven't changed position for a few minutes. If your puppy gets underfoot, command "move," and shuffle your feet toward him, being careful not to step on his toes. He will see your feet coming and he will naturally move. If he does not move by the sight of your feet, command "move," and gently touch his toes. Praise your puppy when he moves, and continue with your work. If you accidentally step on your puppy, do not make a fuss. If there is no fuss to reward your puppy for getting underfoot, he will be motivated to get out of your way. Tying your puppy to your waist for twenty to thirty minutes, a couple of times a day, is probably more than enough activity for the young pup.

To keep an eye on your pup, tie him to your waist as you go about your daily chores.

Door or baby gates are also effective for keeping your puppy in the same room with you where you can watch him and prevent him from sneaking off to do his business in another room.

Puppy Cues

Ideally, life would be very simple if your puppy would just give you a cue every time he had the urge to eliminate. Some puppies naturally cue by whining at the door, while many do not give any overt signals. To train your puppy to cue you, always let him out the same door. Every time he passes the door, whether he has just been out or not, pair a word such as "outside" to opening the door. If you open the door every time he is by the door, he will learn to go to the door to signal you. He may even find going to the door and getting you to open it a game. Play the game with him until you are sure that he's got the idea that when he goes to the door, you open it, even if he wants out every few minutes. If your puppy signals to go out and does not eliminate, that's okay. More important than a few unnecessary trips to the door is that your puppy learns how to get the door opened when he needs to go out. If you stop opening the door before he has made a strong association, he will stop cueing you.

To get your puppy to bark at the door, talk excitedly with your hand on the door knob until he makes a sound out of excitement. Any sound from your puppy should be rewarded by opening the door. Each time thereafter, talk excitedly and require louder sounds or finally a bark before you open the door. Save this type of training until your puppy is old enough to hold his bladder for more than a few seconds.

SUBMISSIVE URINATING

A puppy that urinates when he greets people is urinating submissively. Bitches are more likely than males to do this. The puppy that urinates when he greets people is not to be considered unhousebroken. Disciplining your puppy for submissive urinating will only intensify and escalate the problem. Harsh tones and looming over your puppy will produce urination. While stooping down to your puppy's level and petting her under the chin prevents submissive urinating for some puppies, for others, the level eye contact may still produce wetting. Encourage these puppies to jump up to be petted. If your puppy jumps up, her body is not in a urinating position, and wetting is not as easy as when she is in a squat position. Once the submissive urinating disappears, usually with age and confidence building, your puppy can be positively taught not to jump up.

Do not encourage submissive behavior by scratching your puppy's belly if she rolls over. Eliminate all emotional and happy arrivals. Instead, acknowledge the presence of your puppy with only a monotone voice while you calmly walk her outside to the yard. Do not pet her in the house or before she empties in the yard. After she empties, let her into the house, go about your business, and then after several minutes when the excitement is over, you can greet her. Beware—even after your puppy has been outside, she may still have enough liquid left to wet if you make a big fuss or give an emotional greeting.

Beach adored my husband and dribbled every time he looked or talked to her when she initially greeted him. Every night after work, I would attempt to bring her through the house to the yard, and instead of following me, Beach would run to find my husband. Instead of saying "Hi, honey, I'm home," like normal people, I would yell, "Here comes Beach! Don't look at her or talk to her." Unable to resist greeting Beach, he resorted to trying all sorts of greetings, such as a short "hi" with a pat on the head, a whispered "hello," or even just a smile and a pat. Regardless of the greeting, Beach would dribble on the carpet. While Beach cuddled up to my husband, I cleaned up the carpet. This went on until one late night when Beach greeted my husband in bed and *he* had to change all the bedding. From that day forward, my husband stopped sneaking in whispers and pats of greetings until Beach had been taken out-side, and Beach stopped dribbling on the floor. Most puppies even-tually mature out of submissive behavior, particularly if you help the process by not getting your puppy too excited during greetings. Obedience training also helps curtail submissive urination by building your puppy's confidence. Beach has just turned two years of age, is obedience trained, and can now tolerate calm greetings, even from my husband, without dribbling all over with excitement. Unemotional greetings are best for dry carpet, beds, and feet.

Physical Difficulties and House-Training Problems

There are a variety of physical ailments, infections, and ill-nesses that can cause a puppy to lose control and void in the house inappropriately, and they can be difficult to detect. If your puppy is not catching on to house-training or suddenly has a series of accidents, consult a veterinarian to rule out illness or physical problems.

The Improperly Trained Dog

If you do not find a pile or puddle for a few days, you may make the serious mistake of assuming that your puppy is house-trained. Toy breeds leave such a small amount of waste that the puppy may eliminate in the house unnoticed for months before there is enough volume or odor for you to see or detect. Check the house and furniture carefully for any signs of unwanted presents before you allow your puppy the freedom of the house without a watchful eye. If you do find a problem, you will need to retrain your puppy using the crate and a lot of vigilance. A puppy that wrongly gets the freedom of the house and is not corrected for messing in the house before he is reliably house-trained does not learn that such behavior is unacceptable.

Problems with House-Training

Occasionally, regardless of your vigilance and strict regimen, some puppies refuse to house-train and continue to mess in the house or crate on a regular basis. Puppies raised in an unclean environment or where their droppings fall only a short distance from their cage, such as in a pet shop, adapt to being close to their feces or urine without discomfort. These puppies become accustomed to uncleanliness, and to them, a clean den may not be worth the extra effort required to communicate the need to get outside. These puppies need special treatment and a very strict feeding and water schedule. Feed your puppy in the crate, but do not leave food or water in the crate for more than fifteen minutes. Food left in the crate will be eaten a little at a time and will provide something to get rid of on a frequent basis. On the other hand, puppies don't like to eat or drink near their waste, and feeding your puppy in the crate may discourage eliminating there. Keep the puppy in his crate or tie him to your waist and take him out every hour. When the crate remains clean for three days, extend the time by taking your puppy out every one and one-half hours. Increase the time that your puppy is left in the crate by half an hour, every three days if the crate is dry, until he is maintaining a dry crate for several hours at a time. For some puppies, the schedule may have to change at a slower rate. A professional day-care that can meet this frequent and rigid schedule of outings is a good option for the busy household.

House-soiling problems also develop when you expect or assume too much from your puppy. After a couple of dry nights or days, you might expect that your puppy knows not to eliminate in the house and you do not watch him as carefully or do not let him out as often. You may even view a transgression as spiteful behavior from the puppy to get you back for something that you did, such as leaving him home when you went out for ice cream. A puppy that eliminates when you leave is not being spiteful—he is not totally house-trained. A couple of dry nights or days does not constitute a thoroughly housebroken puppy. Even if your puppy has been maintaining clean standards for months, there are many reasons why puppies may regress in their elimination habits, and spiteful behavior would be the least likely factor.

If you have disciplined your puppy for accidents in the house, he is smart enough not to eliminate in front of you. On the other hand, he is also smart enough to take the first opportunity during your absence to relieve himself when the urge strikes. Even if your puppy just relieved himself outside before you left, he may have become anxious with your departure, and the stress may have precipitated an urge. If your puppy is relieving himself when you leave the house, he is not ready to have the freedom of the house. If your puppy soils and is not caught in the act, he will learn that when no one is home, soiling is okay. Unless your puppy is corrected during or immediately after an act, he cannot possibly know what is inappropriate behavior. This is why you must use the crate—to prevent unintentional training.

House soiling may recur when you have a schedule change and cannot let your puppy outside to eliminate at the same time of day, yet you do not think to change his feeding schedule. Your puppy may therefore not be used to or capable of waiting until you get home. Make any schedule changes gradual by asking friends to let your pup out or by taking advantage of daycare services.

Some dogs are never trustworthy enough to be left in the house alone, and the crate may in fact be a lifetime facility. The crate option is still a lesser evil than the negative emotions that can develop in your relationship with your puppy as a result of problem behavior. The crate, an effective tool for positive house-training, along with good communication, is the key to fostering good behavior and preventing behavioral problems from developing.

CHAPTER 11

Communicating Proper Behavior to Your Puppy

 **E**very new puppy owner has certain basic expectations about how his puppy is to behave. For instance, you expect your puppy to relieve himself outdoors, to reserve biting for his food and toys, to respond to your commands, and to bark when strangers approach. Contrary to your expectations, puppies naturally mouth, bark, and relieve themselves whenever they have the urge unless they are taught proper behavior. Puppies are not born knowing your desires, how to behave, or the meaning of your commands. Puppies have to be taught how to behave through positive interactions and clear communication.

POSITIVE INTERACTIONS

Positive training and interactions are imperative for promoting correct behavior and a happy relationship. Negative interactions increase avoidance behavior and prevent a good relationship from developing. For example, if you kick or smack your puppy for jumping up, your puppy learns to fear you and mistrust you. If you do not want your puppy to jump, avoid a negative interaction by teaching your puppy to sit when you come in the door. A puppy cannot jump up if he is obeying a command to sit. Another example that demonstrates a negative experience is calling your puppy to you for an unpleasant activity. Few puppies beg to have, or for that matter

*Positive training and interactions are imperative for promoting
correct behavior and a happy relationship.
Puppies learn very quickly to avoid unpleasant interactions.*

enjoy, their nails being cut, and if you call your puppy over to cut
his nails, you create a negative interaction and association with
coming when called. The puppy that obeys the command to come
and is grabbed to have his nails cut associates the negative experience with going to you when he is called. Puppies learn very
quickly to avoid unpleasant interactions by not obeying the command to come. If you call your puppy to you, he must always be
rewarded with praise. Even if you proceed to cut his nails after
you praise him, he will associate coming to you with praise rather
than with the unpleasant nail cutting.

GOOD COMMUNICATION

The commands that you teach your puppy must communicate a specific idea in order for your puppy to have an opportunity to respond appropriately. For example, if you teach "down" to communicate the prone position and you use "down" when your puppy jumps on you without insisting that he be lying on the floor, your puppy will become confused. The alternative is to teach "down" for the prone position and "off" to communicate not to jump up.

The best example of a command that does not communicate a specific idea is the word "no." Typically, "no" is used for every misbehavior, such as accidents, barking, chewing, and nipping. One command used for every behavior too frequently loses its meaning and effectiveness. Complicating communication even further, "no" is often used improperly before a command. Denise was practicing "come" with her puppy and stepped away to call her. The puppy started to run to Denise and halfway across became distracted, veering off in another direction. When Denise saw her puppy change direction, she yelled, "No, Lucy, come!" "No" is used so often that most puppies think that the word is their name! Teach your puppy a large vocabulary. Instead of yelling "no" when your puppy is barking, use "quiet." Rather than admonishing your puppy when he jumps on people with a harsh "no," teach him "off." Every behavior needs a specific command to clearly inform your puppy about how he is to behave. A puppy cannot possibly respond to you correctly if the commands are unclear or the rules change from day to day without prior notice.

When Mary first got her puppy, he was not allowed to sleep on the bed. Mary's husband left for a business trip, and Mary decided to let her puppy sleep in bed only when her husband was out of town. The puppy became very fond of the bed, and subsequently, when Mary's husband returned, they all jumped into bed. The puppy was promptly met with a hard boot off the bed, because he had no idea that he was allowed in bed only when Mary's husband was gone. Confused about what had changed from the day before, the puppy tried jumping up onto the bed again, only to receive another kick to get off. He wasn't allowed on the bed for several days until Mary's husband left for another trip. Mary lifted her puppy up onto the bed, and he quickly learned that sometimes he was allowed on the bed and sometimes he was not. Not sure whether he was going to be petted or booted for jumping into bed, Mary's puppy became reluctant to approach the bed and the husband. Mary was instructed to teach her puppy "up," which invited him onto the bed. Mary also taught "off," which informed her puppy to keep his paws on the ground. With clear commands for these specific behaviors, Mary's puppy learned what to expect and no longer acted fearful around the bed or Mary's husband.

Clear communication involves teaching your puppy a command for each desired and undesired behavior. For example, if you don't mind your puppy jumping on you when you come home in your play clothes, you can teach a jump-up command that tells your puppy that jumping up is acceptable. If you don't want your puppy jumping up on you when you arrive home in your Sunday dress clothes, you can teach him "off" or "sit," which instructs him not to jump up as you walk in the door. Good communication teaches your puppy the proper behavior and how to earn your praise for obeying. When messages are confusing, a puppy can neither establish a pattern to earn your approval nor predict your reactions. The puppy that does not know how to predict his owner's reactions becomes fearful, mistrusting, and avoidant.

Communication problems can be prevented by teaching your puppy rather than just assuming that he knows what is right. If you assume that your puppy knows what to do without training him to behave in different situations, you may even punish him when in actuality he really didn't know that his action

Puppies must have training to know what or what not to do. Your puppy cannot read your mind.

was wrong. While Patrick was training his puppy to retrieve, he would motivate Jordan by playing keep-away with a toy. Patrick would move the toy back and forth quickly and would praise Jordan when he jumped up and grabbed at the toy. One day during a family barbecue, Patrick's nephews and Jordan went into the yard to play with a Frisbee. As one of the boys started to throw the Frisbee, Jordan jumped for the toy as he had been taught and knocked the boy down. Patrick was furious and reprimanded Jordan severely because he assumed that Jordan knew better than to jump on children. Patrick was worried about Jordan's behavior until we talked about the incident and he realized that he had never taught Jordan how to play with children. If you assume that your puppy knows better, you will be disappointed or, worse yet, angry when he does not respond as you expect. Puppies must have training to know what or what not to do. Your puppy cannot read your mind. Puppies must be taught how to behave in different situations with praise and appropriate discipline.

CLEAR PRAISE AND DISCIPLINE

Teaching a puppy how to behave involves positive reinforcement and discipline. Positive reinforcement or praise encourages behaviors that you want repeated, and discipline or punishment discourages behaviors that you do not want your puppy to repeat. Your puppy will be motivated to perform behaviors that earn praise and avoid behaviors with negative consequences. Praise and corrections must occur during a behavior or immediately following for your puppy to correctly associate his action with the reward or consequence. A puppy associates praise and correction with the last event or action that occurred before he was praised or corrected. If you come home, see a mess on the floor from hours before, and discipline your puppy, your puppy will only develop an unpleasant association with homecomings and will learn nothing about the mess on the floor. Discipline must never be too harsh or your puppy will become fearful. The ten-week-old puppy that hasn't quite grasped the idea that the outdoors is the only place to relieve himself will become fearful and avoidant if he is yelled at or beaten for an accident.

Any time you discipline your puppy, give him the opportunity to earn your approval and learn proper behaviors. While I was placing a collar on a six-month-old Blue Heeler by the name of Buck, he decided to use his teeth to request the removal of my hand from his collar. After I corrected Buck for his improper choice of using his teeth, I commanded him to sit. After Buck sat, I praised him and went back to adjusting his collar. Buck kept his teeth in his mouth, and I praised him for sitting. Giving a command after a correction clearly distinguishes between the behaviors that produce correction and those that are rewarded. There must be a command between the discipline and the praise so that your puppy does not get confused.

Josie, a Dalmatian, would get very excited and would nip or snap at Georgia when she was attaching his lead. Every time Josie snapped, Georgia corrected her. Georgia felt so bad about correcting Josie that she would praise her right after the correction. Well, the minute Georgia praised Josie, she would get so excited that she would start snapping all over again. Wanting to earn Georgia's praise more than anything, Josie continued to snap and suffer the correction. To break the cycle, Georgia was instructed to correct Josie for snapping. After the correction, instead of praising her, she was to command Josie to sit or down. Once she obeyed, she was praised. Josie learned that snapping elicited a correction and obeying a command produced praise. Josie found the praise more pleasurable than the correction and learned that she could earn praise by obeying commands and avoid correction by keeping her mouth closed.

Discipline for misbehavior and praise for performing on your command clearly inform a puppy about how to behave. Merely praising a puppy for not misbehaving is a very hard concept for him to grasp and does not promote concrete and clear communication. The puppy that is ignored when he barks inappropriately, and then praised when he is quiet, will not easily associate that he is being praised for being quiet. However, if a barking puppy is commanded "quiet," and is either corrected for continuing to bark or praised for stopping after the command, he learns that barking after your command produces a negative consequence and to cease barking earns praise. A puppy naturally wants to avoid negative consequences, and therefore, he quickly learns appropriate behavior to earn praise.

*Chasing is a fun game for dogs and children at first
until the puppy grows up and has bigger teeth.*

POSITIVE TRAINING

Sometimes you may unknowingly and erroneously communicate the opposite concept that you intend. A good example is during a fearful episode. The puppy encounters a frightening object, event, or person and displays a variety of fear reactions, which may include shaking, barking, and backing away. Realizing that your puppy is in distress, you attempt to comfort and assure him with loving strokes and words of sympathy to communicate that everything will be all right. Although you only wish to communicate that the situation is not threatening, the puppy thinks that acting and being fearful is pleasing to you. Stroking or petting a puppy when he is fearful rewards him for fearful behavior. Instead

*Instead of rewarding fearful behavior, encourage your pup
to investigate a seemingly threatening situation so he
learns to cope with his fear.*

of rewarding fearful behavior, you must encourage your puppy to investigate a seemingly threatening situation so that he can learn to appropriately cope with his fear. One evening when my puppy was outside in the yard, I decided to rearrange a couple of pieces of furniture and moved my carousel horse across the room. After the furniture was moved, I let my puppy in from the yard. She walked around for a few minutes, suddenly noticed the horse in a different place, and flipped out. Instead of consoling her, and thus rewarding her for fearful behavior, I walked over to the horse and touched it. By touching the horse, I encouraged her to approach and sniff the scary monster. Once she realized that I didn't get eaten by the horse, she sniffed it and decided that it was not going to eat her either, and she walked off and found something else to do. The strong temptation to lovingly comfort the fearful puppy must be avoided lest you unintentionally communicate that acting frightened produces reward with attention and stroking.

UNDERSTANDING YOUR PUPPY'S COMMUNICATION

Puppies are very communicative through their body language. Observing and understanding your puppy's body language can prevent many problems before they happen. The puppy that sniffs the carpet after finishing dinner is probably looking for a place to empty his bowels. The puppy that stops chewing on a toy when you pass may be signaling his intention to protect his prize from you. Protecting a favorite toy is an extremely important message that you do not want to miss. Protecting toys or food easily escalates to growling and even biting.

As a young child, I was given a Basset Hound mix named Happy, who thought that heaven was having a bone. Happy always took his bone into my bedroom and chewed it under the nightstand where no one ever bothered him. One day after school, I opened the bedroom door to drop something off and Happy sprang across the bed and attached himself to my thigh with his big teeth. In retrospect, I realized that I not only missed Happy's

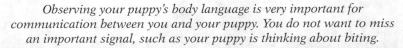

Observing your puppy's body language is very important for communication between you and your puppy. You do not want to miss an important signal, such as your puppy is thinking about biting.

cues but did not understand his body language when he would stop and stiffen as someone passed his food bowl. When cues or body language are missed or ignored, as in the case of people walking by a food bowl, the puppy perceives that he was successful in chasing away the intruders. The puppy learns that his behavior is acceptable, and he will become more confident and aggressive near his possessions. Generally, the first hints of aggression are very subtle, and an inexperienced owner can easily miss the signals. To prevent undesirable behaviors from being reinforced unintentionally, you must understand your puppy's reactions, monitor them closely, and handle them appropriately to quickly discourage problem behaviors before they become inappropriate behavioral patterns.

Dogs have a social order; there is typically a leader, while the rest are followers or underlings.

HIERARCHY VERSUS ANARCHY

The canine is a social animal that possesses a natural desire to establish a social order. The social order is usually comprised of one individual on the top and lots of underlings. Because the individual on the top enjoys benefits not available to the underlings, few dogs miss the opportunity to take charge. If your puppy's attempts to take charge go unchecked, he can easily become demanding and aggressive. An uncorrected grumble from a puppy that protests being removed from the couch may intensify to a snap the next time he is physically moved. Each time an aggressive or dominant act goes uncorrected, your puppy will become more confident about controlling your behavior. Until my dogs pay the mortgage and buy the groceries, the top position in the household is mine, and there is no room for negotiation. Serious ambition must be snuffed out if you and your puppy are to live safely and harmoniously in the same household.

PERSISTENCE MUST PREVAIL

One discussion about who is in charge or a sign on your desk displaying the title "BOSS" may not be enough to convince your puppy to give up trying for the top position. Your puppy may persist in taking opportunities to be boss and will very definitely take advantage of your lack of persistence. If you give in, your puppy will learn quickly that his persistence is rewarded.

My Portuguese Water Dog, Scuba, loves to do tricks for treats. Every night at the dinner table, he starts his repertoire of tricks in front of my husband. The pattern is always the same—my husband tells Scuba to take a hike and never enforces the command, so Scuba just continues his display. About halfway through the meal, my husband becomes annoyed with Scuba pestering him, and his solution is to give Scuba a tidbit and tell him, "Now go away—that's all you get." Scuba is not a stupid dog, so he goes through his tricks all over again and the meal continues until Scuba and my husband have finished their dinner. Instead of being persistent and making Scuba go away from the dinner table, thus teaching Scuba that begging does not pay off, Scuba is rewarded for being a pest at the table and learns not to give in first. If you give in to your puppy, instead of correcting a behavior,

Understanding your puppy's body language and vocalizations will inform you about his emotions or intentions in the context of a situation.

he will learn to endure even longer the next time. Conversely, if you are stubborn and refuse to give in until you get the proper behavior, you will be richly rewarded when your puppy concedes to authority and obeys your commands. Obedience training is the key for learning how to communicate, understand body language, and positively resolve or prevent behavioral problems.

CHAPTER 12

Understanding Body Language

Understanding your puppy's body language and vocalizations will inform you about his emotions or intentions in the context of a situation. A yelp, which may signal pain, or a stiff body and raised hackles after someone passes your puppy's food bowl, are clear messages that you do not want to misinterpret or ignore. If you observe and recognize the cues that communicate that your puppy is running for household tyrant, or that he is fearful of children and may bite, you can intervene before the situation gets out of control.

VOCALIZATIONS

Growling

An uninterrupted loud, throaty, sound which seems to stem from the innermost part of the puppy is an unmistakable warning. The sound conveys strong irritability, annoyance, fear, or anger, and the intention to bite. Growling backed up with aggressive body language should never be taken lightly or ignored.

Barking

Learning how to differentiate and interpret your puppy's barks can be a helpful communication tool. A bark at the back door to go out takes the guesswork out of when to let your puppy outside. Barking can be a valuable alarm system, and the different-sounding barks can alert you to whether a familiar person is arriving versus a stranger. Puppies also bark when they are playing, hungry, and lonely, to name just a few.

Yelping

The yelp is a sharp sound, comparable to a human's "ouch!" and usually indicates surprise and pain. The yelp may also signify a cry of "uncle" or submission. Ironically, the sound of a yelping puppy often brings on more attackers if other dogs are in the area. Puppies also yelp when they are extremely excited.

Whining or Whimpering

Whining is a high-pitched sound that may be analogous to human crying. Puppies often whimper or whine when they are confined or left alone. The sound definitely projects the notion that your puppy is unhappy or uncomfortable.

Dog Talk

Puppies often vocalize with a mixture of growling, barking, whimpering, and whining. Growling and barking are often heard when two dogs play or during a game of tug-of-war. Growling during play and in the absence of aggressive body language is not directed as a threat to the opponent. A short growl as a puppy warms up for a big bark when he is playing does not usually indicate aggression. In some instances, growling and whining may be mixed if your puppy is experiencing conflicting emotions or confusion over a particular situation and is uncertain about how to respond. Mixed vocalizations should be evaluated within the context of the situation and the presence of other body cues.

BODY LANGUAGE

During the litter experience, the first level of communication between puppies is usually based on size and strength. The largest and strongest puppy is usually the most dominant of the litter. A puppy displays his strength and willingness to fight for position through dominant body language. Puppies that are willing to submit to the top dog will also display body language that communicates their submission or lack of desire to fight for a certain position.

Biting and pouncing are natural dog behaviors between littermates and should not be allowed when a puppy interacts with people.

Body Language of the Dominant Puppy

The young, confident, dominant puppy appears to be fearless, and his interactions within the litter are as revealing about his position as his body language. A young, dominant puppy uses physical strength to secure his position by pushing to the first in line, bowling over his littermates, and struggling and snapping when he is restrained. As he gets older, he learns that he can conserve his physical energy and use body language to communicate dominance. When he chooses to display dominance, he may use any number of signals, such as standing erect and tall, displaying a stiff body with an arched neck and a high head and tail carriage, appearing to walk on the tips of his toes in a very slow and deliberate manner as

Generally, the largest, strongest puppy in the litter is the most dominant.

if he owns the place, and raising his hackles on the top of his shoulders and rump. The annoyed dominant puppy will give direct eye contact, curl his lips to expose his big pearly white canines, and rumble or growl. The dominant puppy has no reservation about biting or snapping to get his way.

Body Language of the Fearful Dog

Unlike the dominant puppy, the fearful puppy communicates his position very early by cowering or slinking close to the ground as if trying to melt into the scenery or become invisible. He rarely takes part in new activities and is often observed off in a corner or huddled next to a passive littermate. A fearful puppy will be the last to come up to people or investigate new stimuli. Generally, the fearful puppy moves or darts in different directions to find an escape route. He avoids eye contact and either throws quick glances or looks at people from the side of his eye as he indirectly watches and notes changes, moves, or advances. A fearful puppy holds his ears flat, close to his head, and his tail is usually held tightly against his rump or between his rear legs. If the puppy does expose his teeth, it is usually because he cannot get away and is making an attempt to defend himself.

Body Language of the Submissive Dog

The submissive puppy often urinates during his approach as he either scoots along the ground in a sit position to get closer to you or rolls over at your feet to expose his belly and genitals. The submissive puppy may begin his approach with a lowered, tipped head and his lips curled, exposing his teeth. As a rule, the exposed teeth displayed by the submissive puppy do not pose a threat and are termed "smiling." Although the submissive puppy turns his head and eye contact is generally avoided, he watches body language in his peripheral vision to determine protocol in each social situation. In an attempt to appease, the submissive puppy darts his tongue in and out to lick the mouth and face of those whom he is greeting. The same licking gesture is observed when a pup approaches his dam.

Interpreting a puppy's body language may be difficult if a puppy mixes signals or does not display the classical body language associated with dominance, fear, or submission. Many Northern breeds, such as Malamutes, are very vocal and often mix growling sounds with submissive displays. The puppy that is separated from his litter too early and has not had the opportunity to learn or perfect his body language may erroneously mix body postures that muddle interpretation. If you mistake the submissive exposure of teeth for aggression and correct your puppy, the submissive behavior will only become more intense. If you mistake the body language of a fearful dog and correct him, you will intensify his fear. Consequently, evaluate both body language and vocal communication to gauge your puppy's mood or intentions so that your subsequent interaction with him will be appropriate for the circumstance.

YOUR VERBAL COMMUNICATION AND MEANING

Words do not have meaning for puppies until you attach specific events to them. For example, "cookie" has meaning for your puppy only after you repeatedly say "cookie" and give him a snack immediately following the word. Any word can be taught in the same manner. Puppies form associations or learn the meaning of your words when you pair an action or an event with a particular word(s).

Tone of Voice

Your tone of voice informs your puppy of your mood and intentions. Puppies interpret your sounds within their own frame of reference. Therefore, if you scream, a sound similar to the yelp, your puppy will very likely and correctly interpret the sound as a signal of surprise and pain. A yell or harsh voice is comparable to a growl for your puppy, and he may predict that a correction or dominant gesture is forthcoming. A low, coarse, harsh voice backed up with eye contact and a firm correction will always inform your puppy that you are not happy and will not tolerate his present behavior. Puppies interpret happy tones of voice as praise and reward, while they perceive fear or pain in a screeching voice. Commands sent with the intention to control or correct your puppy from biting must never be delivered in a fearful-sounding, shrill voice. Likewise, do not praise your puppy in the same low, harsh voice that normally communicates dominance. Tone of voice is a powerful communicator and should be used in proper context to help your puppy learn.

YOUR BODY LANGUAGE

Confidence and control must be communicated in your body language when you handle your puppy. If your handling communicates an unsure or tentative attitude, your puppy may very well challenge or question your leadership and authority. A challenge from your puppy that goes unchecked may be likened to climbing a ladder, one rung at a time. Every successful challenge for your puppy is a step up the ladder for him and a step down for you. There is no room for two at the top of the ladder.

A real leader maintains a confident stature and direct eye contact during interactions. Avoiding eye contact with your puppy during a challenge telegraphs weakness as leader. Although you do not need to spend the majority of your time glaring at your puppy to establish leadership, you must use direct eye contact to communicate undisputed authority when your puppy either challenges you or you are correcting his behavior. If your puppy does not believe that you are serious about enforcing the rules, he will not obey you. The importance of earning and maintaining dominance over your puppy cannot be stressed enough. While the thought of your puppy running the household—for instance, having control over the refrigerator—can be amusing, it can also be very scary. Commanding a puppy to get off the couch and being answered with a snarl is not a laughing matter. Whether the challenge arises from a dispute over a favorite chair or a discarded chicken carcass, you must be the victor in the confrontation. If you are not, the challenges will become more frequent and will escalate in intensity until someone is physically harmed.

MYTHS ABOUT DOMINANCE PROBLEMS

Earning leadership and authority does not mean that you have to be a tyrant or deprive your puppy of closeness or affection. There are many theories about managing dominance issues, which include maintaining control by avoiding confrontations that you may not win. Confrontations are avoided by implementing strong sanctions for your puppy. The short list of sanctions commands that you do not feed your puppy before you eat, pet your puppy unless he obeys a command, allow your puppy to sleep on the bed or furniture, permit your puppy to go into a room or out a door first, play tug-of-war, or feed scraps. According to theory, allowing your puppy certain comforts will produce a spoiled puppy and create a monster, dominant dog.

Dominance problems are not caused by "spoiling" your puppy. Aggression and dominance problems are generally caused by training improperly and not enforcing your authority. The puppy that gets fed before you eat dinner will not make a quantum leap to appoint himself leader because he ate first. Petting and touching

are important in the human-canine relationship, and to limit petting for fear of losing dominance is a horrible and unnecessary
restriction. Imagine being instructed not to kiss your child when
you have the desire, or worse yet, make the child earn the kiss by
doing something. Your puppy should not have to perform all the
time to get a pat on the head or a stroke on the back. Your puppy
will not become aggressive because he gets too much petting or is
allowed on the furniture. The puppy that is allowed on the couch
only becomes aggressive and dominant if you don't respond correctly if he growls or snaps while he is on the furniture or after
you tell him to get off. Avoiding certain games or insisting that
your puppy be the last one out the door does little to prevent dominance. The only method for preventing dominant behavior is to
understand your puppy's body language, confront issues when
they arise, discipline appropriately, and communicate positively,
consistently, and sensibly to teach your puppy the rules through
obedience training.

CHAPTER 13

Disciplining
Your Puppy

The form of discipline that you use to correct your puppy for misbehavior greatly affects his confidence and the quality of your relationship with him. Discipline must be timely and not too harsh if you want to raise a mentally healthy and sociable puppy. When discipline is necessary, you must carefully choose corrections that are associated with the misbehavior and that are appropriate for your puppy's temperament.

PROPER DISCIPLINE

Discipline is only effective when you catch your puppy in the act of misbehaving. Puppies think in the present, not the past or future. Your puppy does not think, "If I do this, then this will happen," or, "I stole the bread this morning and that's why I'm getting punished this afternoon." Puppies are linear, sequential thinkers—"There's food, I can reach it, boy it's good." Puppies cannot make a connection between the punishment and crime unless the correction occurs simultaneously or instantly after the dirty deed. Late corrections that are not connected to a specific event will make your puppy meek, unsure, fearful, and reluctant to venture past the familiar. Your puppy must understand which events trigger a correction so that he can avoid correction, and he can only make that connection when the correction is delivered during or immediately after a behavior. Late and/or harsh corrections destroy a puppy's confidence.

Lori was determined that her new puppy would not jump on people. At ten weeks of age, Lori's puppy received such a hard correction for jumping that he fell over backwards. The correction made such a harsh impression on Lori's mild-tempered puppy that he subsequently approached people in a submissive slink. Although the correction cured jumping, Lori's puppy lost confidence around people. A softer correction with positive reinforcement for sitting when greeting people would have been more appropriate for this puppy's temperament and would have eliminated jumping without destroying his confidence. Discipline should begin with the least amount of force or negative consequence and gradually increase until the behavior is discouraged. If Lori's puppy had disobeyed the sit, Lori could have intensified the correction gradually, gauging her puppy's response so that the correction only accomplished discouraging the crime and not destroying her puppy's confidence with unnecessary roughness.

On the other hand, a puppy that receives corrections that are too mild, or that never receives corrections, becomes a tyrant. Passive corrections, such as holding a grudge for a long time or depriving your puppy of social contact (time-out method) by locking him in a room alone or turning your back to him, are ineffective and do not teach your puppy proper behavior. Puppies do not comprehend grudges and isolation. At most, the isolation distracts them and they wind up barking or destroying the room and resenting the confinement.

Matching the punishment to the crime comes easier if you are aware of why puppies do what they do. Puppies do not steal your socks to make you angry or watch the contortions on your face. Retrieving is part of being a puppy, as is investigating new stinky items, carrying them around, flipping them in the air, pouncing them to death, and ripping their guts out. If you can remember that your puppy is not trying to make you angry when he steals a sock, but instead, he is stealing socks because that's what puppies do, your corrections will be more rational and effective. Delivering a tough correction would discourage future retrieving. A proper correction for retrieving a taboo item would be to happily call your puppy to you, praise him for coming, and replace the catch with an acceptable chew toy or a treat. Conversely, the puppy that snaps at you does not deserve a trade of body parts and must be corrected.

IMPROPER CORRECTIONS

Any correction should be fast and should require as little physical restraint as possible. Anytime you battle your puppy physically or restrain him with techniques such as pinning him to the ground, shaking him by the scruff, biting his muzzle, or squeezing his muzzle, you invite him to challenge and bite. The only purpose served by restraint techniques is to frustrate and anger your puppy. Think about what you would do and feel if you were restrained. The normal reaction is to get mad and fight back to get loose. Restraint, especially in a situation where a puppy is in a temper tantrum or frenzy or is seriously aggressive, only makes him more exasperated. Tackling or pinning an aggressive fifteen-month-old puppy to the ground (particularly a very large, aggressive dog) requires superhuman strength, and unless you are training for world-championship wrestling, guess who will win the battle.

While restraint methods may be effective when they are delivered by a puppy's dam, your puppy learns quickly that you are much slower and more vulnerable than his dam, who bit back if he got into a struggle with her. You are not your puppy's mother; therefore, correcting him with methods such as growling and biting him on the muzzle as suggested by some theorists, is ludicrous and dangerous and only serves to reduce your status and authority.

AGGRESSION AND CORRECTIONS

Anytime a puppy places his teeth on a person, he needs to be corrected, because there is a risk of injury regardless of how gentle he uses his mouth. If a puppy is not corrected for using his teeth, he quickly learns that his sharp teeth give him the power to control your behavior. In other words, give a puppy a finger and he will eventually take an arm. Innocent puppy play involving teething, nipping, herding, and snapping will gradually increase to serious biting if it is not corrected.

MOUTHING

Teething, mouthing, and nipping are all similar behaviors that must be discouraged. Young puppies commonly gnaw or mouth fingers and hands to relieve the discomfort of teething or just to test what is edible and what is not. Nipping and mouthing are also forms of aggressive play between puppies. Although puppy nipping

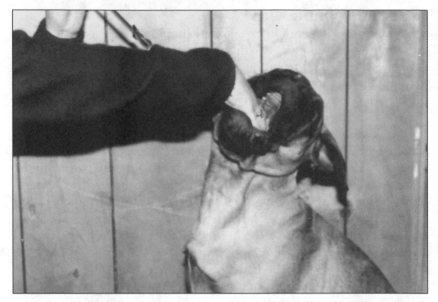

When your puppy mouths or teethes, instead of pulling your hand away, push your fingers down his throat or gag him.

is not intended to do serious harm, your puppy learns that nipping gets people to back off, and it can be a fun game to boot. Typically, if your puppy nips, you yelp (sound of submission) and pull away, and your puppy gets to chase your hand. Certainly, you did not intend to teach him that nipping causes retreat. However, from your puppy's point of view, when you pull back your hand from the painful nip, he has the power and the upper hand, so to speak. As your puppy gets older and attempts to climb the social ladder, or becomes more demanding and dominant, the nipping quickly turns into biting.

The best correction for puppy teething and nipping is gagging. When your puppy teethes, instead of pulling your hand out of his mouth, push your fingers down his throat far enough to tickle his belly button internally. Your puppy will gag and will learn that chewing on your fingers is distasteful. As your puppy is gagging, he will open his mouth wide, and you can remove your hand without getting scratched. Gagging will also discourage chasing and snapping at hands, because smart puppies do not chase things that make them gag.

GROWLING

Challenges often start with a low growl, which is often backed up with a show of teeth. The teeth are your puppy's primary offense and defense, and showing them sends the message to back off. Growling does not mean that your puppy doesn't love you, only that he would prefer a shift in power. In fact, many people who have been bitten by their dominant puppy report that he is very loving most of the time, and particularly after an attack.

If a challenge is allowed to go undisputed, future protests may escalate to bites. If your puppy growls after you tell him to get off of the couch, you must correct him for growling. If your puppy is not corrected for growling, the couch becomes his possession, and the next time anyone attempts to remove him from the couch, he may bite. Other situations in which dominant puppies may readily challenge you include being removed from the bed, having your hands in his food dishes, taking hold of his collar, brushing or grooming him, trimming his nails, and placing him in the down position. The raze correction, explained below, is usually very effective for the start of dominant or possessive behavior in puppies. If several raze corrections do not appear to have any effect in altering your puppy's behavior, beef up the intensity of the correction or switch to one of the other correction techniques.

RAZE

The term "raze" means to level to the ground. The confident puppy that growls and challenges your authority needs to be taken down a couple of levels from his throne if you are to be respected as a leader. An effective correction for growling is a firm "no" paired with strong eye contact as you raise your puppy off of the ground by his loose skin on both sides of his jaw, supporting him under the jaw. He is raised up only far enough for his front paws to leave the ground. Raising your puppy off of the ground makes him feel insecure, slightly intimidated, and less dominant. Once your puppy is off of the ground and your hands are supporting his head and neck, give him another "no" with a light shake to get his attention. Make sure that your forearms are close together under your puppy's jaw so that he cannot bite them. Keep your puppy elevated until he ceases his growling and displays signs of submission, such as turning his eyes away from yours.

The raze correction is effective for puppies
that test your authority with a growl.

Do *not* praise or console your puppy immediately after you drop him the few inches back to the ground; instead, give him a command such as sit, *then* praise him for his good behavior. The raze correction effectively communicates to your puppy that you are bigger and stronger, because removing his feet from the ground places him in a very insecure position. However, if your hard-tempered puppy is not the least bit shaken by the raze correction, the cuff is an effective correction.

SNAPPING

A snap in its least aggressive form is a reflex. For instance, a sleeping puppy that is startled may snap at the closest object out of reflex. When people are startled, they strike out with their hands. Startled puppies strike with their teeth. The bite is usually quick and without enough pressure to leave more than a red mark or a slight break in the skin. If your puppy startles easy, verbally warn him when you are entering the room or moving close. If your household is full of children running in and out, crate or confine your puppy away from foot traffic to prevent tripping on him.

A snap, at its worst, is an aggressive reaction from the dominant or fearful puppy. A puppy's purpose for snapping is generally to get the threat to back off more than it is to do damage. The puppy that is successful in getting people to retreat by snapping will become more confident about his control and may eventually resort to biting. The most effective correction for snapping is a cuff under the chin.

Cuff under the Chin

The cuff communicates to your puppy to keep his mouth closed. The cuff, paired with a sharp "no," is achieved by making a fist and delivering a swat under the snapping puppy's chin. The correction does not need to be hard—just strong enough to make the lower jaw meet the upper jaw. Hold onto your puppy's collar so that he cannot get away, and never swat on top of the muzzle, where many olfactory nerves reside. The cuff, a quick, nonrestraint correction, gets the message across that biting is unacceptable. Rarely will a puppy chase your hand after the correction. If you have ever hit your chin on something hard enough to close your teeth, it is unlikely that you were seriously injured. However, you probably were more careful about where you put your chin, and that is the same message that you want to get across to a snapping puppy. The cuff is a strong correction and should be used for snapping when other corrections have not worked or when you are in a compromising position, such as when a puppy gets more aggressive by a raze or other hands-on correction.

Collar Corrections

Collar corrections, or snaps on the lead, are also good alternatives to the raze correction for growling or snapping. Some puppies become more reactive and aggressive the more they are handled or touched, and a collar correction eliminates having to put your hands directly on your puppy, which he may interpret as

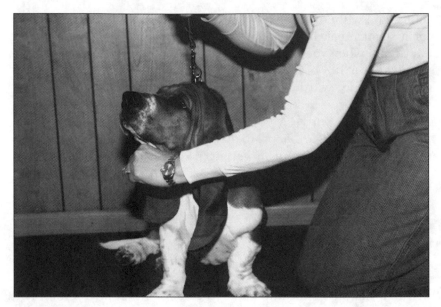

The cuff under the chin communicates to your puppy to keep his mouth closed. Always hold on to the collar before you deliver the correction so that your puppy cannot snap a second time.

aggression or even petting and play. Collar corrections force your puppy to pay attention to you and distract and/or defuse aggressive behavior, especially when the correction is paired with a harsh "no" and a squirt in the face from a water bottle (see next section). Follow your correction with an immediate, strong obedience command such as sit, down, or heel to distract your puppy and give him the opportunity to be praised when he obeys. Of course, if one snap on the lead does not convince your puppy to stop his behavior, give as many snaps as it takes to get his attention and cease the undesired activity. A snap on the lead for misbehavior followed by a command is very effective in directing your puppy's energy or aggression away from undesirable stimuli and toward working with you.

BITING

The difference between a snap and a bite is that the puppy intends to do damage and uses enough jaw pressure to puncture your skin, or worse, crush an appendage. A puppy that intentionally punctures skin, tears flesh, breaks a bone, hangs onto his victim, or delivers multiple bites is considered vicious. This aggressive puppy should not be handled without expert professional advice and help.

Squirt Bottle Correction

A squirt bottle, filled with ice-cold water and set on hard stream, becomes a very obtrusive, nonviolent, effective correction when sprayed at a misbehaving puppy. Few animals, short of a dolphin, like water squirted directly between their eyes. Cold water is shocking, aversive, distracting, and effective for controlling behavior when paired with a strong command. Substances such as vinegar, lemon juice, Listerine, or Bitter Apple should *not* be added to the water. If you wouldn't put a substance in your own eyes, do not spray it at your puppy. Inflicting pain or irritating the eyes is not necessary to get your point across. The principle behind the water correction is to provide an annoying distraction—*not* to impair your puppy's vision.

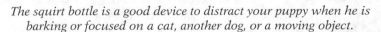

The squirt bottle is a good device to distract your puppy when he is barking or focused on a cat, another dog, or a moving object.

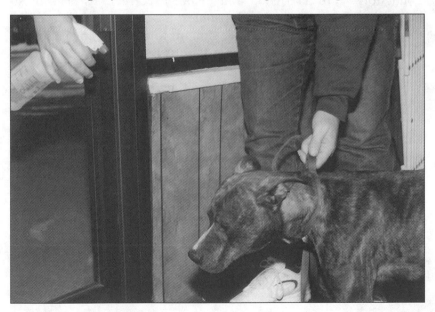

The squirt bottle can be used for many different behaviors, such as jumping up, herding, barking, and chasing cats. A squirt of water in the face paired with a strong, harsh-sounding verbal correction is aversive and distracting. Your puppy will be motivated to halt his actions to avoid another squirt. Be careful not to laugh at your puppy or his reaction. Laughter will only turn the correction into a water game. The puppy that nips at your heels will not find nipping nearly as pleasurable if every time he nips, water is squirted in his face. A battery of bottles can be left around the house for fast and easy access. Once your puppy understands the principle of the bottle (disobey a command and get squirted), a water bottle simply left in your puppy's view is often a good reminder for him not to engage in misbehavior. Water corrections can be used to discourage an array of bad habits from a distance, depending, of course, on how far the water bottle can squirt water and how accurate you are with your aim.

For backyard misbehavior, a power nozzle attached to a garden hose provides a strong, annoying stream of water for long-distance corrections. Battery-operated toy water guns can also send strong streams of water and are more fun for the child in all of us. Loud noises are also good long-distance corrections. The noise might be a pop can filled with pebbles, a cap gun, or a board hitting a hard surface. The noise, similar to a water correction, is aversive and distracts your puppy. If your puppy is digging and he ignores your command to stop, sound your noise to distract him. When your puppy looks up and stops digging, call him to you and give him praise when he reaches you.

Be aware, however, that some puppies are afraid of loud noises, and a surprise noise may make your puppy even more fearful and nervous. You will have to determine for yourself whether the noise correction does more damage than good. On the other hand, a noise correction may become impotent for puppies that grow accustomed to the noises and ignore them. The effects of cold water squirting appear to endure over time. Water corrections will not make your puppy afraid of water. For water puppies that love a good spray, make your admonishment stronger, and make sure that the squirt gets him right between the eyes. Squirt until your puppy responds appropriately or step up to glasses of water. I have yet to see a puppy that thinks that the correction is fun when a splash directly between the eyes is followed by a harsh reprimand.

HERDING

Puppies like to herd, or chase and nip, the heels of children, because children run and scream when chased. Chasing children is much more fun than chasing dull adults who yell "no!" Although chasing is not generally an act of deliberate aggression, a puppy's nipping can progress to bold biting or chasing that could send a child rolling and tumbling to serious injury. Discourage herding with a water bottle hooked to the victim's belt buckle. The water bottle is an effective correction for the wise, hard-to-catch, hit-and-nip critter. When your puppy herds, command "no," and squirt a stream of water straight at his face. When young children are the victims of your herder, do not leave your puppy and children unsupervised. If your children cannot give an effective correction for herding, go out with them and use a hose to squirt your puppy when he chases the children. If children are left to correct the puppy, the affair may become a water game. If your puppy is not corrected properly, he will learn that herding is an acceptable game.

Rolled Paper

The premise behind a paper correction is to distract your puppy from a misbehavior without hurting him. A small section of the newspaper can be rolled into a tube and secured with a rubber band to make a pretty impressive sound to distract your puppy. When your puppy misbehaves, such as jumping on the kitchen counter, command "off," and if your puppy does not obey, pop the rolled paper on a hard surface to make a loud, distracting noise. If your puppy ignores the noise, lightly pop him on the base of the tail with the paper. This is not painful and is far more humane than a choke-collar correction. Like the water bottle, the paper can be left on the counter as a visual reminder to discourage repeated misbehavior.

AFTERMATH

Following a correction, your puppy will look for ways to appease you in an attempt to regain your favor. Do not confuse your puppy by consoling him immediately after the correction. However, the puppy must have an opportunity to appease, and you can provide him with the opportunity by giving him a command that he can obey. Tell your puppy, in a normal tone, to do something simple such as sit. After he sits, and most remorseful puppies will immediately obey, you can praise him. If he does not know sit yet, help him and then praise him for being in the sit position. This clearly demonstrates reward for good behavior and correction for inappropriate behavior without confusing the two issues.

ALTERNATIVES TO PUNISHMENT

A strategy that utilizes behavioral modification or alternative behavioral techniques can be successful in some situations. As an example, teach your puppy an alternative behavior for jumping by commanding him to sit-stay every time the doorbell rings. Your puppy cannot physically sit and jump up simultaneously; therefore, jumping is discouraged as you enforce sitting, and your puppy is praised and petted for sitting or keeping all four feet on the ground. Sometimes corrections can be avoided simply by replacing the maladaptive behavior with an appropriate behavior.

CREATIVE CORRECTIONS

You can also avoid physical corrections by setting up natural-consequence corrections in which the puppy is corrected as a result of the environment. I have a spring-loaded fence gate, and one day I noticed my pup running toward the gate as my husband was exiting the yard. I yelled "back" just as my puppy got to the gate, and it slammed her on the head. Although the slam caused her to yelp and undoubtedly gave her a slight headache, the timing could not have been better. Beach now waits for someone to hold the gate rather than attempting to rush it. Laurie was removing a hot pizza from the oven when her puppy, North, unexpectedly jumped and knocked the pizza out of her hand. North accidentally wound up with a very hot pizza on her head and she no longer jumps on Laurie in the kitchen. Natural consequences are very effective but are unfortunately very difficult to plan.

GOOD PREVENTION FOR PROBLEM BEHAVIORS

While many dangerous behaviors such as biting must be dealt with by correction so that the behavior is clearly discouraged, less serious puppy antics can be prevented with just good environmental management. For example, you can prevent significant damage to your house if during your puppy's teething phase you confine him to a chew-proof environment when you cannot supervise him. Anytime a behavior can be prevented, channeled, or avoided, the relationship between you and your puppy will be more positive. Positive training methods may sometimes take longer, but if they result in the development of a good friendship between you and your puppy, the time and effort will be worthwhile.

*Any healthy puppy can learn, and each day is packed
with new learning experiences that either teach your puppy
bad habits when he is left to his own devices or obedient habits
when you provide good parenting and training.*

CHAPTER 14

How Your
Puppy Learns

One day after class, a man observing my lecture asked me if I could teach tricks to any dog. Without waiting for my answer, he explained that his puppy was the dumbest dog in the world, because after six months of training, his dog still couldn't shake hands on command. Trying to be polite, I told the man to bring the dog in sometime and I would show him how to teach the dog to shake. Two minutes later, the man came back with the dog. Perceiving that this man was determined to have a good laugh at my expense and tell his buddies, "I told you so," I sat his dog and commanded "shake" as I held a treat over the dog's head. When the dog started to reach for the treat, I moved the treat so that the dog had to lean to get it. In the process of leaning, the dog raised his foot, and I praised him. Lucky for me, the dog was a real chow-hound, because after five repetitions with praise and a treat, to this fellow's astonishment (and mine, because this trick usually takes more than five repetitions), the dog lifted his paw on command. The man's only comment was, "So that's how you do it!" and he stormed out. I never really knew if the man was angry because the process looked so easy or because he realized that it wasn't the dog that was stupid. I have yet to meet a stupid puppy!

*When you use treats to shape behavior, your puppy will learn
that obeying produces good rewards and he will be motivated
and willing to obey your commands.*

LEARNING

Any healthy puppy can learn, and each day is packed with new
learning experiences that either teach your puppy bad habits when
he is left to his own devices or obedient habits when you provide
good parenting and training. Without training, the two- to four-
month-old puppy that followed you everywhere without a leash
suddenly discovers a brave new world outside the door and no
longer hears you call him. Without training, your five-month-old
puppy eats everything that doesn't eat him first, and he has no
idea how to direct his enormous energy without getting into trouble constantly. If behavior is not channeled appropriately during
the optimal learning phase—between the ages of two and six
months—serious problems will develop. Whether your puppy is
two months or older, he can be taught appropriate behavior, and
positive training needs to begin the day your puppy arrives,
regardless of his age.

POSITIVE TRAINING

To positively reinforce obedience or ensure that a puppy will repeat a behavior, the puppy must be rewarded. Food rewards give you the opportunity to positively shape your puppy's behavior. The more excited your puppy is about food, the more motivated he will be to perform for the reward. For example, to positively shape your puppy to come to you, show him a treat as you say "come." When he sees the treat, he will get excited and in all likelihood will run toward you. A puppy that associates a tasty treat with obeying a command willingly obeys in anticipation of the reward. When your puppy gets to you, give him a treat and praise him at the same time. Praise, in the form of petting and talking, is an added reward for your puppy, and when given with a tasty food reward, becomes almost as rewarding as food. After several repetitions of showing your puppy a treat, calling, and giving praise and a treat when he comes, your puppy will learn that the word "come," plus running to you, equals praise and a treat. You are motivating—or "shaping"—your puppy to perform a task on his own volition for a

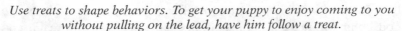

Use treats to shape behaviors. To get your puppy to enjoy coming to you without pulling on the lead, have him follow a treat.

reward. Teaching your puppy to come by pulling him with a lead only teaches him that when you say "come," you will pull him toward you. For a puppy to reliably learn and perform a command, he must be motivated with a good reinforcer and not be physically forced.

Once a behavior is shaped or your puppy associates running to you on command with a treat, you can switch from shaping to the reward system. Instead of showing your puppy the treat to motivate him to perform, your puppy must first perform the task to receive a treat. Hide the treat in your pocket before you call him, and when your puppy gets to you, give him lots of praise and a treat. When your puppy is accurately performing the command and earning praise and treats 100 percent of the time, you can interchange using food and praise, or occasionally just praise. Because praise was pleasurably associated with food, your puppy will perceive praise as a good substitute for food much of the time. If treats are eliminated totally and never again paired with praise, your praise will not maintain the same value of reward. To maintain specific responses and the perceived high value of your praise, behaviors and praise must be reassociated or reinforced occasionally with treats. While positive reinforcement shapes and rewards good behavior, negative consequences are necessary to teach your puppy which behaviors are inappropriate.

NEGATIVE CONSEQUENCES

If negative consequences did not exist for misbehavior, we would all behave inappropriately. If we could walk into a bank and take a million dollars without any consequences, then we would all be millionaires. Lynda taught Sage to come on command with positive reinforcement. Every time Lynda called Sage, he came running—*until* a cute little poodle caught his eye. Lynda called Sage several times, but his mind was elsewhere and he didn't respond. Lynda went over to Sage, gently took his collar to place him back where he started, and tried again. Lynda's reward alone was not motivating enough to override Sage's lust, because he promptly went straight for the poodle. For Lynda to teach Sage to come in spite of distractions, Sage needed a negative consequence for disobeying and a reward when he obeyed. Sage learned to ignore the poodle after he was placed on lead, given a snap on the collar to discourage going to the poodle, and rewarded when he reached Lynda. A combination of reward and negative consequences teaches your puppy a clear distinction between acceptable and unacceptable behavior.

TIMING

Reinforcement must be delivered during or immediately after your puppy obeys for him to understand that his behavior generated the reward. If you command your puppy to down, and an hour later you finally get around to praising him, he will not associate his obedience with your reward. With every second that your reward is delayed, the association between the behavior and reward becomes weaker. After as few as five seconds, your puppy may not make an association at all.

Timing is even more critical for corrections. The correction must occur when your puppy is misbehaving. The puppy that grabs a cookie from a child and

A well-timed treat after your puppy obeys a command will make a strong and positive association between your command and the behavior you desire.

eats it, is rewarded for his trouble, and correcting him after he eats the cookie is not connected with grabbing the cookie. He must be corrected when he grabs the cookie to discourage grabbing food from children.

LEARNING AND TEMPERAMENT DIFFERENCES

Although few puppies fit an explicit temperament model, there are similarities of temperament that allow for some general categorization. Temperament models can be used to predict your puppy's response to different methods of training and possibly prevent some serious mistakes.

The soft-tempered, sensitive, or submissive puppy may become despondent with strong corrections.

Soft-Tempered Puppies

The soft-tempered, sensitive, or submissive puppy may become very despondent with strong corrections. Even everyday household yelling, which may be the normal sound level in a home full of children, can send the soft-tempered puppy cowering into the corner. Beach is a soft-tempered puppy that responds to positive reinforcement. She needs a simple "stop it" to correct her behavior. Anything harsher than a verbal correction causes her to tuck her tail and roll to the ground. The primary method for training the soft-tempered puppy should be positive reinforcement. Corrections should only be strong enough to get the point across. Sensitive puppies can be a lot of fun to train because they are usually very invested in pleasing you.

Hard-Tempered Puppies

Less sensitive, hard-tempered, dominant puppies can also be a lot of fun to train, even though they do not appear to concentrate on pleasing you as much as sensitive puppies do, and they keep you on your toes to maintain a balance between reinforcement and correction. The hard-tempered puppy can tolerate corrections and may even require a fairly strong correction just to get his undivided attention.

Bogie, a fifteen-month-old puppy with testosterone poisoning and a love for the ladies, refused to sit-stay when a new bitch walked into the room. Reinforcement and corrections on his buckle collar weren't enough to convince him to stay. After months of frustration, Bogie's owner replaced his buckle collar with a training collar and staged a female parade past him. After a couple of sessions with a training collar and a few reminders every couple of months thereafter, Bogie learned that courting the girls during a sit-stay was unacceptable. While the soft puppy may only need verbal corrections, the tough puppy usually requires more.

Hyperactive Puppies

The hyperactive or overly energetic puppy requires a trainer who can be firm, consistent, and calm in voice and movement. Fast, jerky movements and animated speech only serve to energize a reactive puppy.

Cody was a hyperactive puppy that nipped whenever he was placed in a sit. After a correction for nipping, Cody's owner would frantically battle to resit him as he screamed, twisted, and jumped in the air at the end of the lead. The owner was instructed to correct him for snapping and then just hold onto the leash until Cody calmed down. Cody would twist and fight at the end of the lead to get loose until he was finally exhausted. Once exhausted, he would sit and pant as his owner calmly praised him for sitting. Eventually, Cody gave up nipping when he was touched and learned to sit calmly because his hyperactivity and temper tantrums were not rewarded or energized by his owner's frantic reaction.

Lethargic Dogs

While the excitable puppy needs a trainer with a calm manner, the lethargic puppy does better with an excitable owner. The lethargic puppy needs to be energized or aroused to a level of awareness that facilitates learning. If your puppy is "asleep," he's probably not learning the lesson that you intended.

Bunny did everything in slow motion and nothing seemed to excite her. Dan, Bunny's owner, didn't really care that Bunny was in the slow track except when he called her to come. To energize Bunny (no pun intended), Dan was instructed to call her and then take off running for a hiding place. The first time that Dan ran, Bunny appeared confused and walked around looking for Dan. After a few sprints on Dan's part, Bunny caught on that she had to react fast or lose sight of Dan. Although Bunny still takes life slow and easy for the most part, she lopes to Dan when he calls her.

For the best training results, evaluate your puppy's temperament and energy level so that you can adjust methods and motivators to help your puppy learn.

CHAPTER 15

Puppy Manners
and Training

Obedience training teaches good manners and is the key to channeling your puppy's behavior positively. Training obedience communicates to your puppy how to behave and earn your approval. To get started with training, you will need the proper equipment.

TRAINING COLLARS

You can effectively train your puppy on a regular buckle collar or on the adjustable Greyhound collar that your puppy cannot slip out of. An alternative to the collar is a head halter. The halter is extremely valuable and is effective for very strong, large puppies that pull you and/or your children.

LEADS

The optimal obedience lead is narrow and should only be long enough to allow a few inches of slack to your puppy when your hand is at your waist and he is in heel position. The more lead you have in your hand, the more difficult it and your puppy become to manipulate. Leather or cotton leads are the gentlest on your hands, and brass clasps are worth the extra cost over chrome, which breaks easily. The lead is used primarily to control your puppy outside.

The best collar is one that is adjustable and one that your puppy can't slip out of but will not choke when it tightens.

HANDLE

Indoors, you will want to use a handle to control your puppy's behavior. The handle is a short lead, six to fourteen inches long, that you attach to your puppy's collar when he is supervised to control his behavior in the house. If your puppy is a chewer, Bitter Apple, tabasco sauce, or ammonia can be sprayed on the handle. If your puppy's palate is not deterred by nasty-tasting substances, a piece of chain can be substituted for the cord or leather.

TRAINING SESSIONS

Training sessions should be long enough to provide several repetitions of an exercise, but short enough not to tax your puppy's attention span. An appropriate training session for the young puppy less than nine months old is approximately fifteen to twenty minutes. You will have a well-trained puppy if you train fifteen to

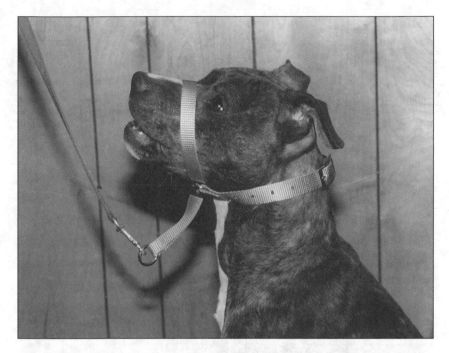

The head halter is very effective for the strong dog, for the hyperactive puppy, or for children to use to keep control of the dog.

twenty minutes per day, five times a week. If you train for fewer days or shorter sessions, you will still get a trained puppy—it will just take longer. As your puppy gets older and learns more exercises, you may want to increase the length of the sessions. The key to maintaining your puppy's attention is to make the training rewarding and lots of fun with treats and praise.

OBEDIENCE COMMANDS

Most obedience exercises or commands did not originate solely to entertain or impress people. Rather, they were conceived to control and direct behavior. Every command should be associated with only one correct response. If you don't want your puppy to chase cats, to be on the couch, or bark, teach him a separate command for each behavior. You can command your puppy to "leave it" for chasing, to "off" for being on furniture, or to "quiet"

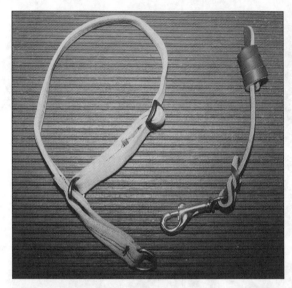

Left: The handle for control in the house; right: A Greyhound-style collar that does not choke and that prevents your puppy from slipping out.

During the learning or shaping phase of training, give your puppy a treat every time he performs correctly. The treat lets him know that he did it right.

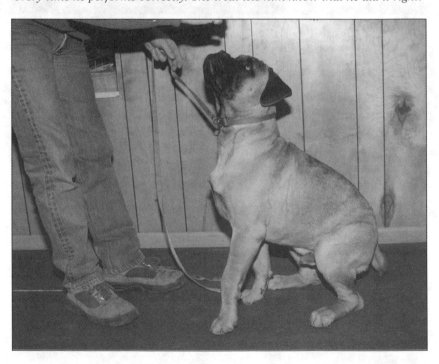

for barking. Teaching your puppy a specific command for each behavior sets up a very clear line of communication that your puppy can understand.

No

"No" is used only for aggressive acts and must be backed up with a meaningful correction to give appropriate value to the command and to discourage repeat behavior. For example, the puppy that lunges at another dog should be quickly admonished with a harsh "no," followed by strong snaps on the collar until he stops lunging. Give him a sit command and praise him when he sits. The next time he starts to lunge and you command "no," and he responds, the command is meaningful and you can praise him without giving a correction. "No" is an appropriate reprimand because it can sound harsh and firm, and in tense situations the word comes to mind very naturally for most people.

Sit

The puppy that dances around with excitement and knocks the food dish from your hand when he is being fed can easily be controlled by teaching him to obey the sit command. Gently hold your puppy's collar to prevent him from jumping or moving backward, and command him to "sit" as you slowly move a treat from above his nose toward his tail. Your puppy will follow the treat and will fall back into a sit. Praise him and give him the treat. After several sessions and repetitions with manipulating the treat, hold the treat still and command your puppy to "sit." Give him praise and the treat when he sits.

Another method for teaching your puppy to sit involves physical guidance and several steps. Train each step for one week before moving on to the next step.

First Step. Place your right hand on your puppy's collar and your left arm or hand across his rear legs directly over his hocks. Command "sit," and gently pull your puppy back by his collar toward your left arm, folding him into a sit. Praise him when he is sitting.

Second Step. Command your puppy to "sit" and, with your right hand on the collar, place your left thumb and index finger on each side of your puppy's spine starting at the shoulder blades.

*Moving a treat above your puppy's nose and back toward his tail
will motivate him to rock back into a sit.*

When he sits, praise him and give him a treat.

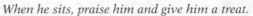

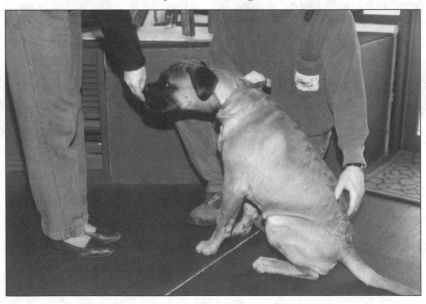

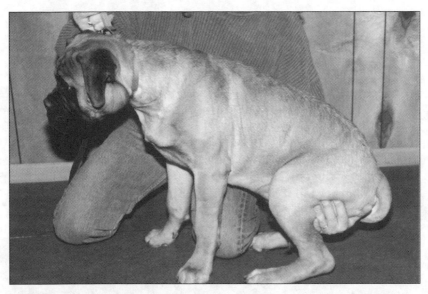

(Above) Step One: With your left hand across your puppy's rump and your right hand at his collar, fold him into a sit. (Below) Step Two: With your right hand on the collar, place your left thumb and index finger on each side of the puppy's spine starting at the shoulder blades. Run your fingers down along his spine with moderate pressure to the base of his tail.

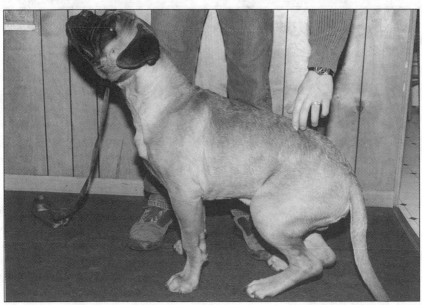

Run your fingers down along his spine with moderate pressure to the base of his tail. Apply pressure at the base of the tail until your puppy sits. Praise him for sitting.

Third Step. Hold your puppy's collar in your right hand to keep him close to you, and command him to sit. If he sits, give him lots of praise and a treat. If you are sure that your puppy knows the sit command and did not obey, tap him on the base of the tail. This clearly communicates that his rump should be on the ground when you say "sit." Do not push your puppy into the sit, because he will only resist a push and will continue standing. Deliver a harder tap if he does not sit after the first tap. The tap on the base of the tail must be hard enough to motivate your puppy to sit on his own. Give immediate praise when he sits.

Ready

The command "ready" tells your puppy to make eye contact with you. If your puppy is maintaining eye contact, he is generally

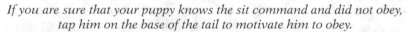

If you are sure that your puppy knows the sit command and did not obey, tap him on the base of the tail to motivate him to obey.

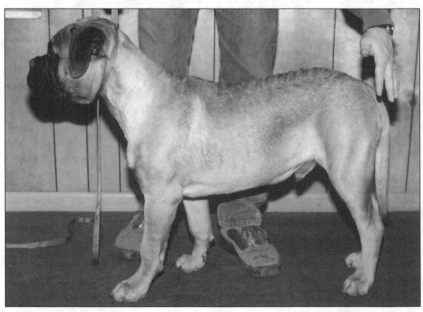

paying attention to you and is ready to learn. You may choose other words, such as "look" or "watch," to get his attention. Use the attention command every time you start a session, have a break in lessons, or lose your puppy's attention.

With your puppy in the sitting position, face him as you hold his collar in one hand and a treat in the other. Command "ready," and move the treat from your puppy's nose to your eyes. Your puppy will follow the movement of the treat to your eyes, and you can praise him for looking at your eyes. You can lengthen the amount of time that you maintain eye contact if you move the treat from your puppy's nose to your eyes a couple of times before you praise him and give him the treat. To determine whether your puppy has made an association between "ready" and looking at your eyes, command "ready" without a treat. If your puppy looks up to your eyes, give him praise and a treat from your pocket.

Come

Your puppy must not be allowed off his leash until he is trained to reliably return to you when you call him. If your puppy

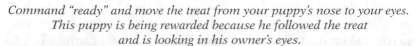

Command "ready" and move the treat from your puppy's nose to your eyes. This puppy is being rewarded because he followed the treat and is looking in his owner's eyes.

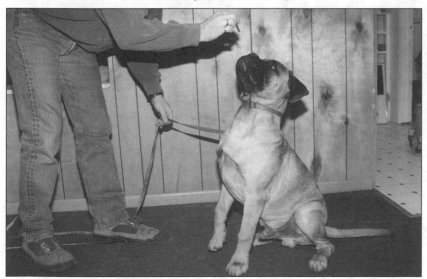

is allowed to run free and you have no way to enforce his return-ing to you, he learns that you are powerless and that "come" is meaningless. You should start training "come" the first day that you have your puppy. The older puppy that has already learned that returning to you on command is not necessary is *not* a lost cause, but it will take longer to train him.

A high-value motivator must be used to teach your puppy to return to you on command. The motivator must be more rewarding than any reward that your puppy would get from not coming, such as the fun of chasing a cat. The best motivators are the two things that puppies love most—chasing something and eating tasty treats.

Puppy Recall

For your young puppy that has not learned to run off yet, start the recall training in the house. Hold a tasty treat right in front of your puppy's nose and call his name with "come" as you run back-wards a couple of steps. When you stop backing up, get down on the ground to your puppy's eye level, praise him, and give him the treat. If your puppy doesn't follow you, don't chase after him—stay on the floor and coax him to you. When your puppy finally comes, praise him and place a lead or handle on him. Repeat calling your puppy, and if he doesn't come, give a gentle pop on the collar as you back up to give him direction and motivation to move your way.

After several repetitions, when you are sure that your puppy is responding to the command, stand a short distance from him as you call him and run backwards. Do not do too many repetitions in one session, because your puppy will get a full stomach and will not put out as much effort for the treat. Continue to increase the distance, maybe even to another room where your puppy cannot see you when you call him. Distractions, such as calling your puppy when he is inattentive or engrossed in playing, can be added after he is responding 100 percent of the time. If your puppy does not come, either find a tastier treat or teach him to come on lead. At least two practice sessions daily will produce a reliable recall from your puppy in the house.

The Recall and the Older Puppy

Attach a lead to your puppy and move to the end of the lead. Regardless of whether your puppy is attentive or inattentive, call

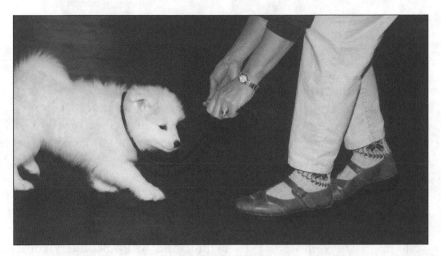

To shape your puppy to come to you, show him a treat, then run backwards a few steps. When your puppy is trotting to you, drop to the ground and give him lots of praise and a treat.

his name and say "come." If your puppy moves toward you, run away about ten feet, being careful not to tighten the lead as you run. If it becomes tight, slow down to leave slack in the lead so that you don't pull or drag your puppy. If your puppy does not respond, give a pop on the lead for direction and motivation before you run away. After approximately twenty steps, turn to face your puppy and continue running backwards a couple of steps until he catches up to you. Drop to the ground as you hold a treat close to your body so that your puppy has to come right up to you for the praise and treat.

When your puppy is coming quickly and reliably on the training leash, take him to different places for practice. Add a couple of feet of rope to your lead after each successful session so that your puppy learns to return to you from long distances. Training should take place in new environments where your puppy will be distracted, or you may add distractions to old training grounds. Teaching your puppy to return to you without a lead should be taught under the supervision of a qualified, knowledgeable trainer after you have completed an obedience course.

Snappy Recall

The snappy recall is my emergency call. One day my puppy slipped out of the gate when someone went through, and she was headed for the road. My first natural reaction was to yell her name, and in response, she tucked her tail and started running faster. If your puppy does not respond to your yell, or if he interprets the yell as trouble, the consequences can be disastrous. The snappy recall teaches a puppy to react appropriately and quickly and desensitizes him to your panicked yell.

When your puppy is distracted, yell his name, give a pop on the lead—or as many pops as it takes for him to turn and start toward you—and give him lots of praise and a treat. Desensitizing your puppy to your yell and teaching him to immediately come regardless of what he is doing may one day save his life.

Wait

The wait command signals your puppy to remain in position until you give another command. For example, as a safety precaution, your puppy can learn to wait at the top of a staircase until you call him so that he doesn't trip you on the way down.

Command "sit," praise your puppy for sitting, and command him to "wait" as you flash your open hand in front of his face. At the silent count of five, call your puppy's name followed by "come," and run away. Vary the time that he has to wait before you call him. If the amount of time between the "wait" and "come" is always the same, your puppy will anticipate when to move. Occasionally, reward your puppy with a treat or praise for waiting before you command him to come.

If your puppy moves before you call him, pop him back to the original position with the lead. Never reposition your puppy with your hands. Instead, use his collar so that he doesn't interpret your hands on him as praise for moving. Even if you were ready to call your puppy, and he jumped the gun only by a second or two, put him back into the original position. Your puppy may move his head or tail without correction, but he should be corrected for moving his feet or body.

The wait signal and the stay signal given with a flash of your hand in front of your puppy's eyes.

Let's Go

A leisurely stroll through the park would not be enjoyable if your puppy pulled or had to heel during the entire walk. The command for your puppy to walk on a loose lead without being in a heel position is "let's go." The command "let's go" tells your puppy: take time to sniff the roses, I will follow you, but do not pull on the lead.

Attach a four- to six-foot lead to your puppy and command "let's go." Walk out and let your puppy go wherever he wishes. If the lead gets tight, command "back," and give a snap on the lead toward the ground. When the lead is slack, praise and reward your puppy. If your puppy does not stop pulling, continue to snap the lead until he stops. Do not walk forward; rather, turn around and retrace your steps and try again. Walk in a circle or retrace your steps until your puppy walks without pulling. Your puppy pulls to

The let's go command is different from the heel command. The puppy does not have to be in heel position; however, he is not allowed to pull. "Let's go" means that your puppy can walk where he wants as long as he doesn't pull.

get to new ground, and if he is allowed to walk forward or to cover new ground when he pulls, he will be rewarded for pulling. Your first couple of walks outside in circles or retracing your steps may mean that you don't get to go to new places; however, covering the same territory for several days is much better than living with a dog for fifteen years that pulls. Once your puppy can walk a few steps without pulling, continue to increase the distance that you walk. However, every time your puppy pulls, give him a snap on the collar, turn, and retrace your steps until he walks without pulling you.

If your puppy is reluctant to walk on lead, encourage him with a treat. Command "let's go," and hold a treat directly in front of his nose. When he reaches forward for the treat by taking a step, praise him and give him the treat. Continue using the treat in front of his nose, and require more and more steps before he gets the

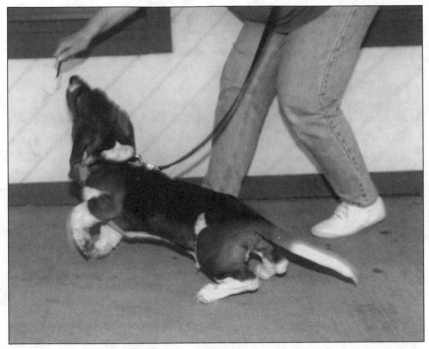

If your puppy does not want to walk on lead, encourage him with a treat in front of his nose and lots of praise.

treat. If your puppy will not move forward for the treat, just hold onto the lead and walk. Your puppy will not like being dragged, and after a few feet he will get up and walk. You must be quick to praise and give a loose lead when he walks even for one step.

Very likely, your puppy will sit down and stop again in spite of the praise. Be tough and walk forward. If you stop when your puppy balks or plants himself, he is the trainer, and he is rewarded for his stubborn behavior by training you to stop. Would you allow your child to stop going to first grade just because he didn't want to go? I remember my first day of kindergarten. My mother first attempted to reason and encourage me to go to school when I stamped my foot, plopped myself to the ground, and refused to go through the door. My mother even resorted to bribery—an ice-cream cone with chocolate sprinkles—when I got home. With arms folded, feet jammed against the door, I screamed "no" as if I were being killed. Without any observable anger from my mother (I am sure that she was fuming), she dragged me into the classroom, set me down, and left. Even after I resorted to screaming, I was ignored. I quickly realized that I had no choice and that I might as well go along with being in school. Although walking on lead may start off with some dragging at first, be patient, don't lose your temper, and just keep walking. Eventually, your puppy will realize that being rewarded for walking on lead is much more fun than being dragged for balking.

Heeling

Once your puppy learns how to walk on a loose lead without balking or pulling, it's time for him to learn how to heel. Heeling is important for keeping your puppy in control and close to you to prevent any mishaps when crossing streets or being approached by other people and dogs. Formal heeling consists of your puppy walking, and sitting when you stop, on your left side with a loose lead. Your puppy's right leg and shoulder should be parallel to your left leg.

Command "heel," and encourage your puppy to be in a heel position by giving him a treat at your left leg. Have several treats in your hand to shape the heel position so that the minute he finishes the first reward, he can look for the second one and remain in the heel position. If your puppy stops to eat the treat, keep walking—he'll catch up and learn to walk and chew at the same time. If he drops the treat, keep walking—he will learn to hold onto it as he walks.

Maintain a relaxed, straight arm. If your puppy moves out of position, away from your left leg in any direction, command "heel," and snap the lead parallel to the ground in the opposite direction. The snap is a motion similar to snapping a whip or shaking out a towel and should only require you to use your wrist and lower arm. Instantaneously after the snap, give the lead slack. The lead is never pulled back or kept tight. For instance, if your puppy is pulling ahead, snap the lead down and back, and when your puppy responds by backing up and walking next to you, loosen the lead. Give the snap just as he leaves heel position, before

Heeling means that your puppy walks on a loose lead next to your left leg.

he is an entire body position away and his body weight is working against you. Teach heeling in a small area or circle, and cover the same ground until your puppy understands the heeling concept.

Sit-Stay

The sit-stay is a useful exercise to control your puppy's movement; for example, in a crowded elevator where he could get underfoot. The sit-stay requires your puppy to sit in the same place until you release him. Common release commands are "okay" or "good," paired with lots of praise. For the sake of consistency, do not call your puppy from the stay position; instead, use the "wait" so that your puppy learns to stay until you release him. The sit-stay is useful when your puppy does not have to stay for more than three minutes. For longer than three minutes, use a down-stay, which is a more relaxed position for him.

To teach the sit-stay, place your puppy in a sit, and hold his collar so that he cannot move. Flash your right hand, fingers

(Top Left) Flash your hand in front of your puppy's face and command "stay" as you hold him in place with your left hand. (Top Right) Holding your puppy in place, step in front and immediately return to heel position at your puppy's side. (Below Left) Step to your puppy's left shoulder, then back into heel position. (Below Right) The final step is to walk completely around your puppy back into heel position. If your puppy tries to move, tighten the collar to hold him in place.

spread, in front of your puppy's eyes, and command "stay." Step directly in front of your puppy, then quickly step back into heel position. Give your puppy calm verbal praise for staying. Repeat the hand flash with "stay," step to your puppy's left shoulder, and quickly step back to your starting position. Praise your puppy. For the third time, use "stay" with a hand flash, step around to your puppy's tail, and immediately return to your starting position. Give your puppy calm, verbal praise for not moving.

The last step involves "stay" with a hand flash and circling once around your puppy to heel position. Once you are back in your original position, release your puppy with lots of excited praise and a treat. If your puppy moves during the progression, place him back into the sit position by the collar, and before you go on through the progression, repeat the part where he moved until he successfully stays.

After a week of holding your puppy by the collar as you perform the four-step progression, leave slack in the lead and gradually increase the distance between you and your puppy as you walk around him. When your puppy stays as you walk around him from a distance of a leash length away, stand in front of him and gradually increase the amount of time that your puppy stays sitting in position. The goal is to have your puppy sit-stay for five minutes without moving his feet or body. When your puppy moves, walk in calmly and correct him by using the collar and lead to pop him back into position. When your puppy remains in position, walk in occasionally and give him a treat to reinforce his good behavior. If your puppy moves for the treat, correct him for moving.

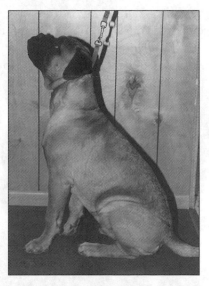

If your puppy moves from the sit-stay, walk in calmly and correct him by using the collar and lead to pop him back.

Puppies are very capable of learning to stay even when a treat is in sight. Practice the sit-stay in different places and with distractions.

Down

The down is as handy as the sit for many situations where you may have to control your puppy's movement. For many puppies, the "down" is a vulnerable position, and placing your puppy in a down may be perceived by him as a threatening gesture that may provoke stress and even aggression. The down is taught in several gentle steps to minimize provoking fear or aggression.

Puppy Down. A positive way to teach the down is to place one hand on your puppy's collar to prevent him from walking forward as you command "down," and slowly move a treat from the front of his nose to the ground, just far enough from his nose that he has to stretch to get the treat. The purpose is to manipulate or shape your puppy to lower and stretch his body on the ground to get the treat. Although shaping is a successful method for teaching the down, you should teach the exercise with physical guidance to ensure that your puppy accepts physical handling and light restraint. There may come a time when you have to physically restrain your dog, and you don't want to wait until he has big canines to find out that he becomes aggressive when restrained.

First Step. Place your puppy in a sit at your left side, and kneel next to him. You can place the end of your lead under your knees

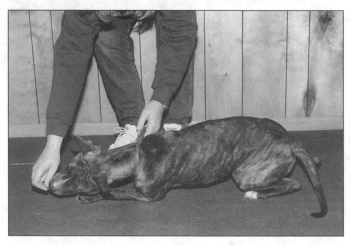

To shape the down, hold your puppy's collar and slowly move a treat from the front of his nose to the ground.

to free up your hands and prevent your puppy from leaving. Command "down," and with one arm over his back, pick up your puppy's left leg by the elbow, and then his right leg with your other hand. Proceed slowly to give him time to adjust to the handling so that he does not become threatened. When you have both elbows in hand, lift your puppy's front a couple of inches from the ground, using your forearm to hold him close to your body to prevent him from pulling away as you stretch him out to a down position on the floor. Stroke him when he is down for a couple of seconds and praise him. If your puppy protests at any time by placing his teeth on your hands, snapping, or growling, discipline him with a cuff, and repeat the exercise and correction until the aggression stops. Licking your hand is acceptable. Repeat the exercise for one week before progressing to the next step.

Second Step. Command "down," and use your right hand on your puppy's collar to guide him to the ground as your left thumb and index finger apply steady pressure to the muscle directly

Teaching your dog to down by placing your left arm
over his back and picking him up at the elbows to stretch
him out into a prone position also teaches your puppy
to accept light restraint without feeling threatened.

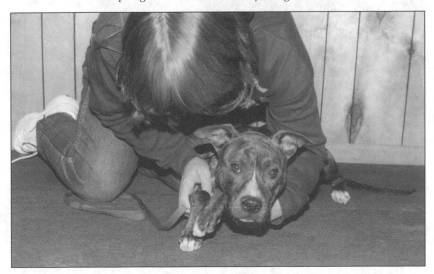

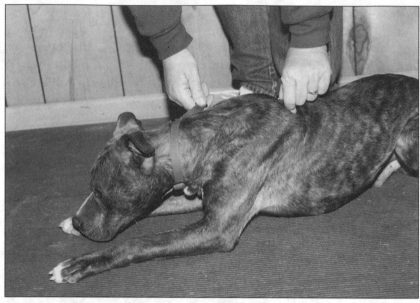

Once your puppy accepts being placed in the down by having his elbows picked up, use your right hand on his collar to guide him to the ground as your left thumb and index finger apply steady pressure to the muscle directly below his shoulder blade.

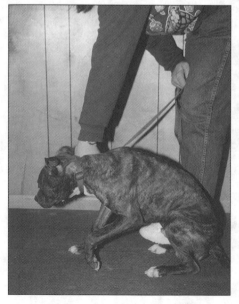

When you are sure that your puppy understands that the word "down" means to be in a prone position, command "down" and apply steady pressure on the collar straight to the ground. Praise your puppy.

below your puppy's shoulder blade. The pressure is applied firmly to the muscle below the shoulder blade so that your puppy will fold his legs and lie down. Once you begin applying pressure, do not let the pressure off until your puppy is down; otherwise you are rewarding the pup for struggling. Praise him.

Third Step. With your hand on the clasp of the lead, command "down," and apply steady pressure straight to the ground. Praise your puppy immediately. The only way that your puppy can avoid being placed quickly to the floor by the collar is to go down on command.

Down-Stay

Once your puppy has learned down, you can use the flash hand signal and command "stay." The four-step progression used for the sit-stay is repeated for the down-stay. If your puppy gets up from the down before you release him, use the muscle-and-collar technique as a correction to place him down again. Use the down-stay whenever your puppy has to stay for longer than three minutes. Gradually increase the length of time that your puppy is on the down-stay until you have taught him to stay for five to ten minutes.

Settle

The "settle" means lie down and "chill out" for longer than five minutes. The difference between the down-stay and the settle is that during a down-stay, your puppy must not move until you return to release him. During a settle, your puppy may move under three conditions—to change positions, to follow you to another room, or to respond to someone at the door.

I use a settle when I'm working. I do not want my puppy to be pestering me or roaming the house and getting into trouble, so I place him in a settle next to my desk. If I use a down-stay and the doorbell rings, he will naturally run to the door before I have an opportunity to release him from the stay, and he will learn that he can choose to break the stay without a release. If I correct my puppy for breaking the stay when he runs to the door, I will be unintentionally discouraging him from alerting at the door. If my puppy gets up and is rowdy for any reason other than alerting me to the door, he is again placed in the settle until he calms down to discourage hyperactive behavior.

To teach the settle, command "settle," and place your puppy down with his lead, your hand on the muscle between his shoulder blades. Tie the lead to your chair so that he cannot run off if he gets up fast. Your first goal could be a five-minute settle. Every time your puppy gets up from the settle, place him back down. Over several weeks, gradually increase the time that your puppy remains in a settle until you have worked up to thirty minutes. When you reach this goal, practice the settle once a day.

Leave It

The command "leave it" instructs your puppy not to sniff or touch an object, or even another animal. The "leave it" can be a life-preserving command considering the objects that puppies may find and eat.

With your handle or lead attached to your puppy, place a forbidden object or treat about two feet in front of him. As your puppy approaches the object, command "leave it," and give him a snap away from the object with the lead or handle. Praise your puppy when he halts his approach toward the object.

For coffee-table manners, enforce "leave it" as you deliver a strong tap on the front of your puppy's muzzle when he reaches

for a piece of food. In my house, the coffee table is off-limits even when I'm out of the room. I enforce the rule by strategically placing a mirror nearby so that I can see my puppy from another room in order to catch and correct him in the act of stealing. One other helpful command is

The leave it command tells your puppy not to sniff or eat the item.

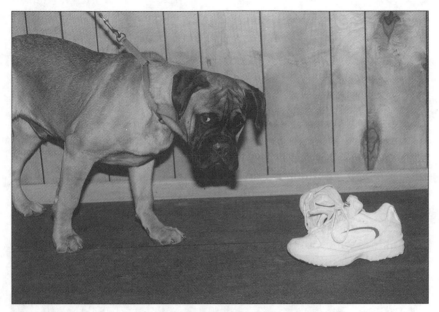

To teach the leave it command, place an object or treat about two feet in front of your puppy. When your puppy approaches, command "leave it" and give him a snap on the lead or handle. The leave it command is very handy when you are walking in the park and your puppy finds discarded delectables.

"vacuum," which lets your puppy know when he may pick up a dropped morsel.

Drop or Give

At some point in your puppy's life—or perhaps every day of his life—he will have an object that you must take away from him. To teach your puppy to drop or let go of an object, first show him a valuable treat when you call him, then exchange the treat for the object with "give." I use "thank you" and give lots of praise when my puppy lets go of an object. If your puppy has already learned to run away with his prized possessions, attach his lead so that you can step on it to stop him and reel him into you. If your puppy does not give up the object, firmly take it out of his mouth even if you have to pry his mouth open. Be prepared to deliver a very strong cuff if he growls or snaps. Repeat the process until your puppy willingly gives up the object. Once your puppy is freely exchanging an object for a treat, keep the treat hidden and command "give." Praise him and give him the treat when he gives up the object.

Off

The command "off" instructs your puppy to keep his paws on the ground. "Off" can be used when your puppy jumps on people or furniture. When your puppy jumps up, command "off," and snap his collar toward the ground by the lead or handle. Give your puppy a "sit" command, and praise him for being on the ground and sitting. If you are working with jumping on people, do not let anyone touch or pet your puppy until he is sitting. If furniture is the lesson, and your puppy growls or snaps, give him a correction. Command your puppy to get on and off the furniture until he obeys without protest.

Move

Walking around or over your puppy when he is in the pathway can be disastrous. Skinner, a very tall dog, taught me an important lesson about walking over him when he was sleeping. I decided to take the proverb "let sleeping dogs lie" seriously, and Skinner woke up just as my leg was in the air. He escaped being flattened, and I had trouble sitting for three days.

Command your puppy to "move," and shuffle your feet toward him. As soon as your puppy moves to avoid your feet, praise him. When your puppy appears to get the idea, gradually reduce the shuffle steps until you can eliminate them altogether. If your puppy does not move on command, touch—do not step on—his paws as you shuffle toward him.

Quiet

There are few things more annoying than a puppy that barks and refuses to stop when you are trying to talk on the phone or answer the door. Teach your puppy "quiet" so that you have the control to stop barking when the noise no longer serves a purpose. The "quiet" does not eliminate or discourage barking at strangers.

Place squirt bottles filled with very cold water, set on hard stream, near the door and in other places in the house where your puppy has a tendency to bark too much or inappropriately. Attach and hold your puppy's handle so that you don't have to run after him when he tries to avoid the water. When you have decided that your puppy has barked enough for the circumstances, command "quiet." If your puppy does not stop barking, squirt him right between the eyes, several times if necessary, until he stops barking. Praise your puppy for being quiet. Be persistent and correct your puppy every time he barks inappropriately or too much. If your puppy is undisturbed by the squirt bottle, back it up with one or several glasses of water in his face. Once your puppy realizes that barking after the "quiet" produces water, he will respond to just the squirt bottle. In short time, if you are consistent and persistent, your puppy will realize that if he stops barking on command, you will praise him instead of drowning him.

TRAINING PROBLEMS

If you are having a problem teaching a particular exercise, you may choose to train only long enough to meet the objective of three successful repetitions for the confusing task and eliminate all other exercises. If your puppy is having difficulty performing three repetitions correctly, end the session the first time he performs correctly, or when he successfully performs part of the exercise. Quit training sessions on a good note. If a session has been going poorly, end it with a simple exercise that your puppy can do to earn praise.

A good puppy trainer is flexible and does not dwell on problems, because it only imprints them in your puppy's mind. Even if your puppy resists a certain lesson, command "sit" and help him obey, so that you have an opportunity to praise him rather than correct him. By helping him perform the exercise, you accomplish two important objectives in successful training: first, the training ends on a positive note with praise, and second, the session ends with your puppy obeying your command. If you end a session before your puppy obeys, he learns that he does not have to obey. This reinforces stubborn, disobedient behavior.

You can be reasonably sure that your puppy understands an exercise when he performs correctly 90 percent of the time. Even when your puppy demonstrates an understanding of an exercise, practice the lessons occasionally to maintain the behavior. The cliché "use it or lose it" also applies to dogs. The more often you and your puppy practice, the more proficient your puppy will become.

When your puppy is fairly proficient at the exercises that you are teaching, change your training location to help keep the sessions new and upbeat. New settings also teach your puppy to be obedient in different places. The location of the training sessions must mimic the environment in which your puppy is expected to be obedient. The puppy that is taught to obey the heel command in dog-training class will not automatically transfer his lesson to heeling in the park or on a city street without practice.

When two techniques are suggested or available for training the same exercise, such as with "sit" and "down," practice both methods. Each method has advantages, and the variety will minimize boredom.

HANG IN THERE

Puppies are naturally good at persistent behavior and are even better if they are rewarded for it. When you give in to your puppy before you get the desired response, your puppy's persistent behavior is strengthened and rewarded. If you correct your puppy for jumping up the first four times and do not correct him for the fifth jump up, you simply are teaching him to jump up five times for the payoff. Likewise, your puppy will not obey if you are not persistent in enforcing commands. The puppy that is told to sit and ignores the command continues to ignore commands unless you are persistent in enforcing your rules.

Do not repeat your commands after your puppy has learned the meaning of them. An obedient puppy responds on the first command. If you must repeat the command before your puppy responds, he is not properly trained. Once your puppy understands what a command means, you must insist that he obey the first command. It is too easy to fall into the rut of giving multiple commands, and with each command your voice gets louder and louder. I used to give multiple commands to my kids, clean your room, clean your room, CLEAN YOUR ROOM! I sounded like a broken record, until one day I decided to test my kids' hearing. I repeated "clean your room" three times, and there was no response. I said, "Let's get an ice cream" once, and they were out the door before me. I realized that not only did my kids have selective hearing, my husband and puppies had it, too. Selective-hearing disease was contagious in my household, and I had to find a cure—quick. The next time my puppy chose not to hear me, I enforced the command instead of repeating it, and the disease was cured. The cure also worked for my husband and kids.

If you command your puppy to do something and he disobeys, enforce the command without repeating it. If you repeat the command, your puppy may interpret the second command as a signal that a new exercise has started. Even if your puppy corrects himself by returning to position as you move toward him to deliver a correction, you must follow through so that your puppy learns that the only way to avoid a correction is to perform the exercise correctly the first time. A good trainer never uses a command that he cannot or does not intend to enforce. Your puppy needs to learn to obey the first command.

REINFORCEMENT SCHEDULE

During the shaping and learning phase of training, your puppy should receive a treat every time he performs correctly. Once you are positive that he understands, based on a 90-percent or higher response rate, deliver the treats randomly to reinforce and maintain behavior. Never eliminate your praise. For example, when my puppy is learning to sit, he gets a treat along with praise every time he sits. Once I am sure that my puppy understands "sit," he is rewarded with praise for each success and is given treats on a random schedule. In one training session I may command my puppy to sit five times, for which he is praised each time he obeys and only rewarded with a treat two times.

To teach my puppy a chain of behaviors, such as to come when called and sit in front, I adjust my treat schedule. Each part performed during the learning stage is rewarded with praise and treats until my puppy understands the commands. To teach my puppy that "come" now means "run to me and sit in front," I eliminate treats in between each exercise. For example, I command him to come, and before I give him a treat for obeying, I command "sit." Now, instead of two different exercises, the puppy learns that in order to earn a treat, he must come and sit in front.

A training schedule that provides random treats instead of treats all the time positively teaches your puppy to obey even when treats are not available. If he thinks that he may get a treat, he will respond and not be disappointed when there is only praise, particularly if he thinks that the next repetition may be rewarded with a treat. Use your treats on a schedule that keeps him guessing. If he's guessing, he's thinking and is going to try harder to earn a reward.

The above exercises are excellent for starting your puppy on his way to being an obedient dog in your home. However, home training cannot substitute for a good obedience class, where your puppy can be socialized and taught to be obedient around other people and dogs.

Rhodesian Ridgeback pups.

CHAPTER 16

Preventing Problem Behaviors

Preventing behavioral problems in early puppyhood is much easier than fixing them when your puppy becomes an adult and is set in his ways. Many behavioral problems can be prevented by good management and early training.

FOOD-RELATED PROBLEMS

Many health and behavioral problems are centered around food and can be prevented with good management.

Food Bolting

Some puppies attack their food as if it were their last meal. To slow down the gobbler, feed your puppy smaller and more frequent portions in a pie pan or any similar large, flat dish to prevent him from picking up large amounts of food to bolt down. Frequent feedings, three or four times a day, take away the novelty and excitement of eating and often slow down the bolter.

If bolting is caused by competition between dogs, stand in the room while they eat so that you can prevent bowl switching. The "leave it" can be taught to eliminate eating from each other's bowl. Feed each dog on the opposite side of the room so that going to the neighboring bowl is not quite so tempting. Feeding the dogs in separate crates or rooms or at different times is another good

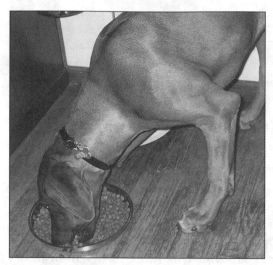

Studies have shown that dogs that gobble or bolt their food down are at risk for bloating, which is life-threatening to your dog. To prevent bolting, feed more frequently and feed from a pie pan so that your dog cannot grab large mouthfuls to swallow.

option. Finally, do not make your puppy wait for his food or watch its preparation. The excitement and anticipation of getting the food will only promote bolting.

The Finicky Eater

There may be several reasons why some puppies are finicky about their food. Finicky eaters may not like the taste or odor of the food, they may not be hungry, or they may regulate their food intake based on the amount of exercise that they receive. Often, puppies will sniff their food and then go off to do something else because they are just too busy to eat.

Switching the mildly finicky eater's food to another brand or flavor from time to time may provide renewed interest in eating. Do not cook special recipes or add tidbits or gourmet delectables to his food. Once you dress up your puppy's food, often with additions that are not particularly healthy for him, he will come to expect the same wonderful diet every day and will learn to hold out for the really good stuff. Feeding scraps to the finicky eater is counterproductive. Scraps are generally more palatable than dog food, and the puppy that does not eat very much to begin with may turn up his nose at dog food if scraps are available. If scraps must be fed to the finicky eater, only feed them in your puppy's dish *after* he has finished his normal meal.

Do not resort to hand feeding or some other ritual to tempt your puppy to eat. When Kathy's busy puppy was young, she stood by his bowl to encourage him to eat so that he would not get distracted. Kathy's puppy learned that part of the eating ritual was her presence, and for fifteen years, Kathy stood near her dog's bowl. If your puppy is not interested in the food, pick up the dish after fifteen minutes and put the food away until the next feeding time. Do not make a fuss over your puppy if he doesn't eat. A fuss is comforting and rewarding to your puppy, and it will reinforce not eating. Your puppy will eat when he is hungry unless he is ill.

A wait or stay command before you place the bowl on the floor for the finicky eater may tempt his interest. For the anxious eater, the command will prevent him from jumping on you and knocking the bowl out of your hand.

Puppies often regulate the amount that they eat according to their level of exercise. The puppy that does not get much exercise may not need to eat as much as you expect. If you suspect that your puppy is too lean and not eating because he is sick, consult your veterinarian.

A finicky eater should not have free access to food all day because there will be no novelty to the food or to being fed. A puppy will be more interested in his food dish if it only appears once a day. When finicky eaters are made to wait or sit-stay for their food, they are sometimes fooled into thinking that the food is a reward. (For owners who want to avoid being mauled by their chow hounds, the "sit and wait" when feeding may be a survival technique.) Try feeding the finicky eater with another dog, because the competition from another dog nearby may motivate him to clean his dish.

Begging

Begging usually becomes a habit when a puppy begs and is reinforced with a tidbit from the table. However, some dogs are just born optimistic, and even though they never receive food from the table, they keep hoping that something will fall their way. If young children drop food from your table, train your puppy to settle or down-stay away from the table so that begging is not reinforced. If you don't want your puppy begging at the table, don't feed him scraps while he is begging. The scraps can be placed in your puppy's dish, or you can teach him the settle. The puppy will tire of staring up at you and will soon fall asleep if he is not rewarded for begging. My dogs only get scraps from the table when they settle at the table. Rather than rewarding begging, I reward quietly settling.

Hand Feeding

Your puppy must never bite the hand that feeds him. To make sure that your puppy takes food gently, teach him "easy." Offer him a treat by holding it in your thumb and index finger, keeping your palm toward your body and your knuckles facing your puppy. Command "easy," and if he grabs for the treat, softly tap the front of his mouth on his lips. After one tap, puppies generally learn to take the food from your hand gently.

Messy Eaters

There are two types of messy eaters—puppies that knock over their bowls and puppies that carry food away from their bowls. To cure the dish dumper, feed your puppy in a large, heavy, ceramic bowl. Ceramic bowls are available in different sizes, and the largest may even be difficult for a Great Dane to turn over. There are also bowls with flanges on the base to make knocking over and picking up the bowl impossible.

For the carryout gourmet, you can use a large dish so that the food is already spread out rather than layered. Do not encourage the behavior of spreading the food by hiding goodies in the bottom of the dish. In addition, stand several feet from the bowl, and when your puppy starts to leave with a mouthful, block his path and send him back to the bowl with a stamp of your feet. If necessary, take him back to the bowl by his handle or collar. You may also choose to feed your puppy in the crate to prevent the mess.

Food Guarding

In a multiple-dog home, food guarding is very common. Feeding time should be supervised so that each dog remains at his own dish. If you cannot supervise your dogs, and they are only guarding their food from each other, feed the dogs in their respective crates.

A puppy that guards food from his owner or other people is behaving unacceptably. Do not feed your puppy in a crate or in a protected cove if you have observed him guarding his food from you or other people. If the feeding area is protected on three sides, he will have an easier time guarding his food.

You must check or test your puppy periodically and throughout his life to determine if he is being possessive about his food. Place your hand in the dish while your puppy is eating and observe his reaction. Your puppy should not display anything more serious than mild interest. Each member of the family, and even visitors, should be able to place their hands in your puppy's dish or pick up his dish without a problem. One of my clients was asked to feed a neighbor's dog when they were out of town. My client picked up the empty bowl and she lost the use of her right hand from the bite. In retrospect, the dog owner realized that

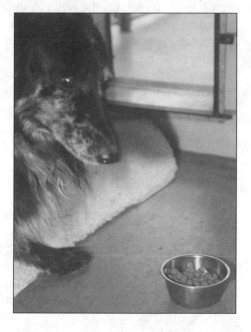

If your puppy stops eating and stiffens and stares at the food when you approach, he is very likely guarding his food.

she was the only one who had ever fed the dog. A training session at the food bowl is a very wise insurance policy.

Training with the Food Dish. Place your hand in your puppy's bowl as if you are mixing the food, and observe your puppy's reaction. Your puppy is probably guarding his food if he stops eating and stiffens, if he starts eating very fast and his tail is not wagging, or if he growls and snaps at your hand. If you observe stiffness or fast eating, food-bowl training is very important. If your puppy growls or snaps, a correction is due along with food-bowl training. Occasional hand feeding is a good tactic to let your puppy know who controls the food.

To train a puppy to accept hands in his bowl, place a tasty morsel in the empty bowl as your puppy watches. Let him eat the treat, and repeat the process several times before you give him a full bowl or his dinner. When your puppy is comfortable with your placing a treat in an empty bowl, place a treat in the bowl while he is eating. If he reacts with a growl or snap, correct him with a cuff. Repeat the process until your puppy does not react. If he just watches suspiciously, keep up the routine until he does not appear threatened. The next step is to pick up the bowl as he is eating. If your puppy growls or reacts negatively, correct him and repeat the process until he accepts the process without aggression. If your puppy does not react, give the bowl back with a treat in it. Periodic checks are important to monitor and cure aggressive behavior over food. Have other members of the household do the same training at the food bowl.

Do not leave the dish on the floor when visitors are present unless your puppy has been desensitized to people handling his dish. If your puppy is very aggressive about his food with other people, you will want to desensitize your puppy to other people at a slower pace to ensure that your helper does not get hurt. With a delectable morsel, such as liver, cheese, or hot dog, in your helper's hand, command your puppy to sit-stay and have the helper hand feed the puppy the treat in front of the food dish. If your puppy does not know sit-stay, hold him in place by his handle during these sessions until you have taught him the command. Your helper should offer the treats closer and closer to the food dish until his hand is in the dish and your puppy is taking the treat gently. Another good tactic is to have your helper feed your puppy by placing the food into the bowl one small piece at a time. Your puppy must learn that hands in the bowl are rewarding. There should be several training sessions a day. The more frequent the sessions, the faster your puppy will become accustomed to his food being handled. Do not feed your puppy anywhere but at his food bowl until he readily accepts handling of his food. Put your hand into his bowl frequently, sometimes with a tasty treat, sometimes without, to reinforce the training and to check whether your puppy is becoming possessive again.

BONE/CHEW-TOY POSSESSION

Bones and other chew toys can turn Jekyll into Hyde. To train your puppy to give up a really delectable bone, condition him to give up other less desirable objects first. Attach a leash or handle to your puppy so that he cannot get away, and start your training with a new toy or with a toy that generates only mild interest for your puppy. Offer the toy to your puppy, and after he takes the toy, offer a very tasty treat, such as cheese, liver, hot dog, or steak, in exchange for the toy as you command "give." Most puppies will give up the toy and take the treat. After several exchange sessions, give your puppy the command, take the toy, then give a treat. If your puppy does not give up the toy, physically take the toy out of his mouth, then give a treat. If your puppy growls, give him a good raze correction. If your puppy snaps, give a cuff correction. Repeat the process until he gives up the possession.

My dogs own nothing in my house. All of their food, toys, and bones are on loan or rent to them by me. Upon notice of repossession, my dogs must give back the items without protest. One night after my class lecture on possessive behavior,

Bone or toy possession is fairly common behavior for dogs unless you take the time to train them to give up their possessions.

a client confessed that her five-year-old Rottweiler growled at her when he had a bone. My client was fifteen years old when she got the dog, and at the time, she felt that the dog's growling was acceptable because, "after all, the bone was his." Recently, my client excitedly reported that she was much happier, because after two sessions of bone training, her dog would give up the bone without growling or protest. Practice the training frequently, and gradually work up to the objects that are really valuable to your puppy, ending with the bone. I was very astounded to hear one trainer tell clients not to give bones so that the dog wouldn't have anything to protect. I certainly would have hated finding out that my dog was possessive the day I took the chicken bone from him that he found in the park. *Avoiding confrontations does not resolve problems.*

BARKING

Barking is a communication system and is a functional behavior for your puppy. Appropriate barking can let you know that your puppy has to go outside, that people have arrived, and, in my house, that one of the other dogs is doing something that he shouldn't be doing. Piper was barking nonstop. I looked out the window and saw Casino chasing something. I went out to find that she had caught a bird. Although Piper's barking was in reaction to the excitement and activity, it did alert me that something was amiss. Barking becomes a problem when it continues past the initial alerting stage or when your puppy does not stop on command. My puppies are encouraged to bark to alert me when someone approaches my door. However, once I am at the door, I expect my puppies to stop barking when I command "quiet." Ideally, you will want to encourage appropriate barking and teach your puppy to be quiet on command when barking is unnecessary or has fulfilled its purpose.

Causes for Barking

While some barking is the result of breed-specific tendencies, it may also develop as a consequence of your puppy's environment. Puppies that are left alone in the backyard for long hours each day, particularly if they are tied or staked, become sensitive to sounds, bored, frustrated, and anxious, which results in barking to express or release their emotions. Puppies also learn to bark by

joining the chorus of neighborhood dogs that bark out of boredom, frustration, and anxiety.

Unintentional Reinforcement for Barking

When a puppy barks in the backyard and no one is home to
correct him when he doesn't stop, he learns that barking is acceptable. Puppies are also reinforced for barking when they are let into
the house after barking instead of being corrected. If you let your
puppy in to shut him up, he learns that when he is outside, the
door key is to bark until someone finally gets tired of hearing him.
Even if you open the door annoyed, he is satisfied, because negative attention is better than no attention at all. The puppy has successfully learned that barking gets your attention. In order to prevent unintentional training when you are not home, confine your
puppy in a crate until he is trained not to bark. When you are
home and he barks at the door, greet him with a correction rather
than with the reward of entry into the house. After several minutes, when your puppy is quiet, let him into the house.

Teaching Your Puppy to Be Quiet on Command

The first step to correct barking is to train your puppy to stop
barking on command. A squirt bottle is the most effective, nonviolent method for correcting barking. Place a squirt bottle filled with
cold, plain water strategically at the front door. Ask a friend or
neighbor to come to the door and knock or ring the doorbell. Allow
your puppy to bark three or four times, or as many barks as it takes
for you to reach the door. Once you are at the door, take hold of
your puppy's handle and command "quiet" with a very firm voice.
If your puppy stops barking, praise him. If your puppy does not
stop barking, squirt him in the face, right between the eyes.
Attempts to dodge the water are squelched if you are holding your
puppy's handle. When your puppy barks again, repeat the squirt.
After about the third squirt, most puppies get the idea to stop barking when they hear "quiet." If your puppy does not respond to the
squirt bottle, water glasses are very effective. If you are concerned
with getting your floor wet, place a drop cloth down to protect your
floors for your training sessions. The squirt bottle can be left near
the door to remind your puppy to stop barking on command. Your

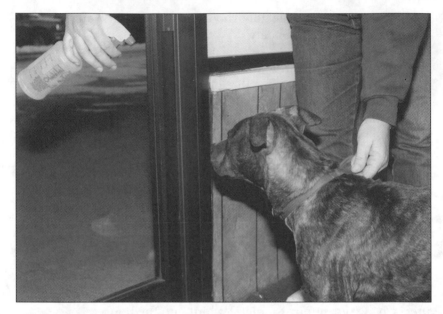

The squirt bottle is the most effective nonviolent method for teaching a dog to be quiet on command. Even if your dog likes water, he will not enjoy being squirted between the eyes with a reprimand to be quiet.

puppy is only being taught to stop barking on command, *not* to stop barking altogether. Your puppy will continue to bark at visitors or intruders but will learn to cease barking on command.

Barking in the Yard

To correct inappropriate barking in the yard, a squirt bottle is not a big enough gun for distance and running targets. Attach a garden hose with a power spray nozzle to an outside faucet, or use a battery-operated water machine gun. Employ the same procedure used at the door; however, you don't have to hold onto your puppy's collar now that you have a long-distance shooter.

Puppies are very clever about testing your seriousness, and you have to stay one step ahead. Jody was thrilled that she had licked her puppy's barking problem. Whenever her puppy barked, she would say "quiet" and then pick up the squirt bottle. As soon as her puppy saw the bottle, he would stop barking. I asked Jody to test her puppy by commanding "quiet" without showing him the squirt bottle. As I suspected, Jody's puppy did not respond to her command—he was responding to her reaching for the squirt bottle.

If your puppy does not stop barking on command, and stops only after you pick up the hose or squirt bottle, follow through with the correction anyway to teach him that the only way he can avoid the correction is to be quiet on command. Even if your puppy runs, follow him with the hose and spray him. If your puppy can get too far away, block off the area so that he does not have the full run of the yard until he responds to "quiet." In order to maintain an association between the behavior and the correction when your puppy is running and you can't get a correction in before ten seconds or so, form a verbal chain by repeating "quiet" until you reach him and deliver the water. The stream of words connects the command to the correction. Persistency and consistency are very important, so keep the water tools conveniently placed and in working order.

Training a puppy not to bark when no one is home requires confining him in the house or crate so that he does not get away with barking. Hire a responsible person or ask a neighbor to help you out by holding vigilance with the squirt bottle or hose when your puppy is outside. Most neighbors would not only be thrilled to drown the barking critter, but would probably pay you for the opportunity. When you do leave your puppy alone, you may want to use a tape recorder to make sure that he is not barking. You may need to repeat the correction process periodically.

Another effective tool to eliminate barking is the high-tech Citronella collar. When the collar is worn by the puppy and activated by his barking it will squirt Citronella into the air. The sound of the spray distracts the dog from barking, and the aversive odor of Citronella further discourages him from barking and activating the collar. The collar should be used under your supervision for two reasons. Firstly, you want to make sure that the collar is working properly and that your puppy responds appropriately. Secondly, you will need to refill the Citronella after fifteen squirts if your puppy is not quick to make the association between barking and being squirted. Do not leave him alone with the collar until you are sure he has learned that barking results in being squirted.

Teaching Your Puppy to Bark

Anytime your puppy barks on his own—during play, standing at the door, or in reaction to a noise—pair the word "speak" with the bark, and praise him. If your puppy does not bark readily, hold a tasty treat in front of his face to get him excited. Motivate him to bark with a jolly, playful tone—"speak." When your puppy barks or makes any sound, give him a treat and praise him. Once you consistently receive a sound on command, raise the criterion where he must make a sound a little closer to a bark in order to get the treat. Many repetitions may be necessary before your puppy learns to bark on command. If he is taught to bark on command, remember to teach him to stop on command also.

CHEWING

All puppies go through a developmental chewing phase to relieve the irritation and discomfort of cutting new teeth. Most puppies stop their seemingly incessant chewing once their new teeth are fully erupted at about nine months of age. The few puppies that do not cease chewing by one year of age either have acquired the habit of chewing from boredom, anxiety, and frustration, or have acquired an unusual gourmet appetite. The chewer should be well supplied with acceptable chew items. You can get him interested in chewing his toys by playing fetch with him. To avoid damage when you cannot keep a watchful eye on your puppy, confine him in a crate or an area where only appropriate chew items are available. Occasionally, "Jaws," the superchewer, is able to work over an airline-type crate. For this truly gifted chewer, a wire-mesh, heavy-gauge metal crate is a good alternative.

Correcting Chewing

When you catch your puppy with a prized possession in his mouth, you must restrain yourself from running after him no matter how tempting it is, or how much you want your item back. If you chase him, he will run and get immense joy from playing keep-away. In the process of the chase, he will also sink his teeth into the item just to hold on tighter. You have a much better chance of getting the prize back undamaged by calmly calling him. Show your puppy a toy or treat, and in your happiest voice—no

All puppies go through developmental chewing phases,
and they need to have appropriate chew toys to relieve
the discomfort of erupting teeth.

To avoid damage or danger of your puppy chewing things
that can hurt him, keep an eye on him or confine him
to a safe place like the crate.

When you catch your puppy with something in his mouth that he is not allowed to chew, use a treat to call him to you and make an exchange.

The exchange is a good way to teach your puppy to give up his possessions when you ask. It is a positive method of teaching your puppy to give.

matter how much constraint it takes to remain calm—call him. When your puppy comes to you, praise him and make the exchange. If your puppy does not drop the item, gently take hold of his handle—do not grab at him—and give a release, such as "drop it," "give," or "thank you," as you take the item out of his mouth. Give him praise and a treat. Even if you have to pry his mouth open, praise him following the exchange of items. If your puppy does not come for a treat, drop to the ground and act very silly. Curiosity will get the best of him, and he will come over to see what is going on. Gently take him by the handle and exchange your treat or toy for the forbidden object. Prudence calls for enrolling your puppy in an obedience course to teach him to return on command. In the meantime, let him drag around a lead so that you can reel him in when he has a forbidden item in his mouth.

The drawback for exchanging stolen items for treats and praise is that your puppy will learn to bring you everything for a treat. Snorkel, the paper shredder, brought me the paper, piece by piece, until his stomach was bursting from treats. If your puppy gets overzealous about retrieving, omit the treat most of the time and just praise him. A puppy that retrieves everything for you is much more enjoyable to live with than a puppy that sneaks an item off to a secluded part of the house and secretly chews it to pieces. The best prevention for fanatic retrieving of household items is to put things away so that your puppy does not have access to them.

DIGGING

Although digging in the yard may do aesthetic damage, the real danger is that your puppy is learning to dig out of the yard.

Why Puppies Dig

Some breeds of dog were genetically engineered and perfected for their ability and willingness to dig. The terrier, for instance, is usually very willing to dig to China to get to the vermin in a hole. My dogs recently finished a home-improvement project for a gopher. They decided to enlarge the gopher's doorway to provide him with an open-door policy to their yard. Digging is a natural behavior for a puppy that likes to store up goodies, such as bones,

Digging is a natural behavior for many dogs;
however, the danger is in them digging out of the yard.

for a rainy day. Puppies will dig in the hot weather for a cool place to lie down, particularly if no shade is available. Puppies also dig out of frustration, boredom, and anxiety and to get out of a fence to roam the neighborhood.

Preventions for Digging

Digging is easier to prevent than it is to cure, because most digging occurs when your puppy is in the yard alone for long periods of time. To prevent digging:

1. Provide plenty of shade.
2. Trim your puppy's nails short. If his nails are short, he will find digging with the pads of his paws very uncomfortable, and he won't dig.
3. Leave play toys outside to keep your puppy busy. If your puppy buries things, avoid giving him toys, bones, or other items that are tempting to bury.
4. Fence off tempting plants and shrubs that are fun for your puppy to dig up.

5. Neuter your puppy as early as possible to reduce his desire to escape the yard.

6. If you cannot supervise your puppy, and as a result, cannot correct him for digging, confine him in the crate or an outside pen. If you choose the pen option, provide shade or shelter against hot or bad weather. A pen only needs to be four feet by eight feet. Of course, a larger pen is acceptable. The pen should not be square or round, because these shapes encourage circling behavior. To prevent your puppy from digging out of the pen, place wire mesh or heavy chicken wire on the ground under the pen. The wire should be just slightly larger than the bottom of the pen so that the excess can be brought up the outside the pen and attached to the sides, providing a floor that your puppy cannot dig through. Leave your puppy in the pen whenever you cannot supervise him closely. If you don't mind your puppy digging as long as he does not escape or destroy property, you can put a sand pile in the pen and let him dig to his heart's content. Hide toys or smelly knuckle bones in the pile to get him started.

7. If your puppy sneaks a hole here or there, fill it with rocks or other hard material. The filler must be large enough so that your puppy cannot swallow it. Dirt can be placed over the filler; however, loose dirt alone will only tempt a puppy to further excavate the site, whereas rock will file down his nails and make digging uncomfortable.

Correcting Digging

Attach a power nozzle to a garden hose. Keep the water on for fast shooting. When your puppy digs, command "leave it," and aim the nozzle right between his eyes. When your puppy looks up and stops digging, praise him. Repeat the process as many times as necessary until your puppy gives up digging when you are home.

While the water procedure will teach a puppy not to dig to avoid a correction when someone is home, it will not teach him to stop digging when no one is home. Therefore, keep your puppy confined in the pen, house, or crate when no one is home to correct or supervise. If your puppy is allowed to dig even once without correction, all of the prior corrections will be meaningless, and he will learn to limit digging to times when no one is home.

You may want to hire a sitter to train your puppy not to dig while you are gone. When you think that your puppy has given up digging, give him the freedom of the yard for short periods—fifteen minutes at a time. If he does not dig, gradually increase the time that he is allowed freedom in the yard. If your puppy resumes digging, confine him to the pen.

JUMPING

Puppies greet people as a show of their affection and excitement; however, jumping can be annoying and can cause damage when your cute fluff becomes six feet tall on his hind legs and weighs 200 pounds. A puppy can easily be taught either not to jump up at all or to jump only on command.

The Sit

When your puppy jumps up, command him to sit, and praise him when he obeys. If he does not sit, gently take his handle and place him in a sit. Do not pet or praise your puppy until he sits. For the older puppy, command "off" in a firm tone, and quickly raise up a knee to waist height, if possible. The purpose is *not* to kick your

Although jumping is a friendly gesture, a dog can injure someone and most people do not appreciate puppies jumping on them.

puppy, but to block him from connecting with your body and make jumping uncomfortable. When your puppy is on the ground, praise him and pet him gently. Too often, people make

*If a puppy is obeying a sit-stay at the door,
he cannot jump on people.*

the serious mistake of correcting their puppy for jumping, but
they forget to praise him for not jumping when he is sitting or
standing. Your puppy can only learn the distinction between
proper behavior and unacceptable behavior when he is corrected
for inappropriate behavior and praised for good behavior. Some
puppies figure out how to avoid the knee and learn to jump up
at your back or side. Be prepared for the modification, and
quickly turn and bring up your knee when your puppy jumps. If
he jumps up at your back, just pick up a foot as if you are
attempting to hop, and your puppy will bump into your foot. Use
"off" and "sit" when entering the door to remind your puppy to
stay on the ground.

Handle Correction

When your puppy attempts to jump up, pop his handle quickly
toward the ground and command "off." Always praise your puppy
when he is on the ground.

Stays and Jumping

Love me, love my puppy does not always go over well with invited guests. Do not wait for people to visit to train your puppy not to jump. Invite someone over for a cup of coffee with the specific purpose of helping you train your puppy. Use the sit-stay at the door to prevent your excited puppy from jumping up on visitors. You can practice the exercise at the door with a helper. The helper should ring the doorbell or sometimes knock. When you and your puppy get to the door, place your puppy on a sit-stay. Hold his handle, and do not open the door until he is positioned. If he moves, pop the collar by the handle to put him back into position. Open the door, and if your puppy moves, concentrate on placing him back into a sit. When your puppy does stay, praise him calmly. Your helper should greet and pet your puppy only when the puppy is sitting. Repeat the process until your puppy sit-stays at the door.

When real visitors arrive, take the time to enforce the stay, even if your visitor has to wait at the door a moment. Waiting at the door is much more pleasant than being mauled or clawed. Allow petting only when your puppy is sitting calmly. Do not release your puppy from the sit-stay or let go of the handle until your visitor has been in the house for a few moments—perhaps after the traditional greetings, and preferably when the visitors are sitting down. The exercise will provide time for your puppy to calm down from the stimulation of the doorbell or knock. When you are ready to release your puppy, use a quiet, unexcited "okay." If your puppy approaches your visitor, he will be calmer, because his initial excitement has been defused by concentrating on staying at the door.

Visiting

The settle can be used to discourage and prevent your puppy from pestering guests once they are in the house. Practice the settle with a helper, whom you invite over specifically to help train your puppy. Tie your puppy to your waist and command "settle." If your puppy gets up, use his handle to pop him down again. Insist that your puppy remain in the settle until he is calm. After some time has passed and your puppy relaxes, he may move to another spot or be allowed to visit. If your puppy reverts to pestering, command him to settle again. Your puppy will eventually learn that pestering is not acceptable, and he will give up trying if you enforce the settle every time. The settle also discourages hyperactivity. If your puppy gets too active, a "settle" every time he is rambunctious will encourage constraint in the house.

FENCE JUMPING

To prevent fence jumping, build a fence that will contain your puppy when he is an adult. A three-foot fence is not much of an obstacle for a Great Dane. An enclosed pen that has a chain-link roof may be a good option when you need to contain your puppy if you cannot install a taller fence.

If you do not want to put up a fence or you live in a community that does not allow fencing, the invisible fence, which delivers a shock when your puppy steps over the boundary, may work for you. An invisible fence can damage your pup's spirit if he is not trained properly and does not understand how to avoid the shock. Your puppy should be trained on lead and must have many opportunities to learn that he should obey the warning signal before you activate the system. If the invisible fence is your choice, read the training instructions very carefully or hire a professional to help you train your puppy with the fence.

There are three significant pitfalls to the invisible fence. First, if your puppy is not thoroughly trained to obey the warning signal and is motivated to cross the line by, for instance, a stray dog running past, the shock may scare him and cause him to bolt away from your property. Second, the fence does not keep other dogs out, and if one gets into your yard, your puppy is as trapped as if he were tied to a chain. And third, if your puppy is taunted by passing children and gets shocked by the fence for accidently crossing the line in his excitement, he may make a negative association with children. Que, a two-year-old Gordon Setter, became very excited by a group of neighborhood children rollerblading in front of his house, and in his excitement, he crossed the invisible fence line. After the incident, Que's owners noticed that he was very fearful and aggressive when children were present. If you choose to install an invisible fence, do not have the fence border the front yard or other area where passing children have access to your puppy.

If you plan to leave your puppy outside unsupervised—regardless of the fence system that you choose—your puppy will be safer in a covered pen close to your house where most people do not venture without an invitation. Aggression may develop when puppies are abused or teased through the backyard fence. Your puppy's space must be insulated from negative interactions and incidents that might prompt aggression when you are not home. A chain-link fence does not adequately protect your puppy when you are at work or away, because individuals or poorly supervised children may have access to your puppy through the fence. Leaving your puppy inside the house in a crate, or constructing a double fence or a run that is far from the street fence, are safer solutions. Protecting your puppy from the environment is your responsibility.

If your puppy attempts to jump the fence when you are home, discourage him by using a hose on the other side of the fence as he is coming over. Catching a dog in the act of fence jumping is very difficult, and you are better off building a fortress from which he cannot escape.

BOLTING

A good way to prevent your puppy from learning that bolting out the door is a bunch of fun is to teach him to sit-stay at the door until you attach the leash and give the heel or let's go command. My dogs are never allowed to exit the front door without a command. They are conditioned to wait for a command at the front door before they go out and do not attempt to bolt, whether we are walking out or I am just answering the door. A sit-stay command at the door not only gives your puppy something else to think about besides dashing out the door, it also teaches him to sit in a controlled manner at the door beside you. A trained dog at your side is good safety insurance when you open the door to strangers. Even if your puppy is not a guard dog and never will be, he will look so well trained, quietly and obediently sitting beside you on command, that people will assume that he is trained to alert, attack, and guard. Storm doors that have adjustable pistons, so that you can set the door to close fast, are also helpful as a safety net to stop your puppy.

If your puppy should learn to bolt out the door, set him up for a bolt and have a helper outside the door with a bucket of water.

As your puppy crosses the line, call him to you from inside the house and praise him if he comes. If he crosses the threshold, your helper should greet him with the bucket of water and chase him back into the house. Precision timing for the correction may be much more difficult than teaching the puppy never to cross the threshold without a heel command.

CHASING

Puppies love to chase anything that runs, and the faster it runs, the better. Cars, bikes, rollerbladers, joggers, and horseback riders are especially fun to chase. Car chasing is most often committed by puppies that have the run of the property and are not exposed to many cars. Expose your puppy to traffic by walking him on lead in your driveway or on a busy street. Command your puppy to remain in a sit-stay as cars pass. If your puppy starts to move or chase, command "sit," and snap the collar back if he moves forward instead of sitting. Praise your puppy when he obeys. Expose your puppy to bikes, rollerbladers, joggers, and horseback riders in this same manner. When your puppy is sitting, ask a passing rollerblader to stop for a second and give your puppy a treat to make the affair positive. Let your puppy watch the person pass by as the puppy performs a sit-stay next to you.

COPROPHAGY (FECES EATING)

This is surely considered by dog owners to be the most disgusting of all habits. Coprophagy is a common behavior for puppies. Boredom is often the cause, as is the presence of undigested nutrients from the dog food. To prevent your puppy from eating poop—whether the problem exists because of boredom or taste preference—keep the yard clean by picking up stools immediately. If taste preference is the cause, you can feed a food that is highly digestible and reduces the amount of waste that your puppy excretes. Quite often that may mean switching to an adult food. There are several good foods on the market that claim high digestibility and low waste. Products to add to your puppy's food to discourage stool eating can be found at pet-supply outlets. Walk your puppy on leash and use the "leave it" if he dives for a treat. After three weeks of walking him on lead, a change in diet, and keeping the area clean, hopefully the habit will be eliminated. If not, you will have to continue to walk your puppy on lead. Consult a veterinarian if your puppy is losing weight or if the stool has an abnormal appearance.

Other Animals' Feces

To prevent your puppy from eating other animals' feces on walks, use "leave it," and discipline your puppy with a snap on the collar if he dives for the feces. A good way to set your puppy up for a prepared correction is to stroll him through a horse corral.

Preventing your puppy from eating out of a cat's litter pan is difficult, because most puppies commit the act when no one, including the cat, is around to correct his behavior. A spray that might repel your puppy from the litter box might also make the pan unattractive to your cat. The best option is to place the pan up high or in an area where your puppy cannot get to it. A barrier for the room where the litter pan is housed is a good snack preventive. A gate with bars that your puppy cannot fit through might be a good choice, because cats are generally smaller and can usually slip through, under, or over gates that puppies cannot penetrate.

EXCESSIVE LICKING

If you want to correct your puppy for licking people, command "leave it" and use a squirt bottle to spray him in the face. The puppy that is licking can be placed in a settle away from the individual whom he is licking. Certainly, if you find licking undesirable, stop petting your puppy when he licks to avoid unintentionally reinforcing the behavior.

SEPARATION ANXIETY

Sometimes a puppy has such a strong attachment to his owner that he becomes extremely dependent on his owner's companionship. In the absence of this companionship, a puppy may become anxious. Anxiety manifests into nonfunctional, excessive behaviors, such as chewing, barking, pacing, and whining. These behaviors are not any different than what people do to relieve their own nervousness or anxiety. Don't we chew our nails, pace, and talk loud and fast when we are anxious?

Separation anxiety is often the reason why dogs chew, bark, whine, and pace excessively. The temptationto get another dog to alleviate separation anxiety should be well thought out so that you don't wind up with double the trouble.

Causes of Separation Anxiety

The primary reason why puppies suffer separation anxiety is that canines are pack or social animals. From the beginning, puppies are in the company of their dam and littermates. In fact, your puppy has very likely never been alone. His first time alone may be when you leave him to run an errand or go to work. Your puppy's first experience with being alone can be quite traumatic if you don't properly enrich his environment.

Acquiring a puppy too young contributes to separation anxiety. The six-week-old puppy is very immature and has not fully developed independence and exploratory behavior. He is merely a component of a collective system and is highly dependent upon his dam and litter. If a puppy is separated from the litter before he is developmentally ready, he may transfer his dependency to you. You will have to help your puppy develop independence through socialization and obedience training.

Separation anxiety may also develop if you never leave your young pup alone. Often, people arrange to get a puppy during a summer vacation or when a member of the family is home all day to take care of him. There is usually someone home with the puppy every minute of the day, or the puppy is taken wherever the owner goes. If there is a schedule change and the family member goes back to work, the puppy that is not used to being alone for several hours a day becomes very anxious. There is a significant relationship between separation anxiety and behavioral problems in dogs. These puppies will whine, bark, dig, escape from the yard, chew, and even cause damage to themselves by chewing on their bodies when they are left alone or without their owners. Puppies need to be conditioned or desensitized to tolerate periods of solitude.

Anxiety can also develop from traumatic events such as thunderstorms. A loud clap of thunder that surprises and frightens your dog as he is comfortably napping in the backyard can cause him to be afraid of being alone.

CONFINEMENT

The best option for providing your puppy with some solitude and keeping him and your house safe is the crate. Your puppy will not be over-stimulated by outside noises and sights that interrupt his sleep and thus give him an excuse to search for things to keep him busy, and there is nothing dangerous he can get into. For further security and comfort, you can leave a familiar-smelling blanket or pad in the crate. Provide chew toys, and leave the radio on to a soft music station to soothe your puppy. Heavy metal, rock, or jazz may be poor options for the puppy that needs to relax. If you are an avid television viewer and your puppy is used to the noise, you can alternate between the television and the radio for familiarity. If there is another caged animal, such as a bird, you might place the crate near the other animal for companionship.

When people perceive that their puppy is lonely, their first inclination is to get a second animal for companionship. Unfortunately, another animal can sometimes present double the problems. Many people choose to get two puppies from the same litter or of the same age for companionship, hoping to prevent separation-anxiety problems. The puppies will go through the same developmental phases at the same time. Two house-soiling, chewing puppies will require double the time. The upside is that both puppies will be through the mischievous stage at the same time. There is always concern that the littermates will bond with each other and not with their owner. You can avoid excessive bonding to a littermate by providing individual time with each puppy on a daily basis. Obedience training both puppies is an excellent opportunity to give each puppy individual, undivided, quality time. The puppies should also be crated separately near each other for companionship, to prevent excessive dependency and bonding. The decision to acquire another animal for your anxious puppy should be well thought out. You may want to borrow a companion from a friend before you commit to a second animal.

You can direct anxious behavior away from self-destruction by placing chew toys in the crate with your puppy. A knuckle bone with the marrow intact may keep your puppy busy for a long time as he relentlessly tries to lick out the marrow. Sterilized bones can be bought at many pet stores, and you can soak these bones in broth and fill them with goodies such as peanut butter or processed cheese spreads. The better the chew toy, the busier your puppy will be, thus channeling the anxious behavior appropriately. Long hours of chewing will keep your puppy's mind off you and will tire him, making him sleep for longer periods of time. Do not give the crate chew toys to your puppy on any other occasion. That way the novelty of the toys will not wear off. Place your puppy in the crate with the toys fifteen minutes or so before you leave the house so he does not associate the crate with the negative emotions evoked by your leaving. Vary the time when you place your puppy in the crate before you leave. Changing your routine and schedule by coming and going at different times will enrich both of your lives.

There must be no fuss when you leave. Commiserating words such as, "Honey, I will be back soon, you poor thing," will only serve to heighten his emotions and imprint your leaving him as negative, and he will miss your comforting presence even more.

Give your puppy a high-value treat and leave with nothing more than a "bye." The purpose of the treat is to make your leaving a rewarding experience. Every time you walk out of the house, your puppy gets a windfall. When you return, there should be no fanfare. If the reunions are emotional and overly rewarding, your puppy will spend the day anticipating your arrival. When you get home, let your puppy out of the crate and immediately take him out to relieve himself. When he comes into the house after relieving himself, go about your business for five or ten minutes. A loving greeting is appropriate about ten minutes after your puppy comes back in from the yard. If the greeting occurs immediately after your puppy comes in from the yard, he will anticipate the greeting and may not empty in his rush to get inside to greet you. If there is an interval between your arrival and your greeting, strong positive emotions will not imprint on your puppy for him to anticipate all day when you are away.

For the dog that is not crated, enrich his environment. Find special toys like a rubber kong and place different-sized liver or beef sticks in it so that he has to bat it around to get them out. Another favorite for my dogs that keeps them busy is the dental plaque bones that I smear with peanut butter or cheese spread. Every few days, I hide special treats around the house. I barely get out the door and they are off and running to sniff out their favorite goodies that may be hiding under a cup or box on the floor. The special treats should only be given when you are away and picked up when you come home.

EXERCISE

Exercise helps reduce anxiety. Scheduling exercise in the morning, such as a game of fetch or a jog in the park, can release a puppy's pent-up energy and help him relax. Limit the amount of exercise to a level that is appropriate for your puppy's age. Too much exercise, such as a two-mile jog for the five-month-old puppy, may be detrimental to his growing bones and joints and may not be appropriate until your puppy is at least eighteen months old. Ask your veterinarian about the appropriate amount of exercise for your puppy. Plan exercise sessions that will be easy and comfortable for you to maintain on a permanent basis. If your

Obedience training is an all-around good exercise for your puppy. You can run your puppy for miles and he will be ready for more. Use his brain for five minutes and he will be exhausted.

puppy becomes accustomed to the exercise and your schedule gets erratic, he will miss the activity and may end up more stressed than he was originally. Obedience training is low-impact exercise and leaves your puppy exhausted. A puppy can frolic all day chasing a ball and never tire, but use his brain for twenty minutes in obedience training and your puppy will be exhausted.

DIET

Devise a diet for your puppy that does not provide more calories and nutrients than he can burn because unused excess energy manifests in anxious behaviors.

DAY CARE FOR DOGS

Doggy daycare has become a popular service for dog owners. The puppy is exercised regularly, socialized with other dogs and people, and sometimes even trained. The puppy is never alone, and therefore he will not experience separation anxiety. Theoretically, the atmosphere fosters a well-adjusted puppy. However, if your puppy is never left alone, he may not adjust well to solitude if being alone later becomes necessary. Daycare can be very costly if the service must continue for the life of your dog. A good way to reap the benefits and avoid the possible pitfalls of your puppy never being alone is to enroll him two or three days a week instead of every day of the week.

OBEDIENCE TRAINING AND SEPARATION ANXIETY

Obedience training can help curb separation anxiety during early puppyhood. Training develops a communication tool that fosters security and trust. Training is also a one-on-one interaction and provides quality time where you and your puppy give each other undivided attention. Quality time can spend pent-up energy and make up for a lot of missed time.

Quality time with your puppy can spend pent-up energy and make up for a lot of missed time.

CHAPTER 17

Multiple-Dog Households

I ntroducing a puppy to another household dog, or to a pack of household dogs, creates changes in the established social structure and status that may provoke fights. Bitches will fight with bitches, and dogs will fight with dogs. Bitches and dogs will also get into occasional altercations, but generally not as frequently and severely as animals of the same sex. The social structure in a multiple-dog home is very likely to change several times as your puppy gets older, when a dog becomes ill, or a when member is deleted or added to the group. If fights and injuries do not result from pack changes, allow the dogs to work out their own social structure. If the dogs are fighting and hurting each other, you must intervene.

DOMINANCE

Dogs maintain a social order that determines how they interact with each other. For example, the dog on the top level is usually the one that possesses the bone and is rarely challenged if only one bone is available to the dogs. Every so often, the social order is challenged, and disputes occur. Most dogs work out the social order among themselves with little carnage and intervention from the outside. Very often, fights between two dogs or an older dog admonishing a puppy produce more noise than injury. You may hear World War III coming from the dogs, only to discover after

241

When a new puppy comes into your home and there is an older dog, it is not always love at first sight. Puppies and older dogs need to be watched carefully to ensure that no injuries occur.

the fight that there are no teeth marks on either dog. (Be extremely thorough in checking for bites, however, because puncture wounds from bites are very difficult to detect until they become infected and swollen.) When neither dog is hurting the other, your intervention may make matters worse by giving attention to the fights and causing more jealousy and rivalry.

Any competitive situation—such as protection of turf or territory, attempting to come through a doorway together, greetings at the door, being petted, and guarding possessions—may precipitate a fight. In a dog's perception, the dog that is in the house first owns the territory, and the dog or puppy coming onto the turf is at a disadvantage. The dominant dog will not miss an opportunity to let the underdog or puppy know that walking on owned turf is dangerous. A fight may start when your puppy simply comes back into the house after going out to the yard to relieve himself. To prevent arguments, both dogs should be sent out together, and they should return together. Be careful that you have the dogs come into the house one behind the other, because bumping or getting stuck in the doorway can also start a fight. If the underdog is in the house first, he will not generally pick a fight, and the dominant dog will generally respect the underdog's position of being on the turf first or through the door first, and will not start a quarrel. Beach is an extremely dominant bitch around dogs, and she tries very hard to be the first one on the turf. If she gets to run up the stairs first, she will wait at the top to attack the other dogs as they come up. I make sure that she is always the last to get to the top, and she always looks extremely disappointed to miss an opportunity to pick a fight.

JEALOUSY

When visitors arrive at the door, have both dogs obey your sit-stay or wait command to avoid pushing for first position. If both dogs get excited and push each other at the door, bark, and jump, a fight will erupt. If your puppy does not know the sit-stay yet, hold onto his handle when you answer the door.

Tiffs can erupt when one dog is being petted and the other pushes his way in. There are professionals who believe that the dominant dog's position should be encouraged—in other words, the dominant dog's position should be respected and you should pet him instead of your puppy. Encouraging dominant behavior empowers your dog even more than does his natural tendency. You can use your obedience "settle" to disempower your dominant dog, or you can place the dogs in a sit or down-stay and pet them both while you maintain control in your own household. You may also just choose to end the petting session and place both dogs in a settle or stay position. Until my dogs pay the mortgage, I determine the rules in the house and ensure that my dogs obey.

If possessions such as bones become objects of argument, each dog should have a bone or toy, or for that matter, you may choose to remove the possessions altogether. Even if each dog has toys, arguments may occur. In that case, you may choose to give your dogs their toys only in their crates. Just as in the situation of food bowl wandering, I supervise and don't let my dogs steal each other's possessions unless fights do not result. Casino loves to pick up toys and flash them off to the other dogs to get one or all of them to chase her. Sometimes she spends fifteen minutes slowly trotting back and forth trying to get the other dogs to chase her. If one of the dogs happens to pull the toy out of her mouth, she never starts a fight—she just chases the other dog. If any of the dogs display aggressive body language, I end the game with "knock it off" or enforced stays.

Puppies are notorious for either ignoring body language or pushing the older dog too far by pestering and barking in a playful mode. When you see your older dog becoming annoyed because your puppy is unmercifully pestering him, this is a good time to command them both to "knock it off." A squirt in the face with cold water is a good way to defuse a potential conflict. Distract your puppy with something to keep him busy, such as giving him a toy. Do not wait to reprimand him after he has initiated an aggressive reaction from your older dog.

MINIMIZING AGGRESSION BETWEEN DOGS

When two dogs fight and injure each other, it is important to monitor their body language and to correct any signs of aggression before the situation becomes a full-blown fight. Correct any signs of aggression, such as staring, raised hackles, leaning over, or mounting, with a verbal admonishment such as "quit it" or "knock it off" before the situation becomes a fight. If you have done your homework with obedience training and enforcing your commands, both of your dogs will obey your verbal reprimands. Do not allow the dogs to become too excited or get into a frenzy in the house or yard.

Games such as fetch may also incite a fight if both dogs are running after the ball at the same time. Play with one dog at a time if the dogs have a tendency to get into arguments, or pick another game that does not cause the dogs to get overly excited. Play sessions can also result in fights if one dog gets pinned or injured. If the dogs have had serious fights in which one was injured or became frightened, do not allow the play sessions to get too rough. Stop the play session with a verbal reprimand before it gets out of hand. If the dogs do not stop with a verbal reprimand, end the play by either distracting them with a new game or by giving each one a toy. If neither the toy nor the distraction works,

Playtime can sometimes turn into a fight if one dog gets shoved or nipped too hard. Puppies can also play so rough that it is difficult to tell if they are playing or fighting. If your gut feeling tells you that the play is too rough, intervene and distract the dogs by a settle or a less rough game.

physically end the play by commanding the dogs to down-stay for five minutes, even if you have to hold your puppy's handle to keep him on a down-stay or place them in their kennels until they calm down.

BREAKING UP FIGHTS

Getting between two fighting dogs is a very good way to get bitten, but few people can refrain from breaking up a fight when their dogs are involved. Generally, when two dogs are of equal size and are fighting, they will not kill each other; rather, they end up needing stitches. However, if you stick your hand in, you may lose the use of your hand if it gets bitten. Fighting dogs are frantic and do not know what they are biting, so before jumping in, try very cold water in the dogs' faces. If cold water does not work, very hot water may do the trick. Although hot water may burn a dog, the burn may be easier to treat than a severed jugular if the dogs are really serious about harming each other.

If water is unavailable, and you feel that your only choice is physical intervention, take time to wrap any handy extra clothing, such as a jacket, around your arm to cushion misplaced bites, and wait for an opportunity where you have a good chance of not getting bitten. Grab one of the dogs by his tail or by the back of his collar, and get him behind a barrier. If the dogs are small enough, you can separate them by lifting them off the ground and holding a dog in each hand by the base of the tail or the back of the collar. The dogs will have a very difficult time biting if they are hanging from their tail or collar. If you grasp the collars, the dogs will have to loosen their grips to gasp for air.

If the fight is between dogs that are too big to lift off of the ground, try to insert something like a stick between them that they can attack rather than each other. The minute the dogs separate, try to get one behind a barrier, such as a door. The barrier is important, because when one dog is pulled off, the other one will continue to attack. Two of my males got into a serious fight, and I was very grateful that they were both obedience trained. Once I separated them, I commanded the attacker to sit-stay while I moved the other dog behind a door. Generally, even the best-trained dog will be so pumped up and involved in a fight that an obedience command will not get processed. I could see that my male was in conflict between wanting to attack again and performing the sit-stay, because he kept shifting his weight looking for a good opportunity to get past me to my other dog. After the dogs are broken up, they should be leashed and made to do a stay until they calm down. When the fights are so serious that physical damage is present, seek professional advice.

MISDIRECTED AGGRESSION

In discouraging a dog fight, be careful not to get the brunt of the dog's aggressive backlash. When a dog readies for a fight, his system is totally charged and cannot be turned off instantly. The dog that is distracted from a fight by a correction may transfer the aggression to you. Dogs also transfer their emotions to other dogs. If you correct one family dog, he may attack the other family dog without any apparent provocation. When more than two dogs are in a household, the other dog(s) will likely join in a fight and attack the underdog or the one that yelps. For safety, crate the dogs when no one is around to supervise. If a dog exhibits anger displacement, take him out to a quiet, distraction-free area or another room, and let him calm down. The best correction for an argument is to stop the conflict before it becomes a fight.

NEUTERING

Neutering often eliminates the aggression and irritability associated with sexuality. Neutering will not change your puppy's personality except for the better. If your puppy is neutered, he will be more attentive to you instead of to other dogs. Neutering bitches will eliminate the heat cycle, as well as the associated behavioral changes, including irritability, false pregnancies, and other emotions that may lead to aggressive behavior. In addition, neutering reduces the risk of cancer greatly for both sexes. Some studies have reported an 80 to 100 percent lower risk of cancer if the dog or bitch is neutered by six months or before the first heat cycle. Neutering will make your dog a much better pet and has been reported to improve trainability.

Sometimes, no matter what you do, the dogs will not tolerate each other and there must be intervention or separation. Intervention may consist of having the aggressive dog wear a muzzle whenever the two dogs are together. Separation may consist of a high, strong, see-through gate between rooms, or for the outside area, separate pens.

While it may not be possible to get two dogs to love each other when they have a personality conflict, teaching them to tolerate each other may be feasible with obedience training and by defusing fights before they get started.

*Games are an excellent and fun way to interact
with your puppy.*

CHAPTER 18

Games and Exercise

Games are an excellent and fun way to interact with your puppy. However, the game must not get out of your control, and your puppy should never be allowed to place his teeth on your body. Even if your puppy is soft-mouthed or never applies pressure, permitting mouthing risks injury. Rio, an eighteen-month-old German Shepherd, and Girard, his ten-year-old human companion, played chase and tug all the time. Rio was never discouraged from playing rough or mouthing. I was asked to work with Rio after he had bitten two of Girard's friends. Although Rio was not mean or vicious and had simply learned that play involved using his mouth on people, the local authorities initiated litigation to have the dog destroyed. Even the gentlest puppy can make a mistake or become rough as he gets more excited and grows older. Licking is acceptable if you don't mind it, but anytime teeth come into play, your puppy must be corrected. Every game that you play with your puppy can be played without permitting him to use his teeth on your body. Rags or toys can be tugged on instead of arms.

TUG-OF-WAR

Puppies love playing tug-of-war, and the game is a good release for pent-up energy. There is no evidence to suggest that your dominance is diminished by playing tug-of-war, as long as

Playing games such as tug-of-war does not cause dominance problems;
allowing your puppy to nip you or to usurp your authority
are the causes of dominance problems.

you do not let your puppy get away with nipping. The overzealous puppy that grabs the rag closer and closer to your hand and nips you accidentally needs to be corrected. Take even an accidental nip seriously, and correct your puppy with a cuff. Your puppy will learn to watch out for your hands. To prevent nipping, play tug-of-war with manufactured tug toys that are easy for you to hold onto and that make it difficult for your puppy to reach your hands. Puppies naturally vocalize with growling and barking when they play tug-of-war. The growling is not directed at you, and even if your puppy wins occasionally, he will not become aggressive toward you.

TACKLE

Tackle is a full-body contact game that may provoke excitement or even aggression. Tackle is probably more fun for you than it is for your puppy, because being tackled or restrained is usually not pleasant for anyone. Restraining your puppy at one time or another may become necessary, and therefore, playing restraint games to desensitize your puppy is a good idea. This is also a good opportunity to desensitize your puppy to rough handling, which he may encounter from children or from special populations that have coordination difficulties. Gentle squeezing of the paws and tugging of the ears, tail, and skin while playing or in a playful manner can help your puppy accept unintentional rough handling. Make sure that you are gentle and that your mood is jovial.

If your puppy struggles too much, becomes frightened, or does not enjoy the game, consider playing another game after you have taught him to accept the restraint without biting. If you allow him the privilege of placing his teeth on you without a correction, he will learn to bite when he doesn't want to be handled. Correct your puppy's biting with a good cuff. If tackle provokes a defensive bite, play the game again, and require that he submit, relax, or discontinue the struggle before you let him up from your grip and end the game.

FETCH

Puppies have a basic tendency to carry things in their mouths. All puppies, even those that are not bred specifically for retrieving, have at some time retrieved something—an old shoe, a sock, or some other item. Fetch with a ball, Frisbee, or stick spends a lot of a puppy's energy. The best way to teach retrieving is by using a toy that your puppy loves.

Place your puppy on a lead, and throw the toy a very short distance as you command "fetch." The first few throws, go after the object with your puppy so that he gets the idea to run after the object and does not accidentally get popped with the lead. Praise him for retrieving. Once your puppy gets the idea to run after the toy, let him chase the object alone. Throw the toy a little farther each time your puppy successfully retrieves it. If your puppy does not naturally chase and pick up objects, contact an obedience instructor to help teach your puppy to retrieve. A knowledgeable trainer can teach any dog to retrieve if it involves lots of motivation and reinforcement.

Most puppies will chase and retrieve a thrown object, but the problem may be that your puppy does not want to bring it back.

Fetch is a fun game for you and your puppy.
All breeds use their mouth to carry things.

Play fetch with your puppy on a long line or retractable lead. Throw the object and command "fetch" or "take" in an excited, happy voice. When your puppy picks up the object, give a light snap on the lead and reel him in close. Command "thank you," "give," or "drop it," and offer him a treat. If your puppy does not let go for the treat, take the object out of his mouth and praise him. Continue to throw the object with your puppy on a line until he is reliably bringing it back.

The first time that you command your puppy to retrieve without the line, do it in a small room or area so that your puppy cannot get away or become distracted and run in the other direction. If your puppy does run off with the object, do not run after him. Few people can catch a puppy that is playing keep-away, and chasing him only reinforces the behavior. The best tactic is to run away from your puppy, and he will naturally chase you. When you run and he chases, the game becomes your game, and you are in control. Praise your puppy when he catches you. Be careful not to grab at your puppy. If you cannot get hold of him, run to a small enclosed area, drop to the ground, and act very silly. When your puppy comes over to see what the problem is, take hold of his handle. This only works once or twice, so get your puppy into an obedience class and teach him to return on command. If your puppy does not run after you, stop playing. He will probably stand bewildered for a while and will then come over and drop the toy at your feet. Resume the game and stop again if he does not bring back the toy.

SWIMMING

Retrieving is also a good motivator to teach your puppy to swim, because most puppies will chase objects into the water. At the start, throw the object near the shoreline to get your puppy used to the water. Increase the distance when your puppy does not seem reluctant about the water. Use a floating line attached to your puppy until you are sure that he knows how to swim and is coming back to you reliably.

My favorite method for teaching my puppies to swim if they don't learn on their own by chasing objects into the water is to carry them into the water just far enough so that they cannot touch bottom. I gently place my puppy in the water and face him toward the shoreline. The first few times, I follow him as I lightly hold him around the sides while he swims to shore. Once he seems confident, I let him go the distance on his own. When my puppy is confident about swimming and enjoys retrieving, I put the two together by throwing objects into the water. To encourage the novice swimmer, I always bring along an

Puppy forging great rivers.

experienced canine swimmer to join in on the fun. Until I am sure that my puppy is physically conditioned to swim distance without exhaustion, I keep a floating line attached so that I can retrieve him if necessary. Swimming is great exercise, and a lot of puppies love it as a game.

HIDE-AND-SEEK

There are two ways to play hide-and-seek. You may hide, or you may choose to hide an object or piece of food, such as a biscuit, for your puppy to find. Start by making the hiding places very simple and in your puppy's view, then place a biscuit under a paper or tissue. If you are hiding, hide behind a chair. Initially, allow your puppy to watch as you hide so that he will catch on to the game faster. Tell your puppy to "wait," or have someone hold onto him. Do not permit your puppy to jump the gun. Command your puppy to "find" or "fetch." When your puppy finds you or the object, give him lots of praise. Make the hiding places a little harder each time your puppy successfully finds the prize. Puppies learn quickly to use their nose on the command "go find." The game could become so much fun, you might want to find a book on tracking or scent discrimination.

TRICKS

The easiest and most enjoyable way for a puppy to earn praise is through tricks. Obedience training can quickly be turned into entertainment for you, your puppy, and many other people. Once your puppy knows the basic obedience commands, these exercises can be modified into tricks.

After my puppies understand the down command, I turn the down exercise into "bang" and they play dead. Cute behaviors can also be turned into tricks easily by attaching a command to the behaviors and praising your puppy every time he performs a certain behavior. You can give a command such as "shake" whenever your puppy naturally lifts a paw, and then praise him. When your puppy finds a behavior that tickles your funny bone or elicits your admiration, you can be assured that he will repeat it. I have taught two of my dogs to sneeze on command. Every time my dog sneezed, I was very quick to say "bless you" and give him a treat. I then held a treat above his head as I said bless you, and the minute he blew air from his nose because of having his head raised and the excitement of seeing a treat, I gave him a treat.

Tricks are a good break from the mundane and can relieve stress in a variety of circumstances. Many times when my dogs want my attention or approval, they will break into their repertoire of tricks on their own. Tricks can endear your dog to the most hardened dog hater. Very importantly, tricks can be a good way for your puppy to willingly earn praise, and they provide a good reason to give your puppy praise.

EXERCISE

The type and duration of exercise that you choose for your puppy should be appropriate to his individual needs. Too much or the wrong type of exercise for a young puppy may strain his growing joints and bones. Exercise that overtaxes your puppy's structure may have serious negative effects on his health, particularly if he is not properly conditioned. Consequently, you must demonstrate good common sense in regulating your puppy's physical activity.

The same principles that apply to humans in their exercise programs also apply to dogs. Warm your puppy up, and condition him slowly and methodically. Jumping and long, forced jogs are not advisable until your puppy is properly conditioned and he is at least eighteen months old, when he has finished growing and is fully developed. Trotting a puppy is better exercise and is easier on his structure than running him. The duration and type of exercise also depend on your schedule and commitment. The plan must be realistic so that you can follow through with the schedule on a long-term basis. The overzealous, well-meaning dog owner who begins a rigorous canine exercise plan may not be able to maintain the strenuous schedule. If your puppy becomes accustomed to a certain amount of exercise, he will suffer from the schedule change. The puppy that is conditioned to a certain performance level will have built up endurance and energy to match the exercise program, and when the exercise is not available, he will have more energy to vent than when the program started.

Devise activities that can be maintained year-round. Indoor exercise that involves retrieving or fetching, tricks, hide-and-go-seek, or jumping over a stick and other obstacles can often be set up in a small area in the house and maintained all year round. Frequently, city dwellers hesitate to get a dog, or they feel guilty for owning a dog because of the lack of space for him to exercise. A city dog can learn to retrieve and jump obstacles to exercise in a limited space. The city dweller who is creative can offer good exercise for his puppy, and thus as good a quality of life as any country dweller could provide, regardless of his puppy's size. If limited space is a disadvantage, it is also an advantage in that your puppy will always be a close companion. In the city, you cannot throw your puppy out in the backyard for the entire day to sleep. The city puppy, because of his environment, is able to constantly interact with family members, if only because the city dog needs to be walked several times a day. Also, because of the close quarters, living with an ill-mannered, untrained, hyperactive puppy is highly undesirable. Consequently, most city people are very conscientious about training and exercising their puppies. A good life for a puppy does not necessarily have to include 100 acres or a large backyard for exercise. Quality of life for a puppy is much more than just room to run.

CHAPTER 19

Puppy Obedience Classes

A good obedience class provides a positive environment for you and your puppy to learn. Puppies are fast learners, and training obedience before a puppy has acquired bad habits, grown a full set of enamel weaponry, gained 120 pounds, and crowned himself leader is sound practice. Every obedience class is different, and you will want to review the class content to make sure that it is appropriate for your puppy.

PUPPY-CLASS BENEFITS

Puppy classes for pups eight weeks to six months old are usually called preschool, kindergarten, or socialization classes. The classes are formatted to socialize puppies, and the class outline consists of lots of games for the puppies to play. Preschool classes can provide positive social interactions with other people and puppies. Puppy classes can be fun for you and your puppy and are good supplements to obedience training at home or a formal obedience course. If you choose to take a class before your puppy is twelve weeks old, check with your veterinarian to ensure that your puppy has the appropriate inoculations to protect him.

CURRICULUM CONCERNS

Many kindergarten classes are set up to include free-for-all playtime. The sixteen-week-old Rottweiler's style of play might not be a good match for your sixteen-week-old Toy Poodle. More than two puppies playing at the same time can turn into a free-for-all disaster. Three puppies playing is very similar to three children playing. Someone gets bumped or shoved, resulting in a tiff and gang-up. An experience with a bully playmate can make playing with other puppies very threatening and can lead to fear and aggression toward other dogs. On the other hand, if your puppy is the bully, he will be empowered and reinforced for being aggressive toward other dogs if you do not supervise or intervene. If the format of the class includes free playtime, keep a sharp eye on the reactions of your puppy and be prepared to intervene.

Until your puppy is reliably trained, you may want to leave your lead on during games that have potential to unintentionally teach your puppy the wrong message. Some games involve letting your puppy play with a group, and then calling him when he is engrossed in play. If there is no lead for you to enforce your command, and your puppy does not respond, he may learn that he does not have to come when you call.

All interactions with people should be positive and not forced. Typically, puppies are merely exchanged in socialization classes rather than taught how to approach people. Puppies need the opportunity to make a choice to approach when they feel comfortable. If a puppy is forced or not given a choice to interact, he may feel apprehensive and may attempt to get away. If the person happens to hold on, the puppy will fight to get loose, and the entire interaction will become negative and will affect his attitude toward people in the future.

Puppy classes rarely socialize puppies with adult dogs. Positive socialization with older dogs provides an opportunity for a young puppy to learn body language and how to approach dogs.

One last concern—puppy classes often do not focus on obedience training and behavioral problems. The ideal time to start obedience training is when your young puppy is naturally prepared to learn, and, in the case of the larger breeds, still of a reasonable weight and size for even the most petite owner to control. In addi-

*In order for your puppy to learn how to behave around other people,
he must be positively exposed to older dogs and people
without being in danger of injury.*

tion, learning how to *prevent* behavioral problems before your
puppy *is* a behavioral problem is easier than fixing him. While
puppy classes have important benefits, your puppy should also
start obedience training before he is six months old.

OBEDIENCE CLASSES

An ideal obedience class that uses gentle, positive methods is
suitable for all ages of dogs. The ideal program teaches basic obedience, canine behavior, systematic socialization with people and
dogs, and problem solving. Not all classes and trainers are equal,
and you should research and observe different classes before you
enroll. A pet professional who teaches effective classes must possess the qualities of an educator and must be an expert on the
topic of canine learning and behavior. Many problem behaviors
start in puppyhood and are difficult for the novice eye to recognize. An expert on canine learning and behavior will be adept at

recognizing problems and teaching you to modify behaviors before serious problems develop.

Bill started obedience classes when his Aussie was four months old. Bill consulted me when his dog was fifteen months old because she was fearful of people. Bill explained that his puppy was fearful in class, but none of the trainers seemed to notice. When Bill consulted with the head trainer about the problem, he was told that his puppy would grow up and get over her fear. Bill needed direction, not false assurance. A good educator and instructor also possesses the ability to communicate ideas and information to others at different paces and levels and is masterful at adapting to individual learning styles, both human and canine. A competent, ethical professional will only teach material that he has mastered personally, and he will train and supervise his staff to assure that proper information is being given. A good training school only assigns experienced assistants to supervise classes.

REFERENCES

Getting recommendations from friends for a good training program is a good start. However, friends may not have the knowledge or exposure to equivocally compare trainers or techniques. Request verification of a trainer's credentials. An incompetent trainer can make the obedience experience very unpleasant. If the experience is negative, your puppy will hate obedience, and you will end up not following through with the training. A good list of references should include character references, people who have attended the class, and other professionals and experts in the pet industry, such as veterinarians, groomers, and breeders.

The decision to enroll your puppy in a particular school should not be based solely upon the location, cost, or glamour of the facility. Prices vary as much as the experience and competency of the instructor, but they are not always representative of the instructor's ability. High prices do not ensure competency, and when the price is low, you often get what you pay for. Although traveling a few more minutes to one school versus another is inconvenient, you will be more inconvenienced in the long run if your puppy does not get the best education.

Observe at least one of the instructor's classes before you enroll, and focus on watching the owners and the instructor. The behavior of the puppies during a one-time observation may not be a good gauge of the quality of the class. Some puppies may have been previously trained, or perhaps the puppy that is pulling on the lead today could not walk on lead at all the previous week. The quality of the class is dependent upon the instructor's ability to obtain and maintain command of the class, communicate, demonstrate clearly, and organize a well-planned course outline in a logical, progressive, sequential format. The instructor must have a professional attitude and comprehensive knowledge about canine behavior and dog obedience. The class format should encourage participation and interaction from everyone. You should feel confident that, even though the instructor does not have all of the answers, he has the resources to find the answers. A trainer who has lived with and trained a diversity of dogs will be more capable of understanding a wider variety of puppy problems than the trainer who has only trained and lived with one single dog and breed.

Finally, it is a good idea to talk with the trainer to uncover any possible philosophical or personality conflicts. Every school should take time to talk to potential participants and allow them to watch a session before they pay their money to determine whether the class is for them or not.

ATTENDING AN OBEDIENCE CLASS

At the start, classes may be frightening for the unsocialized puppy that has never been out of the backyard or around other dogs and people. Eventually, your puppy will not only accept the gentle and firm guidance, he will even grow to enjoy obedience class if the experience is positive and provides gentle methods and lots of praise. If your puppy does not ever appear to enjoy the class, re-evaluate your training methods to determine if they are motivating him adequately.

Obedience trainers expect puppies to be unruly the first night. If your puppy was obedient and well-mannered in all environments, you wouldn't have to pay an instructor. Therefore, be assured that you and your unruly puppy are very welcome to class.

A professional, well-rounded obedience course is very important to your puppy's education. Research different programs to find the best class for you and your puppy.

Don't run or work your puppy before class to tire him. Unless you want to keep running your puppy indefinitely to control his behavior, you should give the trainer the opportunity to see and work with your puppy when he is fresh, energetic, and unruly. If your puppy does not exhibit unruly behavior in class, your trainer may not be able to help you work out the problems. Additionally, the exhausted puppy is not going to learn very much from class if he is thinking more about sleeping than working. Changing unruly puppy behavior is what obedience training is all about, and a competent trainer can help you achieve that goal.

If your instructor requests that you work your unruly puppy off to the side or away from the class so that the class is not disrupted, find a competent trainer next time. Don't give up. Avoiding class because your puppy is unruly or frightened will not teach your puppy to overcome his problems. If your puppy poses a threat in class, a competent trainer may choose to work with you individually, outside of class, until you have enough control to re-enter class. However, if you are asked to permanently work in an isolated area of the class, or you are not invited back, find another school.

Even if your puppy is obedient at home, obedience class teaches your puppy that obedient behavior applies even when other people and dogs are present. A puppy is not trained until he obeys in all environments. One eight- to-ten-week class is not enough to fully socialize your puppy, or train him to respond to your commands under all circumstances. Socialization and obedience are continuous processes. Puppies should attend classes throughout their first two years of life until their adult personalities are permanently formed.

CHOOSING TRAINING TECHNIQUES

Before you choose a particular training technique that you may have heard about from a friend or even a respected professional, carefully examine the method to ensure that it communicates what you intend. Pam was told by her trainer that anytime her puppy nipped, she should fold her arms and turn her back on him. The theory was based on the supposition that Pam's puppy was seeking negative attention and would be punished by the lack of attention. Pam turned away, and she was rewarded with a bite on the butt. If the method does not make sense to you, chances are it won't make sense to your puppy either. If you're not sure exactly how or why a method works, it is probably best to avoid the technique altogether. Vicki was told to spray lemon juice into her puppy's mouth whenever he broke a stay because the method worked for a friend's puppy. Although this correction worked for one puppy, Vicki's puppy became resentful when he was squirted, and instead of learning to stay, he learned the "catch-me-if-you-can" game. Even the most popular methods use techniques that may not be suited for every breed or temperament of puppy. Evaluate each method and trainer, if it applies. Question the associations and motivators in reference to your puppy's temperament to decide whether he will respond appropriately without negative repercussions. Remember—use positive methods whenever you can, and your puppy will be happier and more motivated to obey you.

A puppy is not trained until he obeys in every environment.

Afterword

As I close my last chapter of *Puppy Parenting* during a time in our society when a large faction of dog trainers are taking an extreme negative stand on the effectiveness of discipline in training, I feel compelled to comment on my training philosophy and beliefs.

I tried to be very cautious in not assuaging my views on the importance of discipline at a time when a large majority has been outspoken about terming discipline as abusive. In the typical manner of weak but effective argument, a few isolated incidents where misguided individuals have misused corrections to the extent of abuse, their actions were blown out of proportion and used as evidence that discipline leads to abuse. Discipline used properly, and the majority of loving dog owners will use discipline properly, discourages behaviors such as biting which often leads to the premature death of the dog.

While the use of positive reinforcement is certainly my first choice in teaching people and dogs acceptable behavior, I do not hesitate to use discipline when necessary. The most effective training strategy for dogs has the tools to encourage good behavior and discourage misbehavior when necessary. Discipline is as effective in discouraging behaviors as positive reinforcement is in encouraging behavior.

This book discusses several positive and effective discipline options as a part of parenting a puppy to discourage serious misbehaviors. In this light, although there will be some critics who focus on the negative aspects of my choices of discipline, I wish my readers to know that my disciplinary techniques have been extremely effective. I therefore advocate and emphasize:

1. Preventing and channeling undesirable behavior and reinforcing good behavior.
2. Using forms of discipline that are only strong enough to discourage the reward the puppy receives from the undesirable behavior; i.e., the consequence needs to fit the crime.
3. Discipline should not end before the correct response is produced. This will teach the dog that his incorrect response was unacceptable.
4. No correction or disciplinary technique I describe is to be delivered with such force or intensity to hurt or injure a puppy or adult dog. Any correction I describe that does cause injury to a puppy has been misunderstood and misused.

I would be remiss in my duty and love for dogs to assuage the importance of using disciplinary techniques in parenting a puppy. The majority of dogs are surrendered to animal shelters because of behavioral problems that were not properly discouraged in puppyhood. I am often the last trip before the dog is surrendered to the shelter for behavioral problems when positive reinforcement alone failed.

Empirically, after working with more than 10,000 dogs and their owners, where the successes for rehabilitating dogs that were improperly parented during puppyhood far outnumber the failures, the evidence clearly demonstrates that a balance of positive discipline and positive reinforcement work together in successful parenting.

For the love of dogs.

Other Resources

American Animal Hospital Association
P.O. Box 150899
Denver, Colorado 80215-0899

American Kennel Club
5580 Centerview Drive
Raleigh, North Carolina 27606-3390
919-233-9767
Web site: www.akc.org

American Veterinarian Medical Association
1931 North Meacham Road
Schaumburg, Illinois 60173

About the Author

Gail Clark earned a doctorate in psychology from Colorado State University. She has worked professionally with more than 10,000 dogs of all sizes, breeds, and temperaments. As a canine psychologist, her expertise in solving canine behavioral problems has helped thousands of dog owners over the last eighteen years. Dr. Clark wrote the Gordon Setter column for the AKC *Gazette* for eight years and has been published in several national dog magazines and international scientific journals. Affectionately known as "the K-9 Shrink," Dr. Clark is a renowned dog behavioral specialist, trainer, and obedience and breed exhibitor. Her dogs have earned numerous awards, including breed championships, High-in-trials, and multiple Utility titles. All of her dogs are certified therapy dogs and have been featured in television commercials, books, calendars, multi-media, and on radio. she is a member in good standing with the National Association of Dog Obedience Instructors, Animal Behavior Society, Delta Society, Therapy Dogs International, and the Dog Writers' Association of America. Dr. Clark is dedicated to the humane training of dogs through the use of positive learning principles and believes that owner education is the key to responsible and enjoyable pet ownership.

Index

A

abandoned puppies, 23
    behavioral problems of, 23
accidental breedings, 24
accidents, in house-training, 131
    how to clean, 131
acting, like a dog, vi
age
    and bringing a puppy home,
        49-54
    eight weeks, 52
    nine and ten weeks, 54
    seven weeks, 51
    six weeks, 49
aggression, 14, 17, 161, 232
    body language of, 151
    first signs of, 148
    importance of early
        intervention for, 148
    minimizing between dogs,
        244-245
    misdirected, 246-247
AKC Gazette, 19
American Kennel Club (AKC), 2,
    23
American Veterinarian Medical
    Association, 68
ammonia, 182
anthropomorphizing, vi
avoidance tactics, 105

B

baby gates, 134
backfiring, of a car, 114
baking soda, 131
"balanced" puppies, 48
barking, 151-152, 218-222
    causes of, 218-219
    teaching puppy how, 222
    teaching puppy to be quiet on
        command, 219-220
    unintentional reinforcement
        for, 219
    while in crate, 124-125
    while in yard, 220-222
bathing, a puppy, 92-93
bedtime
    use of crate with, 83-84
begging, for foodd, 214
behavioral styles
    identification of, 40
behavior, problem
    barking, 218-222
    bolting, 232-233
    bone/chew-toy possession, 217-
        218
    chasing, 233
    chewing, 222-225
    confinement, 236-238
    coprophagy, 233-234
    diet, 239

digging, 225-228
excessive licking, 234
exercise, 238-239
fence jumping, 231-232
food-related problems, 211-217
jumping, 228-231
prevention of, vii, 171, 211-240
separation anxiety, 234-236
biting
 among littermates, xi
 a puppy back, vi
 by a puppy, 166-169
 children, 108
Bitter Apple Gel, 55, 167, 182
blood-stop products, 89
body language, of puppies, 36, 37-
 48, 49, 147
 of dominant puppy, 37
 of fearful puppy, 39
 of submissive dog, 39-40
 reading and interpreting, 80,
  151-158
 vocalizations, 151-152
body language, of people, 156-157
 tone of voice, 156
bolting, 232-233
bonding process, 52
bone possession, 217
boredom
 with good, 87
breeder-referral service, 25
breeders
 choosing, 27-36
 novice, 24
 professional, 19-20
 responsibility of, 30, 32
breeds of dogs
 choosing, ix, 1-18
 groups of, 2
breed standards, 33
bringing a puppy home, 69-84
 driving home, 71
 first night at home, 83
 introducing puppy to cats,
  82-83

introducing puppy to family,
 72-74
introducing puppy to new
 home, 72
introducing puppy to other
 household dogs, 74-82
shipping by air, 69, 71
brushing, the coat, 91
bullies, 35
buying a puppy unseen, 32

C
car, leaving dog in, 108
care, of a puppy, 85-95
 dog foods, 85-88
 grooming, 88-93
 visits to the veterinarian, 94-95
cats
 introducing a puppy to, 82-83
chaining, as poor solution to
 house-training, 122
chasing
 among littermates, xi
 cars, 233
 cats, 168
 children, 108
chemicals, danger of, 55
chewing, 222-225
 developmental chewing phase,
  222
 how to correct, 222-225
 toys for, 62
 use of crate for, 222
chew-proof environment, 171
chew-toy possession, 217-218
children
 socializing a puppy to, 98,
  108-111
child safety gates, 56
choke collar correction, 169
choosing a breed, 1-18
 coat type, 1, 9
 energy level, 10
 intelligence, 18

male versus female, 13-18
personality and behavior, 15
sex, 1
sharing favorite activities, 7
size, 1, 7, 9
temperament, 1, 9-13
trainability, 17-18
traits and characteristics, 2-3
choosing a breeder, 27-36
  communicating with a breeder,
    28-29
  first contact with breeder, 27
  interviewing a breeder, 27-28
  observing the litter, 33-36
  puppy contracts, 29-30
  responsibility of breeder, 30, 32
  selecting a puppy, 32
Citronella collar, 221
cleaning products, 64-66
club soda, 131
coat types
  curly-coated breeds, 9
  hairless breeds, 9
  short-haired dogs, 9
collars, 61
  training, 181
come command, 189-190
commands, obedience, 183-107.
  See also each individual
  command
communicating proper behavior,
  139-150
  clear praise and discipline, 143-
    144
  good communication, 141-143
  hierarchy versus anarchy, 149
  persistence, importance of, 149-
    150
  positive interactions, 139-140
  positive training, 145-146
  understanding puppy's
    communication, 147-148
communication
  importance of with puppy, 141-
    143

problems, prevention of, 142-143
  understanding a puppy's
    communication, 147-148
  with breeder, 28-29
Complete Dog Book, 2
confidence, 36, 102
confident/fearless puppies, 48
confinement, 236-238
consequences, negative, 176-177
contracts. See puppy contracts
coprophagy, 233-234
corrections, 159-160
  aftermath of, 170
  aggression and corrections, 161
  creative, 160
  improper, 161
cowering, 154
crates, use of, 58-60, 74, 83-84, 108
  advantages of, 126
  for house-training, 121-128
  long hours in, 127
  schedule, 126-128
  size chart of, 61
  sizes, 59-60
  training, 123-124
  types, 59-60
  where to purchase, 59
  wire-mesh, 60
cues, for elimination, 134

D
dam, 30, 32
day care for dogs, 239-240
desensitization, to noises, 116-117
development
  of a puppy, 49-54
diet, 64, 85-86
  canned food, 88
  how much to feed, 86-87
  scraps and tidbits, 88
  semi-moist food, 88
  to reduce anxiety, 239
dietary changes, 64, 87088
digging, 225-228

at carpet, 17
how to correct, 227-228
in yard, 168
preventions for, 226-227
why puppies dig, 225-226
discipline, vi, 143-144, 159-172
aftermath of a correction, 170
aggression and corrections, 161
alternatives to punishment, 170
biting, 166-169
creative corrections, 170
growling, 163
herding, 169
improper corrections, 161
mouthinbg, 161-162
prevention for problem
behaviors, 171
proper discipline, 159-160
razing, 163-164
snapping, 164-166
distractions, from negative events,
115-226
dog house
to protect a puppy, 56
dog repellents, 132
Dog World, 19
dominance problems, 241-243
myths about, 157-158
dominant puppy, 11, 14, 37, 109
body language of, 153-154
door gates, 134
down command, 141
how to teach, 200-203
puppy down, 200-203
down-stay, 203
driving home, with puppy, 71
drop command, 205-206

E
ear
carriage, 39
cleaning, 90
infections, 90
electrical cords, danger of, 55

elimination, cues for, 134
energy level, of a dog, 10, 11-12
enforcement, of commands, 209
environmental management, 171
escape routes
from yard, 56
events, new, 114-116
exercise, 255-256
importance of warm-up, 255
pen, 130-131
schedule for house-training,
128-130
to reduce anxiety, 238-239
expectations
basic, for proper behavior, 139
discussing with breeder, 28-29
unrealistic, x
exploratory behavior, 54
exposure
of belly and genitals, 39, 155
of puppy to other dogs, 113
eye contact, 39
avoidance of, 154, 157

F
false pregnancy, 17
fear episodes, 111, 145
fearfulness, 36, 39, 146
body language of, 154-155
fearful period, 52. See also
sensitive period
feces, eating of, 233-234
feeding a puppy, 85-88
amount to feed, 86-87
schedule for house-training,
128
fence jumping, 231-232
fetch, 251-253
fights, between dogs
how to break up, 245-246
finding a puppy, 19-26
buying from a part-time
breeder, 24-25
buying from a pet shop, 20-22

buying from a professional
    breeder, 19-20
    humane socoety, 22-23
    rescue puppies, 23-24
finicky eaters, 212-213
fireworks, 114
first-aid kits, canine, 95
first night, of puppy at home, 83
flexibility, importance of, 207
food, 64, 85. See also diet, dietary
    changes
    bowls, 64
food bolting, 211-212
food guarding, 215-216
    training with the food dish,
        216-217
free feeding, 86-87

G
gagging, 162
games
    for interaction, 249-256
    for socialization, 97-98
garden hose, 227
give command, 205-206
grabbing a puppy, 74
Greyhound collar, 61
groomer, professional, 67
grooming, 88-93
    as socialization, 97
    bathing, 92-93
    brushing coat, 91-92
    brushing teeth, 90-91
    ear cleaning, 90
    nail clipping, 88-89
    supplies, 67
growling
    back at a puppy, v
    of a puppy, 107, 113, 151, 163
guarantees, written, 19
Gumabones, 62
gums, color of, 95

H
hand feeding, 214

handles, 182
handling of puppies, 33, 97-98
    proper, 100-101
head halters, 75
head, in lowered position, 39
health
    precautions, 95
    screenings, 19-20
heart rate
    as predictor of behavioral style,
        40-41
heat cycle, 15, 17
    behavioral changes with, 17, 101
heeling
    how to teach, 196-197
herding, 169
    correction for, 169
herding group, 2
hereditary diseases, 3, 5
hide-and-seek, 254
hoofs, for chewing, 63
hormonal changes, 101
hound group, 2
household products, dangerous,
    95
house-training, 52, 54, 121-138
    crating, 121-128
    exercise schedule, 128-130
    feeding schedule, 128
    paper training, 130-134
    physical difficulties, 136
    problems with, 136-137
    submissive urinating, 135-138
humane societies, 22-23
    behavioral problems of dogs
        from, 22-23
hurry command, 129
hybrid dogs, 5

I
independence, 54
inoculations, 100
interaction, positive, 139-140
introduction, of puppy
    to cats, 82

to new family, 72-74
to new home, 72
to other household dogs, 74-82
invisible fence, 231

J
jealousy, between dogs, 243-244
jumping up, 102-103, 228-232
    fence, 231-232
    handle correction for, 229
    squirt bottle correction for, 168
    using the settle, 230
    using the sit, 228-229
    using the stay, 230

K
kindergarten classes, 257

L
leads, 61, 181
learning, by a puppy, 173-180
    negative consequences, 176-177
    positive training, 175-176
    temperament differences, 178-
        180
    timing, 177
leave it command, 183, 204-205
leaving dog in a car, 108
let's go command, 117
    how to teach, 193-196
licking
    excessive, 234
    gesture, 155
Listerine, 167
litter
    interactions among, 35
    observation of, 33-36
    separation from, 49, 112, 155
look command, 189
love at first sight, 32
lunging, 113, 185

M
male puppies versus female
    puppies, 13-18

appearance, 14
intelligence, 18
personality and behavior, 15, 17
trainability, 17-18
manners, puppy, 181-210
    handles, 182
    leads, 181
    obedience commands, 183-207
    training collars, 181
    training problems, 207-208
    training sessions, 182-183
marking behavior, 15
mats, removal of, 92
The Mentally Sound Dog
messy eaters, 214-215
microchips
    for identification, 66-67
mixed breeds, 3-8, 25
mouthing, 161-162
move command, 206
multiple-dog households, 241-247

N
nail clipping, 88-89
nesting behavior, 17
neutering, 247
nipping, 161-162
no command, 141, 185
noise
    desensitization to, 116-117

O
obedience, 116
    classes, 257-263
    commands, 183-207
    training, 150, 181
objects, fear of, 118-119
off command, 103, 141, 169, 183,
    206
older puppies, 23-24
    rehabilitation of, 23-24
optimal learning phase, 174

P
pantyhouse, as poor toy, 63

paper, rolled
    for discipline, 169
paper training, 66, 130-134
people, socialization to, 102-107
persistence, importance of, 149-
    150, 208-209
pet shops, 20-22
physical exam
    for new puppy, 67-68
plants, danger of, 55
plush toys, 62
PMS, 15
popping, of collar, 80, 82
positive
    guidance, vi
    interactions, 139-140
    reinforcement, 143
    training, 145-146
pouncing
    among littermates, xi
praise, as a reward, 140, 143, 175-
    176
preparation for new puppy, 55-68
    grooming supplies, 67
    physical exam, 67-68
    puppy-care essentials, 58-66
    puppy identification, 66-67
    puppy proofing, 55
preschool classes, 257
progesterone, effects of, 15
protecting toys or food, 147
puberty, 101
punishment
    alternatives to, 170
puppy
    care, 85-95
    contracts, 29-30
    identification, 66-67
    mills, 21
    pads, for house-training, 130
puppy classes
    benefits of, 257
    curriculum concerns, 258-259
puppy proofing
    house, 55-58

    yard, 55-58
puppy recall, 190
purebreds versus mixed breeds, 3-7

Q
quiet command, 107, 124-125,
    183, 206
qwicking a nail, 89

R
racquetballs, as poor toys, 63
rawhides, 63
raze correction, 163-164
ready command, 188-189
recall
    older puppy, 190-191
    puppy, 190
    snappy, 192
registration papers, 19, 22
reinforcement, vi, 177
    schedule, 209-210
rescue puppies, 23-24
resident dogs, 74-75
rewards, 175-176
rocks
    eating of, 57-58
rope bones, 62
rubber toys, 62

S
safety, of environment, vi
scooting along ground, 39
scraps, of food, 88
selective-hearing disease, 209
sensitive
    period, 52
    stages, 101-102
separation anxiety, 49, 234-236
    causes of, 235-236
separation from litter, 49
settle command, 203-204
shade
    importance of in yard, 56
shampoos, for bathing a puppy, 93
shedding, 91

shipment
    of puppy by air, 69, 71
show dog, 28
sight/object test, 41
sire, 30, 32
sit command, 185
    how to teach, 185-188
sit-stay, 102, 103, 107, 115
    how to teach, 197-200
size
    of a dog, 7, 9
slinking, 154
"smiling," 155
snapping, 49, 79, 164-166
    collar corrections, 165-166
    cuff under the chin correction,
        165
snappy recall, 192
social hierarchy, 51, 81-82, 149.
    See also social structure
socialization, 97-120
    classes, 257
    desensitization to noises, 116-117
    fear episodes during, 111
    fear of objects, 118-119
    new surfaces, 117-118
    of children and dogs, 108-111
    places to socialize puppies with
        people, 107-108
    positive, 97-99
    proper handling, 100-101
    sensitive stages, 101-102
    socializing puppy with new
        people, 102-107
    to new events, 114-116
    with other dogs, 112-113
social structure, 81-82
soiling
    catching puppy in act of, 132-133
    how problems develop, 137
spay/neuter contract, 20, 22
spoiling a puppy, 157
sporting group, 2
squirt bottle, 82-83, 125
    correction, 167-169

    for quiet command, 206-207
stairs, 117
standards, breed, 33
startle reaction, 102, 114
sterilized bones, 62
stimulus, scary, 115-116
submissive puppy, 11, 39-40
    body language of, 155
supervision, importance of with
        children, 109
surfaces, new, 117-118
swimming, 253-254

T
tabasco sauce
tackle, 250-251
talk, dog, 152
tattoos, 66-67
teeth, brushing, 90-91
teething, 161-162
temperament
    compatibility between owner
        and puppy, x, 1
    differences and how they affect
        learning, 178-180
    hard-tempered puppies, 178-179
    hyperactive puppies, 179
    interpretation of test scores for,
        47-48
    lethargic puppies, 179-180
    soft-tempered puppies, 178
    tests, 36, 40-48
temperature, normal, 95
tennis balls, as toys, 63
terrier group, 2
testosterone, effects of, 15
thunderstorms, 114
tidbits, 88
timidity, 106
timing
    of reinforcements and
        corrections, 177
tooth scalers, 91
top dog, 152

touching chain, 75-77, 105-106
toy group, 2
toys, puppy, 62-63
training
    early, vii, ix, xi
    location, 208
    positive, 145-146
    problems, 207-208
    sessions, 182-183
training programs
    positive, xii, 175-176
treats, 64
    use of to shape behavior, 173
tricks, 173, 254-255
trotting, as exercise, 255
tug-of-war, 249-250
tying puppy to waist
    for house-training, 133-134
    when you have visitors, 230-231

U
United Kennel Club (UKC), 19, 23
urination, submissive, 40, 135-136,
    155
urinating on objects, 15

V
vaccination program, 30
veterinarian
    finding a good one, 68
    first visit to, 94-95

viewing sire and dam
    as part of selecting puppy, 30, 32
vigilance
    importance of in house-training,
        133
vinegar and water solution, 131
visitors
    training puppy to not jump and
    bother, 230-231
vocalizations, 151-152

W
wait command, 192
walks, as exercise, 129, 131
watch command, 189
water
    bowls, 64
    correction, 124-124.
        See also squirt bottle
    guns, 168
weight
    excess, 86
    monitoring, 86
whimpering, 152
whining, 152
    while in crate, 124-125
working group, 2

XYZ
yeast infections, in ear, 95
yelping, 152